HOME

By the same author

FICTION

Darling
Mutton
Comfort and Joy
Don't You Want Me?
My Life on a Plate

NON-FICTION

India Knight's Beauty Edit
The Goodness of Dogs
In Your Prime
The Thrift Book
Neris and India's Idiot-Proof Diet
(*with Neris Thomas*)
Neris and India's Idiot-Proof Diet Cookbook
(*with Bee Rawlinson and Neris Thomas*)
The Shops

HOME

How to Love It, Live in It and Find Joy in It

INDIA KNIGHT

FIG TREE
an imprint of
PENGUIN BOOKS

FIG TREE

UK | USA | Canada | Ireland | Australia
India | New Zealand | South Africa

Fig Tree is part of the Penguin Random House group of companies
whose addresses can be found at global.penguinrandomhouse.com

Penguin Random House UK,
One Embassy Gardens, 8 Viaduct Gardens, London SW11 7BW

penguin.co.uk

First published 2025

005

Copyright © India Knight, 2025

The moral right of the author has been asserted

No part of this book may be used or reproduced in any manner for the
purpose of training artificial intelligence technologies or systems. In accordance
with Article 4(3) of the DSM Directive 2019/790, Penguin Random House
expressly reserves this work from the text and data mining exception

Thank you to the illustrator, Harriet Russell

Illustration credits: Eleanor Crow, *Suffolk Kitchen* (2025); Moses Harris (1730–c.1788),
Prismatic Colour Wheel (1766), photo © Heritage Image Partnership Ltd/Alamy;
Antoine Vollon (1833–1900), *Still Life with Eggs* (1851), photo © The Print Collector/Alamy;
Carl Holsoe (1863–1935), *In the Dining Room* (oil on canvas), photo © Christie's Images/
Bridgeman Images; collage photos, author's own

Text credits: p. 2, excerpt from *Dream Work* by Mary Oliver, published by
Grove Atlantic, Inc., 1986, copyright © Mary Oliver, reproduced by permission of the author c/o
Grove Atlantic, Inc., 154 West 14th Street, 12th Floor, New York, NY 10011; p. 18, excerpt from
Leçons des ténèbres by Clive James, published by the *New Yorker*, copyright © Clive James, reproduced
by permission of the author c/o United Agents Ltd, 12–26 Lexington St, London W1F 0LE;
p. 189, excerpt from *The Bell Jar* by Sylvia Plath, published by Faber and Faber Ltd, 2009,
copyright © Sylvia Plath, reproduced by permission of the author c/o Faber and
Faber Ltd, The Bindery, 51 Hatton Garden, London EC1N 8HN

Every effort has been made to trace copyright holders and to obtain their permission for the
use of copyright material. The publisher apologizes for any errors or omissions and would be grateful
to be notified of any corrections that should be incorporated in future editions of this book

Set in 12.4/15pt Garamond Premier Pro
Typeset by Six Red Marbles UK, Thetford, Norfolk
Printed and bound in Great Britain by Clays Ltd, Elcograf S.p.A.

The authorized representative in the EEA is Penguin Random House Ireland,
Morrison Chambers, 32 Nassau Street, Dublin D02 YH68

A CIP catalogue record for this book is available from the British Library

ISBN: 978-0-241-75743-7

Penguin Random House is committed to a sustainable future
for our business, our readers and our planet. This book is made from
Forest Stewardship Council® certified paper.

This one is for my Substack subscribers,
with love and gratitude.

'He is happiest, be he king or peasant, who finds peace in his home'

Johann Wolfgang von Goethe

'Muv once offered a prize of half a crown to the child who could produce the best budget for a young couple living on £500 a year, but Nancy ruined the contest by starting her list of expenditures with "Flowers – £490".'

– Jessica Mitford, *Hons and Rebels*

CONTENTS

Introduction 1
The Welcome Mat 7

FOUNDATION 1: The importance of charm 9
Knock Knock: First impressions, and the lack of them 13
FOUNDATION 2: Storytelling 23
The Kitchen: Part 1 29
FOUNDATION 3: Lighting 41
The Kitchen: Part 2 45
FOUNDATION 4: A note on taste 65
The Kitchen: Part 3 71
FOUNDATION 5: On paint and colour 97
The Sitting Room 109
FOUNDATION 6: No stuff, or all the stuff? 141
The Loo 149
The Bedroom 157
The *Play* Room 183
The Bathroom 189
The Spare Room 197
Outside 211
Moving to the Country 225
Take it to the tip: The things nobody needs 233
FOUNDATION 7: In praise of imperfection 241
Bonus Chapter: Christmas for the busy,
    and Christmas for the quiet 249

Acknowledgements 255
Index 259

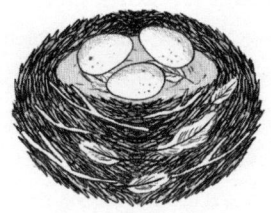

INTRODUCTION

I've been obsessed with domestic interiors since I was a small child. One day, walking home from school in Brussels – something I particularly liked doing in winter because of the warm golden light that puddled out of the houses so invitingly on a dark afternoon – it suddenly dawned on me that there was a whole world behind every single front door. A whole, complete world, with its own people, yes, but also its own sofas and forks and sheets and pets, with different furniture and tablecloths and bathroom products, with different wallpapers and paint colours and crockery and beds. It almost blew my mind, especially in relation to apartment blocks such as the one we lived in. There were whole other worlds *on the same floor as us*!

I still find this thought completely amazing. Who needs magical wardrobes that lead to Narnia when front doors exist? And windows! One of the reasons I really like going to Amsterdam is because its residents don't seem to bother with curtains, and so you can peer into hundreds of little quotidian domestic scenes as you stroll by on your way from A to B – nothing dramatic, just someone laying the table, or someone reading on a sofa, or a woman standing slightly wearily by the cooker, or a teenager coming in and taking off his rucksack. It makes me love humanity, so vast and also so beautifully, endearingly, heart-breakingly tiny.

*

This is partly a book about a feeling. We all know it, regardless of where we live. You know when a toddler becomes tired of his exciting playdate and starts to cry, 'I just want to go home'? There's an adult version, too. Home is when you open the front door and exhale. Home is warmth, safety, comfort, refuge, peace, even if the peace sometimes feels quite chaotic. If you've had a terrible day, just the act of being home improves it. Home is where you are your true self, where you can 'let the soft animal of your body love what it loves', in the words of the poet Mary Oliver, whether that is another person or persons, a particularly charming pet, or, say, custard. It's where you kick off your shoes or take off your bra, literally and figuratively. It is you as a creature in its burrow.

Home is also a kind of yearning. It is a dream of something that is lost for ever, something that a part of you will always miss and long for, even if you have never really known it. It's a flickering, not entirely realistic memory of a sort of idyll where it is always warm, where there is fresh tea in the pot and something delicious in the oven, where there are hollyhocks in the garden, where the days are long and golden and where someone cares for you. That particular idyll is hardly ever completely real – for me it's a complicated composite of real life and, among many other things, television shows, several paintings by Bonnard, children's picture books and *The Cazalet Chronicles* by Elizabeth Jane Howard. But it doesn't matter if the memory is false, real, or somewhere in between. We can all imagine the feeling, whether we've had the good fortune to ever have experienced it, or not. We can all close our eyes and summon up that sense of blissful ease (the picture in my head often involves lying in tall grass and little motes dancing lazily in hazy sunlight, despite the fact that I grew up entirely in cities).

The aim of this book is to help you experience that feeling to its fullest, to amplify it so much and so well that home, whether it is grand or modest, urban or rural, rented or owned, shared or occupied solo, becomes a place of utmost contentment. Your home should not be a functional, soulless place (even if it looks like one when you first move in) – I genuinely believe that living that way

INTRODUCTION

is really terrible for one's mental health. Your home should be an extension of you, in all your multifaceted glory. It should bring you pleasure and a deep sense of well-being. It should be beautiful to you, because few things are better for the soul than the eye alighting with pleasure on items that are loved and meaningful.

I don't mean that your bathroom should be made of marble, or your garden composed of topiary avenues. We live in the real world. In mine, a really good wooden spoon or a cushion with just the right amount of stuffing (not so over-stuffed that it's basically erect, not so under-stuffed that it's depressingly limp) make more-than-acceptable substitutes for that sort of grandeur, which anyway I always find slightly chilly. You know? You go and nose round some grand National Trust mansion and it's all ravishing and jaw-dropping, etc., etc., but I always think, 'But where do you hunker down with a bowl of macaroni cheese on your lap in front of the telly?' and feel a bit (only a bit) sorry for the lack of cosiness. Inevitably I like people's studies the best, because you get an actual sense of the person.

When people say, 'Home is where the heart is', I nod politely but I think, 'Yes, but also home is where the *stuff* is.' More and more of us live on our own, and the suggestion that a home is not a home unless it is filled with a horde of riotously joyful people and children feels outdated. Home is where *you* are, too – you, and all your most cherished and meaningful possessions. Home is your nest, and you're the main bird.

People badly underestimate how much stuff a house needs to feel like a home. Stuff builds nests. Stuff is so important, so meaningful (we'll get to this), and I am deeply mistrustful of a home without stuff. Nine times out of ten, reading an interiors magazine and marvelling at the beauty of this or that impeccably styled house, I'll eventually think, 'But where's your stuff, you absolute weirdo? Why don't you have any stuff?' And then I'll go right off the beautiful house, because it's not a home. It evokes no feelings other than fleeting low-level envy.

Home shapes who we are. So now I'm going to tell you everything I know about living well and making a home. I'm not going to tell you how to make your house look like it's in a magazine – there are loads of books out there that do that, written by experts in their field. I am also not especially interested in turning a house into a magazine shoot. What I am interested in, and moved by, is real life. So I'm going to tell you what I know about making anyone peering in at your home from the pavement think, 'I wish I lived there. That looks such a happy place.' I'm going to go through an imaginary house that's a lot like my own house room by room and tell you everything I feel is valuable and useful about making that room feel a certain way. It might involve the best lightbulbs and the most flattering paint colours, or suggesting what to make when you've asked people to dinner and have forgotten (or maybe never learned) how to cook. I'm going to tell you about pillows and mattresses and rugs, I'm going to show you how to use things you've already got, tell you how to arrange flowers for maximum impact, steer you far, far away from trends and Instagram and help you find, trust – and take pride in – what *you* like. Because when you surround yourself with things *you* like, then *you* feel happy, happier, happiest. My mission in these pages is to try my hardest to make you sigh with contentment the moment you're through the front door. On the way there, I'll tell you stories about the spaces I've lived in, why I feel as I do about home, and what home means to me.

What I am *not* going to do is steer you towards a specific style, or tell you how to decorate for other people. Obviously no one wishes for guests to think 'Oh dear' when they come to supper. But there exists – I blame social media – a certain 'of the moment' style of decorating that is ephemeral, empty, meaningless, reliant on accessories that are fashionable for two seconds and declared passé overnight. That isn't what this book (or the Substack newsletter that inspired it, which you can find and sign up to at indiaknight.substack.com) is about. I'm interested in timeless spaces that are beyond trends and feel occupied by living, breathing people and the paraphernalia of the lives they have made. I'm interested in design, of course. I love design – but not too much of it. I think that very often design is the enemy of charm, and I'm Team Charm.

INTRODUCTION

Home is about *you*. It's also true that sometimes home is about other people. And that sometimes another human being feels like coming home, although I would suggest that another being feels more like coming home if the habitat you end up in after the first flush of passion is deeply pleasing to both of you. Bricks, mortar and decoration matter. *Things* matter.

And yes, it's true that, as per Thomas Wolfe, you can't go home again: that ache for the nebulous feeling of home is out of reach, in part because it has mutated into something that is half-imagined. But what we are going to do together in this book is turn your current home into the thing which that ache hungers for. We are going to make it so delightful, so enjoyable, so nest-like and cosy, so full of memories and joy that you won't yearn to 'go home again' – because you'll wake up one morning and realize you're already there.

THE WELCOME MAT

A word on how this book is set out

This book is in the shape of a house. We'll be going through room by room, and in each room I will share thoughts that I think you'll find useful and/or inspiring. You may have more rooms, or fewer rooms, than the ones I mention, but that's fine: you can adjust the information to fit your own space. There's no dining room chapter, for instance, because I don't have a dining room – but if you do, just refer to the section on eating areas (it's in the kitchen chapters).

Imagine me showing you around my house, as if I was the kind of person who presumptuously said, 'Would you like to see the house?' These are not words I've ever uttered – the idea makes me want to die of cringe – but, hypocritically, I love nothing more than other people saying them to me. Sometimes *all I want* is to see the house – I don't actually need a drink or lunch or supper or whatever else we're supposed to be doing after the tour, because my curiosity (a nicer way of saying nosiness) has been satisfied.

In this tour of *my* home, we will stop in every room, and I'll point things out and tell you stuff. Sometimes we'll just have a conversation – I might say, 'By the way, do you know this chicken recipe? It's brilliant because it works for every single occasion you could think of,' or 'The thing to know about buying mattresses is this.' And, as in life, sometimes we'll go off at a tangent on the theme of home, domestic life and life more broadly – the equivalent of running upstairs and coming back down with something I want to show you.

On our way through the house, we will have places to sit and chat (I imagine comfy, well-placed chairs on landings, though more realistically we would just perch on the edge of a bed or on some stairs, assuming we had stairs). These places are where we pause and discuss the foundations of the house – not literally concrete and wooden frames, but rather foundational principles according to me, like the importance of charm or the pointlessness of constantly striving for 'perfection', before we head off into another room.

One final note: I am using 'house' or 'your house' throughout as shorthand to mean 'the space you live in'. It doesn't have to be a whole house, obviously, but saying 'house' saves me from clunkily saying 'your house/flat/room/the space in which you live' every time the word comes up.

Right – consider yourself welcomed! Let's go in.

FOUNDATION I

THE IMPORTANCE OF CHARM

A house without charm does not feel like a home

Charm is an elusive quality. Charm in a human is what makes you feel giddy with delight. It's what makes a person immediately enchanting and likeable. It isn't about being the prettiest or the most handsome or the cleverest or the funniest, though obviously all those things are desirable attributes. But charm has nothing to do with perfection. On the contrary, charm is slightly wonky. It's ineffable. It's *je ne sais quoi*, it's a little bit curious and off-piste. You know how you say of a charming person, 'I've never met anyone quite like him/her before'?

It's exactly the same when it comes to houses.

Without charm, a house is not a home. It can be perfection on paper, the interiors considered and 'curated' (I do not love that word) to within an inch of their life – but without charm, without that element of wonkiness and originality, it is missing something essential. If you've ever sat in a room and thought, 'I can't work it out, I've got all the kit, it's perfect on paper, so why does it feel . . . not right?', the brutal answer is often, 'Because it is charmless.' (Nobody is ever going to tell you that your home is charmless – it would be a monstrous thing to say – so you alone need to be on top of this issue.)

Like charming people, charming houses – or charming rooms, or charming objects – are few and far between. Why is this? Two reasons, I think. The first is that charm is no longer a quality that is properly valued. We no longer *expect* things to be charming – to really speak to us at a meaningful level that truly delights us. Instead, we skim along the surface. Our charm radar is mostly switched off, replaced by a lesser, more algorithmic radar that is quickly able to 'read' someone or something based solely on their purchases (if a human) or label (if an object). From their haircut to the book they're reading to their candlesticks, our brain goes tick, I saw that on social media, tick, I was influenced into buying the same book, tick, those candlesticks were on Pinterest. The whole thing has become incredibly basic. We no longer take the time to really *look*, and even worse, we no longer take the time to *feel* anything beyond 'It's nice, I want one.'

You can see the problem. The things we're going to be talking about in these pages are the things we surround ourselves with – the things we see first thing in the morning and last thing at night, the things that make up all the visuals of our domestic existence, the things that build our memories of home and the way we feel within our own four walls. Not feeling warmly towards these things, even if they are relatively boring functional things that we use every day, has a demoralizing effect over time. You can use the scratched Pyrex bowl you've had since you first left home as a salad bowl, or you can buy a beautiful wooden one that develops a patina over time (provided you oil it lovingly every now and then – normal cooking oil and a piece of kitchen roll will do perfectly). One of these will make you feel happy when you dish up dinner, and one of them will make you feel nothing. I'm not saying you're going to look at your wooden salad bowl and scream with joy – it'll be more of a microscopic inner peep, if that. But if that microscopic peep applies to most things in your home, then cumulatively all the peeps make a pretty chunky difference to the feel of the place, and to how you feel in it.

The second problem is that you can't mass-manufacture charm. You can't make it in giant factories in China and sell it cheaply online, because charm requires authenticity and originality. This doesn't mean that charm is expensive (it very rarely is, in fact) or that it requires you to have an impeccable eye, magical powers and/or

FOUNDATION I: THE IMPORTANCE OF CHARM

specialist knowledge when it comes to truffling things out in junk or antique shops.

What it requires you to do is to think and to *feel*, far more deeply than we are used to when it comes to thinking about décor. The mass-manufactured thing can be *made* charming. It's a bit like cooking. You wouldn't boil a chicken breast, slap it on a plate and call it dinner. You'd cook it with some butter or olive oil. You'd make a sauce for it, and give it a couple of friends in the form of maybe a potato and a well-dressed salad (there is a vinaigrette recipe on page 54). You wouldn't put these things all on top of each other in an unappetizing lumpen heap – you'd have a very quick think about presentation.

Or think of fashion. The best-dressed people, in my view at least, aren't wearing one expensive label top to toe, like some sort of trophy wife. Instead, they are creative and playful: this is my high-street t-shirt, this is vintage (i.e. from a charity shop), this is my one good expensive thing, here it is all mixed up together and cleverly accessorized.

Like the chicken breast or the basic white t-shirt, the cheap little mass-produced vase that cost £2.50 isn't charming on its own. But it becomes charming if you give it a paper flower, or a little sprig of blossom from a tree you passed on your way back from work, or a froth of loosely arranged garden flowers in summer. It becomes more charming still if you place it in the right spot. These things don't require money – they are either free or inexpensive. What they require is thought, and using your eyes. We will go into much more detail about how to do this shortly.

I know that some of you will be thinking, 'It's all very well for you to say, but I wouldn't know charm if it reared up and bit me on the bottom.' You'd be wrong, though. What you'd be talking about is not trusting your own taste, which is a whole other thing and which we will get into at length later in this book.

But charm – we all know charm when we see it. We immediately *feel* it. Deep down, we're primitive. We sit in a room, unconsciously tap into some ancient folk memory of huddling round the hearth in our rough-hewn garments, a cauldron of stew hanging above the flames, and some little part of twenty-first-century us thinks, 'This kitchen does not feel sufficiently kitcheny.' Allow that thought to expand further, and it might go, 'Maybe too many things are hidden away in this bank of cabinets.' Or 'The walls are really very bare.' Or 'The lighting is harsh, but I need it to see what I'm doing.' Or any number of other things – you will find them all in the kitchen chapters, starting on page 29.

Here's the headline news: the charm is within you. You bring the charm. No matter where or how you live, *you* are authentic and original. The things you are instinctively drawn to are authentic and original *to you*. All you have to do for a home that has charm is to tell *your* story. And we'll come to that later on.

KNOCK KNOCK

First impressions, and the lack of them

I am sitting here trying to visualize the colours and door furniture of all the front doors I've lived behind – there are quite a lot of them in three different countries – and I am failing. I only remember my three most recent own front doors: bright red in Hackney, ultra-bright, a very seventies, almost neon green in Primrose Hill (the shade is Pthalo Green by Little Greene), plain wood in Suffolk. I remember the front door of the modern house my mother and stepfather built in London – black, almost square, with a matte silver doorknob – but I can't for the life of me picture the front door of the house before that, a semi-detached Victorian redbrick that I still think of as my childhood home, despite the fact that it was one of many (my love of home is partly due to the fact that I lived in so many as a child).

This Victorian house has, over the years, acquired almost mythical status in my and my sisters' imagination: it was the Old House, where everyone loved each other and everything was cosy and good. The New House, though spectacular, was where the parental marriage broke up and everything went wrong, though by this point I was in my early twenties and no longer lived at home. My stepfather stayed in the New House for a bit after the divorce, and I got ready for my wedding day from it.

That was a nice and emotionally significant morning, but generally I didn't love the New House. When the building work was finally finished, we had a party to thank the builders – a lovely, thoughtful and really well-intentioned impulse, obviously, but you have to imagine the very, very high comedic potential of some nice people in rarified Hampstead, north London, with their raw plaster-finish walls and Italian furniture and twenty-foot indoor tree and so on, hosting about a dozen blokes who would obviously have preferred to be given some cash to spend down the pub. One day I will do this scene justice in a novel. It also featured my lovely Pakistani grandmother smiling at everyone in her sari and telling these beefy and almost certainly slightly racist men that they were good boys, very hard-working, very strong.

Anyway: I was having a cigarette with one of the builders who was quite close to me in age and he said, laughing: 'Not a subtle message, is it? Your bedroom.' What about my bedroom, I said. 'Well,' he said, looking at me as if I were very dim, 'no offence, but it's tiny. The laundry area is bigger. It's the smallest room in the house. The spare room is about four times the size.'

'Oh,' I said, realizing for the first time that this was absolutely true. You tell yourself whatever story you need to hear, in life, and I'd obviously told myself a lie about how my designated room was... cosy. My much younger sisters had four-poster beds; I had a narrow single of the kind I don't even think exists any more, and one shelf for my hundreds of books. What could this mean? Cosy, is what my brain came up with, trying to take care of itself. Brains do this: they cushion the blow.

I tried to laugh it off, to tell the builder something about how I was in and out because I lived with my boyfriend, but actually I wasn't in and out because this particular boyfriend and I had split up and I had – I thought – gone 'home'. To the smallest room in the house. Smaller than the laundry area. The builder realized that he was responsible for making the penny drop, looked slightly awkward, put out his fag, said, 'See you later,' and wandered off to get another beer (tiny little bottles of Peroni) and an egg-and-cress sandwich. (I'm making the sandwiches up because I can't remember what was in them. Goat's cheese or Parma ham, maybe. On brioche. My parents are lovely people – as I say, the intention was good, and they didn't want to give their guests food other than they'd give any other guests, because that would have been awful. But, yeah.)

If I were writing fiction, I would make the builder say something kind, but really, what must he have thought? He was about two years older than me and earning his living by back-breaking manual labour; he was northern and far away from home, I imagine in temporary shared digs somewhere, with nary a marble tile or cup of Lapsang. I was making a sad face because my parents' room for me in their beautiful house was insufficiently grand. Not so far in the future, my stepfather would buy me a flat of my own. There's not actually much to say, and so he didn't say it.

I can't remember the front doors, but I do remember all the hallways, from my beloved grandmother's flat in Brussels (ancient parquet in the shape of chevrons) to the clean, optimistic pale blond wood of my own first flat. Front doors matter up to a point, but hallways are where the story begins. There is actually something to be said for a really unpromising front door, too. If you live in a flat and the communal front door is nothing to write home about, and if the common areas are a bit grim – cheap carpet, scuffed door, marks on the walls, the inevitable pile of flyers and takeaway menus splayed messily on a shelf, then opening the door of the actual flat and finding yourself in a whole other world is an exciting feeling, like the start of an adventure.

The problem with the hall is that, almost inevitably, it makes the start of the start of the adventure feel like a damp squib (or damp squid, as my kids thought the expression went). Halls are, by definition, long and thin, and most of them don't have any natural daylight unless the front door is open. I am envious of people with really wide, bright halls – they do exist, often in the countryside – and when I was young I was always amazed by, and admiring of, the way the front door opened straight into the sitting room in so many US sitcoms. The practicalities – where did they put their coats and muddy boots and dog leads and random bits of crap? – never occurred to me. All I saw was the zero-seconds journey from outside to inside, the instant switch from weather and traffic to a welcoming sofa without first having to negotiate a narrow, too-dark corridor cluttered up with unphotogenic stuff that tripped you up if you weren't vigilant.

How to avoid this in a normal, non-American house? Here's a piece of advice that I hope you find useful, not just in the context of halls but in the context of houses generally (and of life – it's my number one piece of life advice, in fact). The advice is: DECIDE WHERE THE MESS IS GOING TO BE, AND MAKE YOUR PEACE WITH IT. I am mostly talking to parents here, but to be frank my children left home long ago and I still use the principle elsewhere. One room is always going to have a load of stuff dumped in it, and that room is never going to gladden your heart when you look at it. Let it go. Accepting this mess as a fact of life takes away all the stress of it. But let's stay on halls for now.

On my camera roll there are ten years' worth of trainers in the hall. They started off being manageable – eight- or nine-year-old sized trainers – but they grew and grew, until the floor as good as disappeared under a tidal wave of size 12 Nikes and Adidas. These used to drive me so mad that I started photographing them. Sometimes I'd passive-aggressively text them to my teenage sons, who were having a nice time in their rooms with their many, many huge-footed mates. The mates' giant trainers were also in the hall, either completely blocking access to the front door or, when left in the space to the left of the stairs, requiring you to leap over them to get to the downstairs loo. I really mean leap: you had to take a running jump. The hall, not wide in the first place, narrowed more at this point to accommodate a staircase, and there were coats all down the left-hand side. The combination of the giant trainers and pegs heaving with a variety of five people's winter coats (plus, obviously, mates' coats, these usually being large and puffy) made the whole area barely navigable.

I haven't even mentioned the skateboards. Or the mates' skateboards. Or the bikes. Or the mates' bikes. My children's bikes should really have been wall-mounted, but an artist called Charlotte Mann (charlottemann.co.uk) had drawn one of her beautiful black marker pen murals all along the hall wall and up to the half-landing. It featured all our most treasured possessions, real and imaginary, from the boys' cricket bats to my favourite books to a portrait of Mary, Queen of Scots. When we moved out of that house, leaving London altogether for a life in the country, I was champing at the bit for the new chapter, but truly devastated at leaving the mural behind. It would make no sense to the new owners: it was profoundly intimate, all about our life and our things. But equally I couldn't bear the idea of them painting over it. I don't know what happened to it. I don't want to know because I still feel sad about it.

The fact remains that aside from the front door, the hallway is the first impression anyone's going to get of your home, and it would therefore be nice if the impression was positive. And yes, it's true that there are all sorts of things you can do to try and improve a narrow, busy hall situation if you have children and/or teenagers – clever storage, shoe racks (there are suggestions for these below), strict and tiresome rules that you can try to enforce about A Place For Each Thing And Each Thing In Its Place. You can stand there after school like you're the fun police, directing people to put their things away properly.

But do you know what? During these years, I think it's better to just embrace the chaos. You can't control everything, and you will feel much better if you just decide that your hall is going to be a bit of a mess. Because what is agonizing – for years on end! – is deciding that the hall must be neat, tidy and attractive, and then trying and failing, a dozen times a day, to succeed in making that happen. It grinds you down the moment you come down the stairs, the moment you come in from outside, and during many moments throughout the day and evening. It's not worth the stress.

If you accept the mess, you roll your eyes but you can let it go, because you've accepted that you have a messy hall. If you don't, you feel depressed/let down/cross every single time you set foot in it. The hall becomes the thing you've failed at, the thing that annoys you most about the house – and the first thing that you are seeing every time you come in or go out. It's enough to drive you mad. Give up on it, is my advice. Keep it clean, have a sweep of all the stuff every now and then, thin out the coats once winter is over, but just accept the fact that the hall is a bit of a disaster.

In houses as in life, it pays to pick your battles. I think that if you have to cede control of one area, the hall might as well be it (though it could also be another room). And listen: hard as it is to imagine when you are scooping up twenty-five pairs of shoes in a foul temper with dinner burning on the stove and setting off the smoke alarm, there are people out there who envy you your busy, cluttered hall and all its bits of crap. The crap is signs of life, of activity, of people and things happening. Compare it to a spotless hall where the ticking of a clock is the only audible thing, where dust motes are settling in silence and where the lone elderly occupier can think of nothing nicer than a visit from huge-footed teenagers bringing with them life and noise. Even if they do leave their shoes everywhere.

However: children do leave home eventually, and while this is a poignant moment in more respects than I can name, it does mean that the space – and the hall – becomes your own again. AT LAST! Now you really can work on the first impression you've wanted to create for so long. You can embrace serenity over chaos (you will miss the chaos once the space is serene – it's just one of those things of life, a lesson learned after the event, like in the Clive James poem 'Leçons des ténèbres', which contains the lines 'I should have been more kind. It is my fate/To find this out, but find it out too late').

HERE ARE SOME THINGS THAT WORK FOR ME:

Don't try to overcompensate for a dark hall by lighting it super brightly. Bright light is for big spaces, so it can bounce around at leisure. It doesn't quite work in small or narrow ones – it always feels off, and sometimes it can even emphasize the faintly claustrophobic nature of the space (halls tend to be on the poky side). You want to see well enough to find your keys, but you don't want a harsh unflattering light when you take a last look at yourself in the hall mirror.

Instead, create atmosphere with lighting. Wall lights are good – I like sconces – and so are small table lamps fitted with relatively dim bulbs (see page 42) if you can squeeze one or two in. These immediately create a relaxed atmosphere. A warm, dim light is really welcoming, whether it's first thing in the morning or when you come home from work: it's that glowing yellow light thing that so many of us associate with the word 'home'.

A table or shelf of some kind is always a good idea, whether it's a big table, a narrow console table, a wall shelf or a chest of drawers – whatever you can fit in without making the space feel squashed. My London hall 'shelf' was a piece of wood balanced on top of a radiator. Make this pretty, because it'll be the first thing people see.

My current hall table is a wide, deep, waist-high bookcase – one and a half shelves of books, the other half-shelf a space for my gardening bag (containing my hallowed Niwaki secateurs, twine, ties and so on) and a basket for packets of seeds I need to sow. On top of the bookcase are a table lamp, a jug of flowers, a big, flat ceramic plate where bills and uninteresting brown letters hang out and where things sit if they're waiting to be posted (a quaint concept these days, like saying 'and where I soak my petticoats'), a little stone dish for keys, a papier-mâché tomato I got in a car boot sale, and a small bowl with Santa Maria Novella pot pourri in it (recommended, it makes the whole house smell amazing in a natural and credible way). Above the bookcase is a painting. Past that, the space narrows into the hall proper. Which is fine because we have far fewer shoes lying about these days.

Now, halls are boring, but they do have the advantage of a lot of wall space. Depending on your personal taste, you might want to utilize it to display your less good art (because no one is going to stand in the hall and stare at it for hours). This can be very effective, whether we're talking cheap posters, oil paintings, photographs

HOME

or children's drawings – I will get to what 'art' means in this, or any context, later in this book, and talk about the importance of framing, which makes all the difference.

My own hall is hung floor to ceiling with a mixture of things in frames, but you don't need to go that far. You can of course leave the walls completely bare, but I think it's nice when halls give a taster of the house and sort of lure you in.

Speaking of luring: what we're doing next, rather like Scheherazade/Shahrazad, is making our home tell a story that is so enchanting and compelling that we'd be happy to stay in it for 1,001 nights. Which isn't very long at all, but I'm not going to let that spoil the analogy.

RECOMMENDATIONS

Some practical storage ideas for narrow hallways:

- **Go vertical**. If floor space is limited, as it inevitably is, wall-mount shoe cabinets (I have to say, these never had enough compartments for the kids' shoes and those of their visiting mates, but they're a start). Stacked-up shoe racks take up a lot of room. Wall-mounting them doesn't gobble up precious floor space. I like vintage pigeon-hole shelving or recycled sports-locker type mini-cabinets, but hundreds of different sorts exist at every price point.
- **Use hooks or wooden pegs** rather than bulky coat stands. You can get hooks that fold flat when not in use, i.e. that become flush with the wall (also meaning you won't snag on them). Paint these the same colour as the wall and they more or less disappear. Or make a feature of them, if they're handsome enough.
- **Have high shelves**, meaning above head height. These are good for storing out-of-season items like woolly hats, or other things you don't need daily access to (spare rolls of poo sacks for the dog, say). High shelves also make the space feel taller, which

is never a bad idea. Store the scarves and so on in something attractive and decorative, like pretty baskets, and suddenly you have an additional decorative feature that is actively nice to look at.
- **A very narrow floating shelf** is a handy thing for keys and mail.
- If you have a bit of spare floor space, **storage benches** hide a multitude of sins and you can sit on them to put on your shoes. I like them because in an emergency you can chuck everything inside and close the lid. Out of sight, temporarily out of mind, which is sometimes the best you can do.
- **A mirror** is a friend to halls, not just because you can check you haven't got jam on your face as you head out but because, in the right spot, they double the width of the hall.
- **IKEA picture ledges** are very very narrow shelves with a lip and are good for propping up pictures, in hallways and elsewhere.

FOUNDATION 2

STORYTELLING

Who wants a home that's like a blank page?

We've all been to houses that feel nicer, more comfortable, cosier to be in than others, just as we've all been to houses that make us sit up straight and feel far smarter and more impressive than ours. What's interesting is that the smarter houses – the sort of houses that make you feel like you're not a proper adult, even if you're actually really old – might make you feel envious and admiring for a bit, but it's the cosier houses that make you want to have another glass of wine and sit around until the early hours on sofas that have seen better days. The houses people congregate in are always the houses that feel the most like a home.

Houses need a vibe. And for a house to feel like a home, it needs to tell a story – the story of the person or people who live in it. When I go somewhere, I want to know exactly where I am. I want to feel whose world I'm in, and I want to learn something about the people who live there. If I know the people well, ideally I want to think, 'Of course their house is like this! It's just like them – Oh, and what's this interesting thing over here?' I want the house to be an extension of them. When that happens, I feel happy and comfortable: my friends, in their friendly house, full of things they love that reflect them back to me.

Here is something that is so important that I'm typing it in bold. **99% of life is made up of ordinary things.** Ordinary things – little, tiny, stupid everyday things – are what weave together and make up the fabric of our lives. Most of our happinesses are minuscule: a biscuit and a cup of tea, a sweet dog on the way to the shops, the first tulips of the year. Yes, of course enormous things happen too, and yes, of course there are dramas and triumphs and catastrophes, and they are memorable too, in both good and bad ways. But they're few and far between. The little ordinary things are what we encounter every day of life – all of us, everybody in this whole world. We mostly live in a succession of short stories, I think, rather than in one fat enormous novel – our lives are made up of lots of mini-stories stitched together into one volume.

So many stories! And so it breaks my heart when people think their own stories aren't interesting, or that their life is too quotidian or boring or small to put on display at home. Nothing could be further from the truth. First of all, your life is interesting to you, so why not surround yourself with pieces of it? Second of all, your life is fascinating to the people who love you – yes, even the dullest bits. Third of all, what are you even saying about your life if you hide it all away?

Houses need souls – the souls of the people who live in them. You know when you're moving house and there's nothing left to do except drop the keys off with the estate agent, and you go around the house one last time to see if anything's been left behind and to say goodbye to it? That is always the moment when you realize that it's not your house any more. It's no longer a home. It's just *a* house. Just some bricks and mortar. A carcass, to be bleak about it. Because the heart and soul went out of it the moment your possessions were loaded on to the removals van.

So what I really don't ever want is to feel like I'm in a strange, anodyne show home, no matter how lavishly appointed or professionally designed, and no matter how many boxes it ticks on paper. Being in a room that feels almost anonymous, like *anyone at all* could live there – friends, strangers, aliens, robots – makes me unsettled, as if all the people in the room at any given time could be replaced by a whole other lot of people and it wouldn't really make much difference. Those rooms aren't good. They have no vibe. If they could speak there would be no happy chatter of voices but rather a droning monotone. The story they told would send you to sleep. And when the owners moved out of it, it would feel much the same empty as it did furnished: soulless.

A room is only truly comfortable if the room feels *real*. Otherwise it's like sitting in a beautiful stage set, or like the room is wearing a costume. That's fine if your house is a Grade I listed masterpiece of which you are the latest in a long line of custodians, and the stage set aspect is kind of the point. But for the rest of us, interiors are like clothes: you could be talking to someone wearing the most exquisite, handmade, historically accurate fancy dress, but after a certain point you'd think, 'Do you want to take that off now, or do you not have any real clothes?' If a room feels like it's wearing a costume, you eventually start thinking, 'Why not just show me who you are?' And then the more you think about that and the more stubbornly the room persists in hiding its owner's true self, the stranger the situation becomes.

So rooms need stories. But people are scared of telling their story, because an awful lot of people don't trust their own taste, which we will come back to. Isn't it safer to just do as you're told, buy the things other people seem to like, keep things neutral, not frighten the horses, fantasize about one day being able to afford an interior designer to show the world who you are? (There are many good reasons for hiring an interior designer – not something I've ever done – but to me that is not one of them.)

The first thing to do when telling your story is to understand storytelling itself. The thing about stories – good ones, at any rate – is that they are messy. They veer off in all sorts of unexpected directions. They're full of quirks and twists and turns. They keep you intrigued. What irks me about boring, bland domestic interiors is that they tell boring, bland stories, like a child learning to write: 'I got up and then I brushed my teeth and then I had breakfast and I went to school.' It just about understands the assignment, but it's dutiful and ploddy.

We are adults. We have lived. We either have or are capable of inventing better stories – as does that poor child, who probably longed to write, 'I woke up and cuddled Hester, my hippo teddy. She smells of biscuits and she has a blue dress. I like her ears because they are really soft. When I was a baby I chewed the left one to go to sleep.' That is the story I want! I want to know about the ears! Or rather, I want its grown-up equivalent. I want to know that you love Morocco, hence the pottery candlesticks; and knitted granny squares, hence the throw; and that you are partial to muddy green colours; not too fussed about a bit of dust; that every autumn you peel the casing from the dried honesty in the garden and stick the results in a jug.

Or I want to know that you are sophisticated enough to appreciate the beauty of a lone sculptural vase on a pristine and unadorned surface; that white on white on white floats your boat; that what you love is airiness and space. Or that you really love pigs, as reflected in your mugs, your teapot, your tea towel and that enormous papier-mâché creation in the sitting room. All these things tell me valuable things about you – things that, as your old friend or recent acquaintance, I am interested in, because I am interested in *you*.

Stories are, by definition, at least partly an act of imagination. What this means for us, in this context, is that your story can be straightforwardly autobiographical if you like, but it can also include inventions – flights of fancy. All good interiors tell made-up stories. Without stories, there would be no French farmhouse kitchens, no cottagecore, nothing industrial, no California chic, no traditional Posh English style, nothing mid-century modern (to say nothing of Japanese or Scandinavian aesthetics – and the rest: it's a long list).

Your story can be anything you like because you're the one writing it. As its author, you can make use of what you already know, and make some other bits up wholesale.

The thing to do with telling a story is to put yourself in it, to narrate it. That way, you tell the story, rather than the story telling you. Here is what I mean.

FOUNDATION 2: STORYTELLING

Say, for the sake of example, that you have always wanted a farmhouse-style kitchen, even though you live on the seventh floor of an apartment block. That you are not actually a farmer poses no obstacle. In with the scrubbed wooden table, in with some iteration of a Welsh dresser, even if it's only some shelves on the worktop prettily arranged with mismatched china. In with something approaching a range cooker or Aga. A butler sink, daffodils in a rustic jug on the table, maybe a rug under it – you get the picture. Your story has summoned up the feeling of the farmyard. But you wouldn't now buy so wholeheartedly into the look you'd created that you'd start to wear a gingham pinny and spend your afternoon baking pies in between resuscitating newborn lambs. In the same way, detaching yourself completely from the realities of your lambless twenty-first-century life would turn your lovely kitchen into a parody of itself, a tribute act. We want a story, but not a fairytale (or a room set from the Museum of Rural Life). So always remember to let your real life in. In this setting, a state-of-the-art coffee machine might be more jarring than a stovetop whistling kettle; a rustic straw broom might look more in keeping than the cordless vacuum cleaner propped up against the fridge, but go with the coffee machine and the vacuum anyway. They are real and they are what brings authenticity.

THE KITCHEN: PART 1

All human life is here – and all human feeling

I can't say this without resorting to cliché, I'm afraid, because the kitchen really *is* the heart of the home: the place where people want to linger, the place where everyone spontaneously congregates, the best place for chatting, the place that feels warmest – both literally and figuratively – nurturing and hopeful. If rooms were expressions of emotion – which they are, to me – the kitchen would be a hug. It's the best place to feel happy in, and the best place to cry in (having tea nearby helps).

Kitchens are so full of promise. They are a place of safety – a refuge from the drearier or more agitating aspects of life – and a place of fun, of parties, of big, long weekend lunches and intimate dinners *à deux*, of high chairs, mashed banana and fish fingers and of gatherings with family and friends. They are for celebrating and commiserating and everything in between. This is as true of too many people squashed into a galley kitchen as it is of a larger, roomier space.

I sometimes feel that I've lived my entire life in kitchens, not because I am always cooking – though I do cook quite a lot – but because it's always where, given the choice, I choose to hang out (and where I'm writing this from, as it happens, even though there's a far more comfortable and ergonomic chair at my actual desk). I've lost track of the number of books I've written at the kitchen table.

For several years before I had a desk, it was the only table that was the right height – but that's not the real reason. The real reason is that kitchens are my habitat, the place where I feel most myself. A kitchen is essence of home, and also essence of me. And of you, I'll bet. It is a rare person that feels differently, unless they really hate food (imagine!).

Given all this, there are few things I like less than a sterile kitchen that feels like a lab (-oratory rather than -brador – though -brador if I had to choose). To me, if the kitchen is everyone's favourite room in the house, then it should feel like it. It should feel like the favourite room *because* of how it looks, not despite it.

And yet so many people strive to eradicate the warmth and comfortingness of kitchens by placing their emphases on efficiency and spotlessness, all evidence of life hidden away in a cupboard.

Why is this? It feels so un-modern. I think we, or rather our grandmothers and great-grandmothers, were presented with a blueprint of what a kitchen should look like at some point roughly midway through the twentieth century, and have never deviated from it or questioned why that particular 'vision' was one to stick with for the next hundred years. Obviously the mid twentieth century was a time of progress – all those white goods and brand-new stand mixers! – and also a time where being a fragrant housewife involved keeping things looking pristine, from the worktops to one's lipstick. If you were 'house proud', your kitchen was spotless. If your kitchen was not spotless, then you were somehow a slattern, a failure at being a woman, because you were incapable of imposing order on the domestic sphere. We've got past some of that in terms of how we live our lives, but not so much in terms of what we think kitchens should look and *be* like. Walk into a kitchen that looks like a bomb's gone off, and you – we – still make a quick judgement on the person in it.

Nowhere is women's fear of seeming slovenly or sluttish (in the old-fashioned sense of dirty and unkempt) better expressed than in their attitude to kitchens and hygiene. Now, obviously, I am in favour of hygienic environments – who isn't? But it's important to be able to tell the difference between dirt, ordinary life detritus and the welcome decoration provided by, say, a particularly handsome tin of biscuits. Only one of these needs to be removed in the name of 'tidying'.

In our panicked bowing down to the great god Hygiene, our kitchens have become so wildly over-clean, so ritually scrubbed and sprayed and drenched in anti-bacterial this or that, that our children literally fall ill or develop allergies at the merest sighting of a germ or bit of dirt. This is not sane, and nor, in this age of terrifying antibiotic resistance, is it a kindness to them. Being so over-assiduous when it comes to hygiene that it ends up weakening the immune systems of those we love is the very opposite of healthy. So that's the first thing: we all need to relax about keeping the space so pristine that we could eat our dinner off the floor or countertops. What's the point of that, when we have a table and chairs? Nobody's expected to eat off anything other than a plate.

Whatever your tastes in interiors, your kitchen should feel alive, lived in, occupied. Since it feels special simply by virtue of being a kitchen, it has a head start on the other rooms in the house. For me, creating a sense of aliveness, of a room that lives and breathes – in the kitchen or otherwise – starts with chilling out a bit about the ordinary mess of life. Also, if you have just had a longed-for, brand-new kitchen installed – congratulations! – bear in mind that a spanking new kitchen can sometimes make the space feel a bit like a show house, or indeed a showroom. Unless that is specifically the look you are going for, in which case fair dinkum, you might want to rough it up a bit, figuratively speaking, so that it doesn't look like Grace Kelly in a twinset and pearls at a rave. There are lots of ideas for how to do this coming up next.

I think kitchens should, in so far as is possible, be decorated like any other room in the house. How you do that depends on your taste: obviously if all the rooms in your house are white, spotless and free of anything more than the most minimal decoration, then your kitchen will fit right in, and that's great. For many of us, though, a super-bare, super-tidy kitchen will feel jarring when compared to the other rooms we inhabit, which probably have more life and atmosphere in them. Poor kitchen! It *wants* to be warm and inviting, but sometimes we don't let it. (This is the sad fate of rooms with very specific designated uses – see also bathrooms.)

I *really* let it. My kitchen has rugs, books, table lamps, paintings and a squashy armchair – I wish it were a sofa, but I can't fit one in. It has mismatched crockery on open shelves, cutlery in open jars and food on display front and centre. My kitchen table – a long, scrubbed farmhouse table, on the basis that these never date and look better the older and more bashed they get, not something that could ever be said of the modern alternatives – has on it a jumble of candlesticks, several fruit and vegetable bowls, this morning's newspapers, a little stack of cookbooks, a large bunch of flowers in a vase, and whatever the day's requirements bring: today it's a set of headphones, my laptop and the novel I'm reading. And no, the general effect is not one of pristine tidiness. That's why I love it so much.

HOW TO MAKE A KITCHEN FEEL JOYFUL

- Treat the kitchen like any other room in the house. If yours is anything like mine, it's the most used and the most lived-in. The feel of the room should reflect that.

- Lighting is the most important thing in *every single room*. You can't have only one source of light because the room will look flat, overlit, unwelcoming and dreadful – a particular disaster in a kitchen. You always need layers, i.e. different sorts of lighting at different heights. In the kitchen, table lamps on the worktop instantly bring atmosphere and cosiness. Don't immediately kill it by using a super-white bulb! See page 41 for more on lighting and for an in-depth explanation of bulb temperatures, and page 112 for more on layering generally. I have several table lamps in my kitchen and only use the overhead spotlights if

I'm chopping things or paying forensically close attention to whatever is on the hob.

- Those wretched overhead spotlights unfortunately come as standard in most kitchens. They are incredibly unflattering, both to the room and to any humans unfortunate enough to be seated under one. The trick is to put them on a dimmer – any electrician can do this for you – and to then, crucially, buy dimmable bulbs for them (otherwise they'll make a weird buzzy noise) in a warm colour temperature – see page 42. Warm, dimmable bulbs are a revelation if you're stuck with spotlights anywhere in the house. They force the dreaded spotlights to give out a cosy – sexy, even – and intimate glow.

- Candles immediately create intimacy. I have dinner by candlelight every night, even if I am by myself eating instant ramen. I know – it sounds slightly mad, but I can't tell you how lovely it is. It's instantly peaceful. Relaxing, too, because candlelight forces you to unwind, whether you want to or not. If you work from home, as I do, it also very clearly demarcates the end of the working day. Sometimes in the absolute depths of winter, we have candles at breakfast, which I also strongly recommend. The only problem with candlelit brekkers is that it's really not conducive to rinsing your mugs, cracking your knuckles, snapping your heels and briskly getting on with the day's tasks. It makes you want to go back to bed. Best at weekends, maybe.

- Kitchens love rugs. Depending on the number of messy people/children/pets you have, you might want to consider something washable (though I haven't yet met a stain that can match the powers of neat Fairy Liquid). Washable rugs are not created equal. My own favourites are below.

- Don't hide all your food away. Generous bowls of fruits and vegetables look beautiful on the kitchen table and have the tremendous advantage of reminding you of what you need to eat before it's past its prime. Before I put my greens on display, cabbages and kale leaves would die a slow death in the crisper drawer of the fridge. Now I have them where I can see them – and admire their beauty – I eat them when they're still perky.

- I also keep longer-lasting fruit and veg, like lemons, onions and garlic, in wooden bowls, and keep them near the chopping boards. Obviously this depends on how much worktop space you have, but decorating with vegetables is cheap and practical, as well as highly effective. See page 79 for more on this in a table-dressing context.

- You don't need to hide your crockery away either. Mine is on open shelving, immediately to hand. It's also a visual reminder that this is a place of conviviality and pleasure. I have stacks of serving platters and dishes on the sideboard – not only are they nice to look at, but it saves me from ferreting about in cupboards once dinner is ready.

- A kitchen is a good place for living things, be they herbs on the windowsill, a bunch of flowers, house plants, or all three.

- I really love open shelves with displays of rice, pasta, spices, etc. on them, decanted into glass jars, or whatever kind of jar you like. Again, the impression is convivial and generous, plus it's easier for the cook to have everything to hand.

- On cabinetry: having chunky, rectangular cabinets both above and below your worktop takes up a lot of visual space. We all have to work with what we have, but if you're installing a new kitchen, consider having cupboards below and open shelves above. Yes, dust. But also yes, airiness and beauty.

- Obviously you can't have *everything* on display. There's just one rule here: if it's ugly but necessary (some non-daily-use appliances, mostly, and the more battered pans) it goes in a cupboard; if it's nice to look at and friendly-seeming, it stays out, whether it's a toaster, a teapot or a handsome pan that lives

THE KITCHEN: PART I

permanently on the hob. This is contrary to what a lot of people do, which is have hideous black plastic appliances permanently on show and the lovely things – the dishes, plates, mugs and glassware – hidden away. Wrong way round!

- On pans: buy, for example, one handsome, fancy cast-iron one from a normal shop, a charity shop or eBay, and buy all the other more workaday pans from a catering equipment shop like Nisbets. Great pans – designed to be used commercially, so very robust – at great prices.

- On appliances: if you use something all the time – a food processor, say – it is really worth seeking out one that is aesthetically pleasing. This is why people so love KitchenAid stand mixers: it's not necessarily because they're obsessive bakers, but because they look so nice out on the counter. Apply the same principle to anything that has to live there, not just food processors but kettles, toasters and the like. Even microwaves can be relatively attractive (see below).

- Consider soft furnishings. Most of us don't have the space for a giant sofa in the kitchen, more's the pity, but the right blinds or curtains have a wonderful softening effect on a room and can take it from overly functional or overly clinical to something more relaxed and comfortable-feeling. This applies to anything fabric-related, down to tea towels and oven gloves. You can create a whole mood with little bits of soft furnishings.

- You can also create a whole mood by paying attention to tiny things like spoons and containers.

- As ever, textures matter, as does the interplay of textures (see page 129). If you have a modern, slightly wipe-clean-looking fitted kitchen that you don't especially like but can't afford to replace, detract from the cabinetry by adding accessories in contrasting textures. Wood is your friend here, because it is an immediately warm, tactile material that can detract effectively from a sea of rectangular cabinets. Add table lamps, candles and lots of interesting things for the eye to land on and the unlovely units recede as if by magic. You can go mad here: sheepskins on chairs, fabric lampshades – anything that is more pleasing to look at than an unbroken row of kitchen units. Even linen tea towels have a softening effect.

- The less you like your kitchen – your actual kitchen, i.e. your kitchen cabinetry – the more the sorts of accessories described above will help. Fill those worktops! Decorate that table! Don't let the units dominate, even if they unavoidably do in terms of the space they occupy. Give people – and yourself – something else to look at, and they will look at it.

- Take the doors off a couple of the lower units and put a fabric curtain there instead. Not only does this break up that blocky 'too many units in a row' feeling but it adds instant cosiness. The curtain can be anything from something reminiscent of Brambly Hedge to something neat and modern. It's also a good way of introducing pattern in a room that is often composed of large blocks of colour, again because of the units.

- Colour is really important. Go for something warm on the walls, is always my advice, since the whole point of kitchens is warmth.

- If you hate your kitchen cabinets (we've all been there), don't paint the room in a sharply contrasting colour – it will only make them stick out more. Go for something complementary instead: a rich cream if they are white, perhaps, or something dark and foresty if they are black. Dark paint can be incredibly effective in kitchens, though obviously they're never going to look particularly sunny and summery. But they *will* look like places you want to hunker down in.

- You can paint any surface, including cabinetry. The brand you want is called Zinsser. They make a variety of primers to suit any non-paintable-seeming surface, down to UPVC window frames. Apply normal eggshell once the surface is primed, or a kitchen-specific paint that's been formulated to resist scuffs.

- In a rental, don't discount peel-and-stick (removable) wallpaper or vinyl wrap for units. These can both look fantastic – it's down to really careful application.

- If there is a table and it is ugly, put a tablecloth on it. Now it is beautiful!

- It's really easy to change kitchen door furniture and it makes a surprisingly big difference. Handles and drawer knobs can be the things that make a kitchen feel dated. Often you find that the units themselves are fine, being fairly anodyne, but that it's these other bits that age your kitchen in an unwelcome way. Swap them out. If you're in a rental, it's easy to swap the old ones back in when you leave.

- If the kitchen feels too modern for your taste, add vintage. If it feels too vintage, add modern elements.

- Art is a wonderful way of making any room feel loved and comfortable, and that also applies to art in the kitchen. Don't put anything too near the cooker or sink, obviously, in case it gets splashed, and don't put your most precious painting within reach of clumsy people carrying soup. My kitchen is junk-shop finds only.

RECOMMENDATIONS

Some good suppliers for kitchen decorating:

- **Washable rugs: Weaver Green**, weavergreen.com, make wonderful, thick, well-designed woven rugs out of recycled plastic bottles. They feel like wool – soft, warm and springy underfoot and lovely on bare toes – and are a luxe experience. They are not inexpensive, but in my (considerable) experience as well as being indestructible they are the best quality and the most beautiful. Many options, from patterned kelims to stripes to plains. They wash like a dream and are smart enough for any room in the house. Bonus: you can drag them outside on a sunny day. **Ruggable** have cornered their side of the market. These are much thinner rugs that adhere to a sticky layer – only the top rug bit gets washed. They've improved their designs a lot recently and are worth a look. The patterns are printed on rather than woven. **La Redoute**, laredoute.co.uk, have a ton of attractive washable rugs at a keen price point.

– **The Braided Rug Company**, braided-rug.co.uk, sell individually made Appalachian braided rugs that are cosiness in rug form. I have one by my cooker – they are very, very hard-wearing, hide stains brilliantly but are also machine washable on a cool wash with very little detergent.

– **Flatwoven jute** is a good material for kitchens too. You can't wash it, but it's really robust and I find a squirt of Vanish gets rid of even spilled tomato sauce. Widely available, including from **Dunelm** and **John Lewis**, but my own two favourite sources are **Maison Bengal**, maisonbengal.co.uk (who supply many a smart retailer – buy directly from them and swerve the markup) and **The Braided Rug Company**, as above, for their lovely coloured versions. **IKEA**'s Lohals jute rug is classic for a reason – it's all over my house – and **Nordic Knots**, nordicknots.com – my top recommendation for every kind of non-vintage rug – make jute rugs of utter perfection.

– **Reasonably attractive microwaves, kettles, toasters**: **Haden**, haden.com, are good for all three. I also like microwaves from **Sage** and **Russell Hobbs**, specifically their retro-but-not-too-much Scandi Compact model. Nice kettles from **Kitchen Aid**, **Dualit**, **Dunelm** (the Contemporary model comes in a lovely ochre colour, with a wooden handle; **Next** do a similar one called Bronx), **Salter** (via Amazon) and **Swan**. These brands

also all make appealing toasters, though see page 61 for a note on toaster ovens.
- **Good tea towel brands: Charvet** (posh but everlasting), **Ulster Weavers, The Linen Works**, and the excellent tea towel offering at **Nisbets**, nisbets.co.uk, and other professional catering stores.

FOUNDATION 3

LIGHTING

Lighting is EVERYTHING. Nothing, not even paint, changes the feel of a room better or quicker. If you're after instant cosiness, it's all in the lighting. I can't bear light that isn't warm, particularly in a sitting room. There is no faster shortcut to the sort of gloomy-ass room you never want to hang out in. It could be the most beautifully put together room in the world, but bad lighting undoes all the good work.

As I wrote in the introduction, I vividly remember walking home from school in deep winter and the houses I passed having that very inviting yellow glow. I still love to see it as an adult, especially in cities in the rain near Christmas. But you have to work harder at achieving the yellow glow these days because obviously those were filament bulbs, and we live in an LED world.

For that perfect kind of warm light, you need the right bulb. I go for amber, as dim as possible, but here I feel obliged to tell you that in winter my house is then so cosily, sexily lit, like some sort of rustic speakeasy, that *I can't actually see to read* and need to use discreet, additional reading lamps. The lighting situation is aesthetically heaven but incredibly impractical – a normal person might be happier with something marginally less extreme.

For me, the colour temperature of the bulb needs to be between 2000K and 2800K, absolute max. My personal sweet spot is 2200K, bearing in mind I like it *extremely* warm. Anything of 3000K and over (still considered 'warm white' by some retailers, even though this is a barefaced lie) says dental surgery to me. Here is an explanation of how colour temperature works:

Colour temperature in lightbulbs refers to how 'warm' or 'cool' the light appears to our eyes. It's measured in Kelvin (K). The higher the number, the cooler and bluer the light. Therefore, obviously, the lower the number, the warmer and more yellow/orange the light.

Warm light (technically 2000K–3000K, though as noted this is a terrible lie)
- At the lower end, appears yellowish or orange, similar to candlelight or sunset/golden hour.
- Creates a cosy, relaxing atmosphere.
- Common in living rooms, bedrooms and restaurants.
- At the lower end, the most like the soft glow of traditional incandescent bulbs.

Neutral light (3500K–4100K)
- Allegedly balanced white light.
- Good for kitchens, workspaces and bathrooms.
- Provides good visibility without being harsh – again, allegedly. I find this range blinding.

Cool light (5000K–6500K). Yeah, I wouldn't unless you do at-home dentistry
- Appears bluish-white, is meant to be similar to daylight on a clear day, even though I've never thought of daylight as being bluish-white.
- Good for detailed tasks, reading and workspaces.

The cosier you need the room to be, the lower the K rating you should go for. If you need really bright light, go for the higher end. Also, don't get confused by the way the Kelvin scale seems back to front, with the higher numbers giving a cooler, bluer light and lower numbers giving warmer yellow light. (It comes from physics: when

FOUNDATION 3: LIGHTING

heating metal, it first glows red – lower temperature, then white, then blue – higher temperature).

A NOTE ON SPOTLIGHTS

The boring need-to-know detail here is that the angle of the beam is relevant – the smaller the number, the narrower the beam. So if you want the light to shine only on your chopping board, for example, you can get away with a narrower beam, say 10 degrees, than if you need the bulb to illuminate a wider area, in which case obviously go for a higher number. Zico bulbs, as used in various very luxe hotels and venues, are the crème de la crème of lightbulbs. (You're either reading this going 'what on earth is she on about, my lightbulbs are perfectly fine' or you are weeping with gratitude.)

One last thing: white plastic switches are not beautiful and stick out if the rest of the room has clearly been put together thoughtfully. You can get all sorts of alternatives, from see-through ones (good on wallpaper as they don't break up the pattern) to brass ones to black ones, and so on. There will be a switch that is right for your interior – one that complements it rather than jars. While I'm at it, the extension cables we all rely on all the time if we live in an older house with insufficient sockets are not beautiful either: no one really needs thick white plastic snaking across a room. But you can now buy beautiful extension leads made of woven fabric cord in every colour under the sun. Being actively attractive, they are a game changer.

RECOMMENDATIONS

- **Fabric extension leads: Lola's Leads**, lolasleads.co.uk. See also **Dowsing & Reynolds**, dowsingandreynolds.com, and **Caradok**, caradok.co.uk
- **Fabric cable: Urban Cottage Industries**, urbancottageindustries.com.

- **Handsome wall switches in brass, etc.: Jim Lawrence**, jim-lawrence.co.uk, **Pooky**, pooky.com, **Dowsing & Reynolds**, as above, **Corston Architectural Detail**, corston.com, and **B&Q** for brass effect.
- **The best lightbulbs for atmosphere if you are as fussy as me**: **Zico**, zico.lighting. The bulbs cost a fortune but come with a three-year guarantee.

THE KITCHEN: PART 2

Eating

My paternal grandmother was Belgian, a keen eater – like I say, Belgian – but not a cook. She'd never learned because her family was rich and didn't do their own cooking. Her father, my great-grandfather, owned what became the largest wallpaper factory in Europe (in 1921 it employed a young René Magritte as a graphic designer).

In 1979 the factory, which had always provided the family with a lavish income, went bankrupt. My grandmother, unlike her four sisters, had married a not-rich working-class man – a bookish, extremely good-looking soldier who she'd met during the war (objective opinion. That my grandpa looked like Adonis is a fact of life). By the time of the bankruptcy, he had a whole chestful of medals and an army pension, and that was it.

If this were a novel, after the initial shock of the money being gone my grandmother would dry her eyes and stiffen her spine. She would go into the kitchen (in those Ferragamo shoes with the grosgrain bow) after decades of barely setting foot in it. She'd peer around curiously. She'd open the unfamiliar cupboards and hold up, say, a whisk, with a puzzled look on her face.

And then, slowly, egg by egg, she would find not just herself but her true calling. Within a year or two she would be producing absolute feasts. Word would spread far and wide. Her dinners would become legendary. And then . . . Maybe a little bistro? Maybe two or three? Maybe a chain of them! Family finances restored, daughter of privilege morally redeemed through hard work, many lessons learned, narrative arc completed, et voilà.

This is not what happened.

She mourned the loss of her fortune intensely and at length, and the fact that my grandfather was not materially minded became a constant irritation. She was never at home in the kitchen, and remained completely inept at cooking – she could slice the saucisson and cube the cheese to have with drinks, but that was it. She was, she said, too old to learn.

Her remaining asset was the apartment she and my grandpa lived in. She sold half of it and they squashed up and lived off the proceeds, in much reduced circumstances but hardly destitute. She re-hired her old cook, Anny of blessed memory, one day a week. This was Wednesday, a half day at school, when Anny would make a huge lunch for all of us children and grandchildren – always roast chicken, frites, the most delicious dark brown chicken sauce (but thin and intense, not like gravy), green salad, cheese, tarte aux pommes – still my platonic ideal of a perfect meal.

On the other days, my newly frugal granny went shopping for food, very locally, with her basket. After moving to London – which Anny had warned against because English people ate jam with meat – I still regularly went to Brussels to stay with my grandmother, whom I loved passionately, until her death in my twenties. We always ate like kings – because of the shopping.

She became really, really good at buying food. She was picky. She asked to try things. She was happy to trot about – here for the lemon tartlets (they said Citron on them in thin chocolate italics), but here for the baguette. She didn't go anywhere smart. The grocer across the road, who had hair like Tintin, sold good butter, good coffee, excellent vegetables. He had a small display of ready-made things – vegetables à la Grecque, glazed baby onions, mushrooms in olive oil – and his wife made a couple of pâtés every week.

THE KITCHEN: PART 2

The fish shop had ready-made coquilles St Jacques au gratin, among a ton of other things. The butcher had big, fat stuffed tomatoes that only needed to go in the oven, and hachis Parmentier, like a more refined cottage pie, and always waterzooi, a delicious kind of Belgian chicken stew. And so on and so forth. All this before she even got to the proper *traiteur*.

Can't cook? Hate cooking? Judicious shopping is the answer. Actually, it's part 1 of the answer. Part 2 is feeling no embarrassment about not cooking. It doesn't matter. What matters is giving people nice things to eat. Who cares who made the things? Cooking is of course great, but there is an almost equivalent skill in shopping well for food.

Now, obviously, the food culture of Belgium and France was at the time – and largely remains – completely different to the food culture of the UK. *Traiteurs*, shops selling only ready-made food, have existed since the eighteenth century. After we moved to London and I went to see my Belgian family in the school holidays, my mother would send me to Wittamer in the place du Sablon to bring back a couple of quiches Lorraines. Unlike my granny, my mother is an excellent cook but I can't tell you the reverence and ecstasy with which those quiches were greeted and eaten (I feel the same way about the chef and cookery writer Sally Clarke's tarts. Sometimes I gingerly transport them from Westbourne Grove to rural Suffolk as if they were treasure, which they are).

Before I got okay at cooking, I'd cross London to buy two of these, make a salad and call it a dinner party. Perfect meal. Growing up, there was absolutely zero shame attached to producing a lunch or dinner that has been entirely bought in, though you'd be expected to make a decent green salad. In my entire Belgian life, I don't remember a single one of my great-aunts, aunts or cousins ever serving a home-made pudding – why would you, when pâtisseries existed and charged fair prices? The two coastal great-aunts who split their time between Brussels and the seaside produced endless unbelievably delicious croquettes aux crevettes (number two platonic ideal, with deep-fried parsley on the side) that they bought from the fishmonger and reheated at home. On Christmas Eve and New Year's Eve everyone served lobsters and home-made mayonnaise. Literally no cooking whatsoever. Lobsters aside, none of this food was expensive. Sure, some *traiteurs* were grander and smarter than others – but most were just normal, frequented by ordinary people on their way home from work.

No one cooked if they didn't want to – and everyone who came round had a lovely time and went home feeling they'd eaten wonderfully well. The idea that anyone would sniff disapprovingly and mouth 'shop-bought' would have struck people as hilariously mad, and yet some people do still sniff in the UK. I always thought this at school bake sales when my children were little – like, I'm busy, I work, I'm tired enough, why would you sneer at a perfect lemon drizzle from a shop when my own lemon drizzle would be significantly inferior? You don't get extra points for sending your child to class in a home-sewn uniform. Why would you over cake?

Sometimes, especially in summer, everything we eat has been bought from a shop, ready to unwrap and eat. I buy cheese, bread or crackers, smoked fish, anchovies, and pick salad from the garden. I buy chicken turnovers, sausage rolls, olives, mozzarella (to have with tomatoes) and Greek yogurt. I buy thinly sliced salami to put in a baguette with a slab of butter, this being my favourite sandwich in the world.

On the other hand, I love cooking. Whether you do too, or whether it is your idea of hell, or whether you are somewhere in between – for me the hellish part came in the years when I had to produce breakfast, packed lunch, child tea and adult dinner, year in, year out, every single fricking day – I want to share a handful of recipes with you. Why?

Because they are dishes I have cooked for eons and are still the ones I turn to on autopilot when I have to feed people and my mind is a blank. They are easy, unbelievably delicious, and I honestly think I'll still be making them when I am a really old lady. To me – and I think to my now-adult children – they are still what home tastes like.

THE KITCHEN: PART 2

A really good roast chicken that isn't just roast chicken

This is my adaptation, barely tweaked, of a Diana Henry recipe that appears online and in her brilliant book *From the Oven to the Table*. It is a fantastic recipe for any occasion, including having people over – not only because it is amazingly delicious and amazingly easy, not only because it tastes unusual enough to feel special, but also because all you need on the side is a green salad. Have it *à deux* and feast on the leftovers, have it with friends, have it for celebrations – it works every time and in every context. I'd be happy to have this for Christmas lunch, if one of my kids wasn't so obsessively attached to roast turkey. You can riff on it – I also make a version with lemon zest and fresh thyme instead of tomatoes and oregano.

- 1 big chicken, the best you can afford, weighing about 1.8kg
- 1 packet of feta cheese, roughly crumbled
- 2–3 ripe tomatoes, roughly chopped, or 3 torn plum tomatoes from a tin
- 75g or about one medium slice, coarse country bread or sourdough, torn roughly into chunks, crust included
- 4 tablespoons extra virgin olive oil
- 2 fat garlic cloves or 3 smaller ones, finely grated
- 3 teaspoons dried oregano
- ½ teaspoon, more if you like heat, cayenne pepper
- 225g orzo
- 500ml boiling chicken stock (from a cube or pod is fine)
- a few sprigs of chopped parsley

Preheat the oven to 200°C/180°C fan/gas mark 6. Put the chicken into a large oven dish. Mix the feta, tomatoes and bread with the olive oil, half the grated garlic, 1½ teaspoons of dried oregano and some salt and pepper in a bowl. Stuff this into the chicken cavity, really packing it in.

Rub the chicken – breast and legs – with the cayenne and sprinkle with the rest of the dried oregano, then season it with salt and pepper and drizzle it with olive oil.

Roast in the oven for 50 minutes.

After 50 minutes, sprinkle the orzo around the chicken and pour on the boiling chicken stock. Return to the oven for 20 minutes. Check during this time to make sure the orzo isn't becoming dry: there should be enough stock in it, but top it up with a little boiling water if it's needed.

Check the chicken is cooked by piercing it between the leg and body – the juices that run out should be clear.

Stir the chopped fresh parsley into the orzo and serve the chicken straight from the dish.

My puttanesca recipe

Please forgive the charmless bragging, but I make the best puttanesca I've eaten in my life. This is not a claim I make lightly, and I certainly don't make it about anything else I cook. But I make it like this because I find other puttanescas boringly timid and underpowered. The dish is supposed to be spirited and punchy. It's not supposed to be *polite*. It's the sort of thing you eat with kitchen roll to hand, not napkins. It's very good if a group of you come back hungry from somewhere; it's excellent at a normal time of day if there's nothing in the fridge; and it's the perfect thing to eat in bed at 2am in the early (or late!) stages of a relationship.

The point is, it's an adult dish, full-bodied and ripe. It's not an ingénue. It should taste a bit unruly, and mine does. The other thing I love about it is that it tastes of summer even in the depths of winter, but not in a jarringly weird way, so unlike e.g. anything that requires fresh basil in January. I should also say that one of my children, who claims to 'hate' anchovies, invariably has thirds of this.

THE KITCHEN: PART 2

For 4 people with normal appetites

Fill an enormous pan with water. The bigger the better – like all of us, pasta needs room to express itself in. Add some salt, but not as much as you'd usually use because anchovies are salty. Put that pan on a high heat.

Put a shallow, wide pan – any kind of deep frying pan, skillet or shallow round casserole – on a medium heat on another burner. Add a glug of olive oil.

Slice 2 fat cloves of garlic.

When the shallow pan is hot, add the garlic and stir. Give it 30 seconds and then tip in 1 whole can or glass jar of anchovy fillets in olive oil – the whole contents, including its oil. Stir so it's not sitting there in a clump.

Add a pinch or two of chilli flakes. I don't know how hot your particular chilli flakes are, but you do. Add enough for the heat to make itself felt.

The anchovies will quickly start dissolving. The garlic and chilli will sizzle. Give it all a stir again.

Once the anchovies have dissolved (moments), add a 400g can of best-quality chopped tomatoes, or whole tinned tomatoes that you crush through your fingers as you put them in, and stir that in. Then get the empty tomato tin, three-quarters fill it with water, and add that too.

When the pasta water starts boiling, add 500g of spaghetti, bending it round with a wooden spoon so no bits stick out.

To the shallow pan, add a generous tablespoon (or two – I love capers) of capers and as many pitted black olives (halved if you want) as you like, drained if they're in brine.

The sauce will look watery but will quickly thicken. If it starts looking too thick before the pasta is done, take it off the heat.

When the pasta is cooked, fish it out with tongs and swirl it straight into the pan of sauce. The water clinging to the strands is the sauce's friend, so don't worry about it. Toss very well (the olives will try to migrate to the bottom).

Dish up and eat, with Parmesan to grate on the side.

PS If the pasta is ready before the sauce, just drain it and leave it sitting in the colander for a couple of minutes while the sauce thickens (turn it up if needs be to hurry it along) before adding it.

Steamed fish and greens

Cooking fish freaks people out, but it's affordable, sustainable and really good for you. It also cooks in minutes. Depending on the flavourings you use, you can take it in any direction you like – make it classic, make it East Asian, make it South Asian: it is incredibly versatile. It can taste either pure and wholesome, or luxurious and decadent. I love fish. What a sentence to write – but I do!

Buy some firm to medium-firm white fish fillets, such as sustainably fished cod, haddock, coley, pollock, sea bass, bream or plaice. You want them all roughly the same weight, 150–180g, and of a similar thickness. This is so they all cook at the same time.

Now you have two really easy options.

To pan fry: Pat the fillets dry with kitchen paper to help them go brown and slightly crispy when they cook. Season them on both sides with salt and pepper. Heat a non-stick or well-seasoned pan on medium-high. Add a couple of tablespoons of neutral oil (like sunflower). It's hot enough when it starts shimmering.

Add the fish to the pan (don't crowd the pan – do it in batches if necessary), skin side down. Cook for 3–5 minutes, depending on thickness. Observe the fish: the edges will turn opaque. Flip tenderly and give them 2–4 minutes (depending on thickness) on the other side. Before the fish is quite done, add a generous knob of butter. When it starts to foam, spoon it over the fish. You're done. You could sprinkle it with chopped parsley and squeeze lemon juice over it at the table.

For East Asian flavours: Add 1–2 cloves of sliced garlic and a few thin slices of fresh ginger to the hot oil for about 30 seconds before adding the fish (be careful not to burn the garlic). After cooking, drizzle the fish with a little soy sauce and a few drops of sesame oil, then scatter over some chopped or shredded spring onions.

For South Asian flavours: As well as just salt and pepper, season the patted-dry fish with ½ teaspoon of ground turmeric, ½ teaspoon of ground cumin and a pinch of chilli powder before frying. After cooking, squeeze over fresh lemon or lime juice and garnish with chopped coriander.

To roast/bake (easier when cooking for more people):
Preheat the oven to 200°C/180°C fan/gas mark 6.
Pat your fish dry, as above. Put the fillets on a lightly oiled baking sheet or in an ovenproof dish. Drizzle with olive oil and season with salt and pepper. For a classic European version, top with lemon slices, garlic slices and fresh herbs (thyme/rosemary/dill).
For an East Asian vibe, sit the fish on slices of ginger, and drizzle with sesame oil and a touch of soy sauce. Or use ready-made chilli crisp.
For South Asian, rub with a mix of salt, turmeric, cumin and chilli powder and drizzle with neutral oil.
Bake for 10–15 minutes, depending on the thickness of the fillets. The fish is done when it is opaque and flakes easily. At the table, add any of the further seasonings as outlined above, so lemon juice, lime juice, spring onions, sesame oil or whatever else you like.

For the greens, but this method works with any vegetables

This is what I now do with any kind of greens, but you can use carrots, broccoli, pretty much anything provided it's sliced into pieces. You melt a bit of oil or butter in the pan, let it heat up, add your veg in one layer, season, and leave them alone until they brown. Then you flip them over, add half a small glass of water (max, start with less) and clamp the lid on. The brown-ness makes the veg delicious and the steaming bit means they cook through properly. Feel free to add stuff to the butter or oil, like garlic, herbs or spices, but they don't really need it – vegetables really taste of themselves cooked this way. If the water runs out before the veg are cooked, just add a bit more.

Finally, here are some favourite salad dressings. The first is my best extra virgin olive oil + salt + lemon juice to taste, tossed with your leaves more thoroughly and for longer than you would imagine necessary (optimally with clean hands). That's it – no recipe needed.

Classic vinaigrette with variations

Enough for 3–4 salads

The thing to know here is the 3–1 ratio of oil to acid.

1 tablespoon red wine vinegar, white wine vinegar, cider vinegar, balsamic, sherry vinegar or any other good vinegar you fancy
1 teaspoon Dijon mustard, though again you can play around with your mustard flavours
¼ teaspoon fine sea salt
a good grind of black pepper
3 tablespoons extra virgin olive oil

Charlotte Mann's marker pen mural in our London hallway

My kitchen, painted by Eleanor Crow

Put everything into a jam jar with a lid and shake until it's emulsified (i.e. thickened and come together). Taste and add more of anything if you feel it needs it.

Variations: you can add a tiny bit of minced shallot or minced garlic to your jar before you start mixing. Or try a tiny bit – like ¼ of a teaspoon – of honey, sugar or maple syrup.

Once the vinaigrette has emulsified, you can add chopped soft herbs like tarragon or basil, or dried oregano, which sounds gross but is nice. If you want to turn it into something creamy, add a tablespoon of mayo, plain yogurt or, for nuttiness, tahini. If you want to make it piquant, add a pinch of chilli flakes, a chopped anchovy or two (or use anchovy paste), or about 1 teaspoon of white miso paste. Play around with flavours you like: you really can't go very wrong.

All these versions keep in the fridge for at least a week.

Julia Turshen, whose books I also heartily recommend, has a sublime dressing for sturdier leaves like Little Gem, which is equal quantities, say three tablespoons, of soy sauce, sesame oil, olive oil and tahini, all mixed together. This dressing makes eating salad as moreish as eating crisps.

What about pudding? The truth of the matter is that I almost always buy it in. I don't have a sweet tooth and I'd always rather have cheese, except in summer when I might have a scoop of vanilla ice cream on the side of the most basic (but delicious) fruit galette imaginable, which I learned from Debora Robertson's book *Notes from a Small Kitchen Island*. You buy a ready-rolled sheet of shortcrust pastry, ideally all-butter, and lay it on some baking paper on a baking sheet. You sprinkle it with about 3 tablespoons of ground almonds mixed with 1 tablespoon of sugar. Then you pile about 600g of summer fruit, sliced or chopped, into the middle of the pastry, leaving a wide border. Then you fold this border back over some of the fruit. Brush the border with beaten egg or a bit of milk and bake at 180°C/160°C fan/gas mark 4 for 45 minutes. Serve warm or cold.

And now here is some of my **favourite kitchen kit** – favourite not just because I like using these things, but also because I feel that these are items that genuinely make my cooking life much easier. Specific brand suggestions are below.

1. **A giant pot**. I find coloured enamel ones irresistible. They're (relatively) inexpensive and you can cook anything in them. Get a big one – mine is 5.5 litres. Such a useful size if you've got people round – there's nothing more annoying than trying to cram stuff (especially spaghetti) into a too-small pan, plus it won't have the space to separate out and so will stay in a wodge and not cook properly. This size can also hold the Christmas Ham, or an entire chicken. If you're squashed for storage space, this is the kind of pan you'd happily have living on the cooker, semaphoring warmth and good cheer whether it's in use or not.

2. My most used and most beloved cooking vessel, namely a **roughly 30cm shallow casserole with a lid**. Because it's really wide, more food is in contact with the heat source, meaning things cook perfectly evenly, brown better if you're trying to brown them, and cook more quickly. I actually credit this style of pan for making me a better cook. It's just so versatile – ideal for everything, from scrambled eggs to curries to stews and braises to risottos and pilafs to roasting a chicken in the oven with some grain/orzo/veg around it (if your vessel is ovenproof). I use mine constantly. Mine is old and from Le Creuset, which has sadly become unaffordable unless you find some second-hand. These shallow pans are also great for sear-steamed vegetables, as described above.

3. **A mini-chopper (unless you have a hand blender)**.
   I *love* my mini-chopper. There are loads at all price points.

Yes, full-size food processors are great, and I remain loyal to my elderly Magimix, as you would be to something that could slice, chop, grate, shred, make batter, dough, etc., etc. But food processors are really big, come with lots of extra blades and discs that you have to store somewhere, take up a lot of counter space, and are heavy enough to be a pain to lug in and out of the cupboard if you hide them away. They're fantastic if you want to chop a massive amount of onions or slice kilos of carrots, and if I was still cooking for a lot of people on a regular basis as opposed to sometimes, I wouldn't even have looked at mini-choppers. But getting out the giant Magimix to chop two onions is silly (I don't like doing it by hand because since having my eyes lasered the crying/extreme redness situation is off the scale). Grabbing the mini-chopper, by contrast, is easy. It makes short work of chopping or mincing the trinity of onion, garlic and ginger, or the other trinity of onion, celery and carrot. It whips feta or ricotta in moments (put roast vegetables on top of a generous smear of either, drizzle with a little bit of olive oil, eat. I have whipped feta on toast for breakfast at least twice a week, with chilli flakes on top). The mini-chopper also makes tahini sauce, pesto, mayonnaise and all sorts of dressings. It chops up nuts and chillies, makes a single-serving smoothie, makes bread-crumbs out of stale bread – it is just massively and endlessly useful. You might want a mini-spatula for scraping.

4. A **cast-iron skillet** for cooking steaks, skin-on, bone-in chicken thighs and the sturdier vegetables, like slabs of cauliflower. Obviously you can cook a steak in an ordinary frying pan, but I eat steak about three times a year (with frites, béarnaise and a green salad, a Death Row dinner) and I need it to be as close to perfect as I can get. Plain cast iron is the best surface for cooking large pieces of meat, and gives the best sear/caramelization/brown crust. Very handy also for shallow-frying. You can also stick them on the barbecue

or on an open fire – they are indestructible. They are not expensive. They're also naturally non-stick, and get more and more non-stick the more you use them, to the point where things just glide about like swans. People sometimes think keeping them that way is mysterious or complicated, but it's not. Here's what I do:

- Unpack new pan.
- Put some vegetable oil on a piece of kitchen roll and rub it all over the sides and inside of the pan.
- Put the oiled pan on the hob, low-medium heat, until it starts to smoke.
- Turn the hob off and let the pan cool. Wipe off any leftover oil.
- The pan is now ready.
- After cooking, clean with hot water and dry carefully – it must be bone dry or it may rust (in which case rub the rust off with oil).
- If it's too dirty for rinsing, use a bit of detergent but oil it again afterwards.

5. **A really thin, super-flexible fish slice.** I'd always had quite thick, square-headed fish slices, which were a faff to slide under anything, like fish, pancakes or fried eggs. You want a pliable, ultra-wieldy version. They're cheap and lots of people make them.

6. **A spider**, massively useful for fishing things out of boiling liquid, be they dumplings, tortelloni, ravioli or just regular pasta when you still want it a little bit wet, like when you need a smidge of pasta water to help the sauce along. I find that anything that is a delicate stuffed parcel, like dumplings or ravioli, gets bashed too much when drained directly into a colander – at least a couple burst and the filling escapes. Spider them out and they emerge pristine. Also handy for lifting pakoras, fritters or anything else out of hot oil.

THE KITCHEN: PART 2

7. **Enamel roasting tins.** When I tided the kitchen cupboards recently, I found I had a vast pile of stainless steel roasting tins, most of which hadn't been used in months. The ones I use all the time are Falcon ones in sizes 37 and 31cm, depending on how many I'm cooking for. I roast things in them, make lasagne and parmigiana in them, use them for gratins (which I used to make in earthenware dishes), make fish pie and apple crumble in them . . . you get the picture. They're in constant use.

8. **Flattish roasting trays.** As I have already noted, their lack of depth maximizes browning and crispness, making them perfect for things like roast vegetables or sausages, among many others.

9. **A handsome salt pig.** For years I under-salted everything I cooked because 'salt is so bad for you'. Which it is, in excessive amounts. But salt used in home cooking isn't what harms people – that would be the grotesque amounts of salt (and sugar) in ready-made food. Home cooking that uses salt liberally isn't going to hurt anyone, and salt makes things *dramatically* more delicious, particularly vegetables and meat. Like, to a crazy extent. If your food tastes flat, salt it more. Salt changes everything. Which means you need a salt pig by the hob. The interior of salt pigs is unglazed, meaning the salt won't clump.

10. **An Instant Pot or similar.** This is an electric pressure cooker, though it does other stuff too, like make yogurt and cook rice, but never mind that for now. Instant Pots had their moment of viral fame in 2017. This made sales go through the roof but it also did this noble machine a disservice, because its very virality suggested transience, like it was just another fun gadget that would end up shoved at the back of the cupboard. I am not at all a gadget person and the Instant Pot remains, nearly seven years later, one of my most used

kitchen items, meaning two to three times a week year-round and more in winter. I *love* mine. It perfectly cooks things that would normally take hours – stews, braises, casseroles, ragù, black dal, beef rendang, etc., etc., etc. – in roughly half an hour, give or take. Ditto tough cuts of meat that would take forever to become melty and tender cooked normally. Soups and vegetables are near-instant. Pot-roasts take a hilariously short time. The textures are great, the flavours are pure and less diluted – you don't use much liquid in pressure cookers – meaning everything tastes more concentratedly of itself. It's not just for hefty, wintry things, or for things that would otherwise take hours – it poaches chickens, steams whole fish, makes perfect greens and the best quick orange and yellow dals. Curries! Ramen! Phō! Stock! Risotto! Custard! And if you cook dried beans from scratch, i.e. soak them overnight, replace the water, boil them, simmer them, yada yada yada – well, in an Instant Pot they go from dried to cooked in under half an hour, plus however long it takes for the pressure to drop. I would not be without my Instant Pot if you paid me.

The other thing is that it's so well built that you won't need to replace it. This has actually proved a problem for the company that makes Instant Pots – it nearly went bankrupt at one point – because these days 'gadgets' have obsolescence built in. This one doesn't. It's a total workhorse. It's also very economical to run.

Pick a size and go for the basic, cheapest model – you don't need bells and whistles. It does what it does *perfectly*. It's all you need. And don't be put off if you don't have children that need ferrying about, or a big family – I guarantee you will use this all the time even if there's only one or two of you, just get the smaller model.

Two things to note: trust the timings in the recipes for Instant Pots – at first I thought 'it can't possibly be done in that time' and whacked on an extra five minutes for safety, but there's no need. Also if you're new to pressure cooking, as I was, then Catherine Phipps's book *Modern Pressure Cooking* is the bible. And don't fear 1970s-style pressure cooker explosions – it's electric, so no risk of that.

11. **If you have the space, a countertop oven**. Talking of economical to run: this, which is called a toaster oven in America, is hardly essential, but it is cheap to run and very hard-working, to the point where I don't often use my normal oven when it's two of us. They heat up amazingly quickly and do a brilliant job of cooking everything. If I *do* use the normal oven – when I have people over, or for things like Christmas – then this extra oven is invaluable: it can do an extra batch of roast potatoes or parsnips while the normal oven is rammed with everything else.

As its name suggests, it's also great for making vast quantities of toast at the same time, for reheating, for keeping things warm, for small things like roasting nuts – it is absurd to turn on the giant oven to roast some nuts; for grilling stuff – basically everything a normal oven does, including baking cakes or bread and roasting a whole 1.8-ish kg chicken perfectly. As well as this, mine can slow-cook, has special settings for toasting bagels (no more trying to cram them into the toaster slot), for cooking ready-made pizza, for crumpets (a civilized setting) and for baking biscuits. It is perfect for two people, or maybe two people with one or two very small children who eat teeny portions. You set the amount of time you want something to cook for and it turns itself off when it's done – handy for the forgetful.

Some favourite cookbooks

I have a couple of hundred cookery books. These are the ones that I use the most, or at least the ones I use the most at the time of writing. Some are new, some are old, all of them are fantastic and none of them are fussy or over-complicated. These are in no particular order. The authors' other books, where applicable, are also recommended.

- *Cooking*, by Jeremy Lee (Fourth Estate)
- *A Table for Friends*, by Skye McAlpine (Bloomsbury)
- *Dinner*, by Meera Sodha (Fig Tree)
- *Make It Easy*, by Jane Lovett (New Holland)
- *Nothing Fancy*, by Alison Roman (Hardie Grant)
- *Feast*, by Nigella Lawson (Chatto & Windus)
- *Canal House Cooks Every Day*, by Christopher Hirsheimer and Melissa Hamilton (Andrews McMeel)
- *Ultimate Curry Bible*, by Madhur Jaffrey (Ebury Press)
- *You're All Invited*, by Margo Henderson (Fig Tree, out of print but findable second-hand)
- *The Art of Friday Night Dinner*, by Eleanor Steafel (Bloomsbury)
- *House & Garden: A Year in the Kitchen*, by Blanche Vaughan (Mitchell Beazley)
- *The Secret of Cooking*, by Bee Wilson (Fourth Estate)
- *A Cook's Book*, by Nigel Slater (Fourth Estate)
- *Home Cookery Year*, by Claire Thomson (Quadrille)
- *Modern Pressure Cooking*, by Catherine Phipps (Quadrille)
- *Market Cooking*, by David Tanis (Artisan)
- *On the Side*, by Ed Smith (Bloomsbury)
- *Small Victories*, by Julia Turshen (Chronicle)
- *Live Fire*, by Helen Graves (Hardie Grant, the only barbecue book you need)
- *Ottolenghi: The Cookbook*, by Yotam Ottolenghi and Sami Tamimi (Ebury Press)
- *The Weekday Vegetarians*, by Jenny Rosenstrach (Random House)
- *The Green Cookbook*, by Rukmini Iyer (Square Peg)
- *Service*, by Anna Hedworth (Quadrille)
- *One Pot, Pan, Planet*, by Anna Jones (Fourth Estate)
- *The Good Cook*, by Simon Hopkinson (BBC Books)

THE KITCHEN: PART 2

KITCHEN EQUIPMENT: SOME RECOMMENDATIONS

- **Enamel cooking pots**: The Ukrainian ones from **Objects of Use**, objectsofuse.com.
- **Affordable cast-iron casseroles**: **Sainsbury's** and **IKEA**, both excellent.
- **A 30cm-ish shallow casserole** (the most useful pot in the kitchen). **Judge** Vista Sauteuse Pan. **Kuhn Rikon** All-Round Shallow Casserole. **Our Place** Always Pan (the Large is 31.8cm). If you have strong wrists, **Netherton Foundry**'s beautiful, naturally non-stick, spun iron 30cm Prospector Casserole is perfection and can be used anywhere, including on an open fire.
- **Mini-chopper**: Much of a muchness given how little horsepower is required. Mine is by **KitchenAid**.
- **Handsome and still-unbeatable food processor**: **Magimix**.
- **Everyone's favourite stick blender**: Any by **Braun**.
- **Cast-iron skillet**: I can't understand why so many of them are so expensive: my absolute favourite, **Judge** Speciality Cookware Skillet Solid Cast Iron Frying Pan 24cm, is just over £20 at the time of writing. These weigh a ton, I'm afraid, but they're so, so good, plus the depth means you can cook one-pan dinners in them, and obviously they're entirely happy in the oven.
- **Enamel roasting tins**: **Falcon**, falconenamelware.com.
- **Toaster ovens**: I researched this very comprehensively when I was buying one. **Sage**, every time. **Our Place** if you're after something tiny.

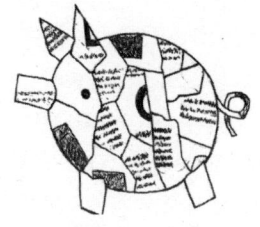

FOUNDATION 4

A NOTE ON TASTE

How to become confident of yours

The very first thing to tell you about taste is to always ask yourself this very twenty-first-century question: **Is it my own taste, or is it the algorithm?** When you don't quite trust your own taste, you think the algorithm is your friend. And it can be, some of the time. But despite appearances, it doesn't know you as well as you know yourself. It knows what you've bookmarked, it knows your Pinterest boards and Instagram and TikTok favourites, it follows you about all day thinking it's really got the measure of you.

But really, all it knows is what you choose to *consume*. It does not know what you *feel*. It doesn't know the naked you, as it were – it only sees the more polished surface. And the two aren't the same. The algorithm does not know your soul – and, as we have seen, successful houses are all about soul. So always ask yourself whether your taste is guiding you, or whether it's the algorithm. From the heart, or by numbers? Forever wonderful *to you*, or fashionable to everyone for the next thirty seconds? Only you know the answer to the question of whether you really love something, or whether you are merely hungry for external validation (it's not your fault – it's what the internet does to all of us. But it is really worth bearing in mind).

Sometimes, of course, it will be both taste *and* the algorithm that point you to a particular purchase or a particular style. But the question remains worth asking, because sometimes the two get enmeshed: are you decorating for yourself, or (not even necessarily consciously) for social media approval from complete strangers? I don't think anyone should decorate their house in a particular way because their phone told them to. Plus, as we all know from people all suddenly wearing the same trainers/carrying the same handbag/drinking the same smoothie whether they're in London, Beijing or Brisbane, the algorithm has killed individuality. 'Obedient follower of trends' is not the look anyone should be after. Clothes and smoothies are one thing – but your entire home? No.

Here's a good rule: if it isn't trendy, it will never date.

I think people worry needlessly about their taste being judged. Does your taste have to be my taste for me to appreciate and value the story, the ambience, that you have created in your house? Do I also need to love papier-mâché pigs or farmhouse kitchens to love the feel of your home? Of course not, just as your clothes don't have to be the clothes I would wear, or your taste in husbands overlap perfectly with mine. How boring would that be? You can truthfully say 'That looks absolutely amazing on you' of your friend's new jacket while knowing that the same jacket would look terrible on you. You can admire her fantastic, incredibly flattering new haircut while wanting to laugh out loud at the idea of it suiting you.

People love – really *love* – looking at and spending time in all sorts of interiors arrangements while knowing that they personally couldn't live in them. It's why we like going to each other's houses! It's why we like Pinterest and interiors magazines! I am maximalist in my approach, but I adore – and truly admire – very pared-back, soothing, minimal interiors when they're done well (meaning when they have enough texture and interest – see page 129). I personally prefer reds to blues in an interior setting, but that doesn't mean I hate the sky or the Aegean sea, or that I can't appreciate the ravishing loveliness of Farrow & Ball's Cook's Blue. My kitchen might be very far from your idea of dreamy when it comes to your own kitchen, but that doesn't mean you wouldn't enjoy sitting in it.

FOUNDATION 4: A NOTE ON TASTE

There isn't a unifying theory of taste – and nor should there be. We like what we like for ourselves, and we like and appreciate all sorts of things for other people. Understanding this should take away some of the fear of being judged for how we decorate our homes. I think that fear of being judged really inhibits the choices people make when they decorate, and that this makes them sad, like marrying the nice, dull man and wondering for ever more about the interesting hottie that got away.

Or the other thing that happens is that people decorate entirely by algorithm, as above, and then feel compelled to constantly redecorate – which aside from anything else can become very expensive – once the trend that they copied has died. These days, trends can die within weeks, if not days. So if you're worried about being judged, then taste via algorithm will ensure that your taste is deemed out of date within mere moments. As I was just saying, that's one thing if the trend is for eating cabbage or wearing tall socks, but what we're doing with our homes is aiming for timeless (to us) appeal – something that is beyond fashion or trends. You're never going to get timeless appeal if your style doesn't speak to your heart. Or if it's somebody else's style entirely. If you're going to buy into trends, which is a fun thing to do occasionally, make sure you love the item regardless of its fashion status – despite it is much better.

People often also worry because their taste isn't consistent, meaning they like more than one style and more than one look. We're always being encouraged to go all in – to fully embrace every single aspect of this or that decorating style when it comes to a room. Again, this is a so-called rule that nobody needs to obey. It makes for very boring interiors that are wholly without friction. Friction? Yes, friction. Friction is an important thing, in this context. You want a few things that don't necessarily 'go' to rub up sexily against each other – to eye each other up and conclude they make a fine pair. Again, this is to stop the room feeling obvious and dull. It's like texture, but more to do with objects. So, for example: the main part of my house was built in the sixteenth century. I have a number of low-ceilinged, beamed rooms. You know what looks good in those rooms? A sudden jolt. A gold 1970s lamp shaped like a mushroom. A modern, abstract painting. A glass coffee table. A slash of hot pink. Not all the time, and not everywhere – but every now and then. This is friction: the rubbing up of something atypical in a room that otherwise looks much as you would expect it to look. It keeps things both interesting and modern. So if your maximalist heart hankers for a bit of pared-back Scandi furniture once in a while, try incorporating it. Only, style it *your* way. So many styles of decorating play nicely together. Again, it's very like fashion: the accessories that make the outfit are rarely the obvious accessories but rather the ones that provide a jolt and make you think of the clothes in a whole different way.

The jolts and the friction protect against 'ghastly good taste', a phrase coined by the late Poet Laureate John Betjeman in an essay of the same name, published in 1933. He was writing about architecture, a subject about which he was passionate. In it, he gives Modernism both barrels and extols the beauty and grace of Victorian and Edwardian architecture, both profoundly unfashionable at the time. He also has a pop at the fetishization of antiquism, the sorts of houses lived in by modern people so keen to honour the period of the house that they're basically cosplaying. Both approaches, Betjeman argues, are not only timid but appallingly unimaginative. 'Ghastly good taste' basically means taste that is so obviously desperate to please, so fearful of offending anyone, that it is unforgivably dull and bland, and thus 'ghastly'. I agree, and would add that copycatting a room that you saw online without adding a single element that is individual to you is the contemporary version of ghastly good taste. For me, it is basically any room that is devoid of any kind of individuality: a room that could belong to absolutely anybody. But it doesn't belong to anybody. It belongs to you. Where are you in it?

There's a lot of ghastly good taste about, because people – then as now – are eager not to be seen as weird outliers that offend against the norm. But who, exactly, would they be offending by filling their rooms with things they truly loved instead of by-numbers 'tasteful' items purchased not because they make the heart beat faster but

FOUNDATION 4: A NOTE ON TASTE

because they're a safe bet? I'm all for safe bets in some contexts: you want your mattress to be a safe bet, your fridge, your cooker, your vacuum cleaner. But your table lamps, your dinner plates, your rugs and pillowcases and decorative objects too? It's a recipe for boredom – and, more to the point, dissatisfaction, because sitting in rooms filled with nothing but ghastly good taste will never make you feel truly contented. There is an emptiness about them, because they're for show. They're hollow.

This isn't an attack on neutral interiors. Neutral interiors can be absolutely ravishing. If you like whites and creams and beiges, knock yourself out: they're beautiful. I'm not saying 'have a purple room with a red sofa and green walls' (though do, if that's what your heart wants – congratulations, you are basically a Fauvist). Instead, I'm saying that if the stripy blue vase makes you smile in the way that the plain taupe vase doesn't, buy the stripy blue vase. Don't always play it safe. Listen to your desires. These things may not seem very important, but they have the power to alter the way you feel within your own four walls, and that really matters.

Whatever your taste, remember that every successful room needs something in it that is jarring, or even something that arguably constitutes bad taste (provided you love the item in question). That's not just my view but the view of every interior designer worth their salt. You need a bit of tension to jolt the eye out of complacency; you need the occasional something that makes people go 'hahaha, what is *that*?'; and you need something to remind you that are a playful person rather than a martyr to Good Taste, which can start feeling oppressive and suffocating if there's too much of it. Nancy Lancaster (1896–1994 – 'I've lived too long and I've lived too well'), a towering doyenne of interiors who owned the pioneering design company Colefax & Fowler, said that 'if every piece is perfect the room becomes a museum and lifeless'.

Surrounding yourself with things you love matters. It is a really sane and anchoring move in a lunatic world. I can't emphasize this enough: the whole point of the exercise is to come home and exhale, to sigh with contentment, to think, 'I am home and home is *lovely*.'

One final point: some people think they don't have any taste at all. But they do. Everyone does. It lives inside us. It is an intuitive response to the way a certain thing makes us feel. It is not the same as quite liking something – it is a KAPOW, a *coup de foudre*, a dead certainty: 'I love it.' That sort of reaction is not necessarily the same as the one you have when you find something pleasing, or even beautiful, and are able to appraise it coolly, without that jolt of longing. I'm talking about a visceral response. When you know, you know. Trust yourself!

THE KITCHEN: PART 3
How to have fun eating

The kitchen table is the table you eat at – it can of course also be a dining table in a dedicated dining room. Two names for the same thing: the place where you sit down and tuck in – though also the place where the children do homework, friends have a cup of tea and, later in the day, where the adults have a relationship-saving glass of wine when the kids are in bed. The kitchen table is the most versatile item of furniture in a house, I think – everything of significance happens there. You might work from it, too.

I have a kitchen with a big table in it and that's where we eat, whether there are two or twelve of us. But if you have a more open-plan, knocked-through situation, then the trick is to make the eating area feel as inhabited as the kitchen part. Often it can feel slightly apart from it, and somehow less loved. The issue with dining tables, whether they are part of the kitchen or in a separate room, is that they look a bit abandoned when they are not in use – a big, slightly looming rectangle (or circle, or square) of empty furniture.

If people tend to congregate at the kitchen end, leaving the eating end feeling a bit chillier, you need to make sure that the eating area is as welcoming as the rest of the room. It often isn't because it's more formal, and formality doesn't invite conviviality. This is also often the case if you have a separate dining room.

This, for me at least, is the problem with separate dining rooms: there is something of the 'for best' about them. I strongly believe that there is no such thing as 'for best' in any context (clothes and jewellery included) and that there is simply no point in having lovely things and not using them every day. I consider it a terrible, almost sinful, waste. Who buys special things to keep hidden away in a cupboard or wardrobe? It defeats the entire purpose of the enterprise.

If you are lucky enough to have a separate dining room, consider whether you really need it, or whether it would be more useful repurposed as an extra living area. If the answer is that yes, you absolutely need and want it, then lavish as much attention on it as you would any other room. Often dining rooms are quite bare, with a big table and chairs, maybe a couple of other bits of furniture, and that's more or less it. You find that people seem reluctant to move from the much friendlier kitchen.

What helps a dining room dramatically is roaring logs in a fireplace, but we can't all have one of those. The next best thing is recreating that intimate, almost confessional atmosphere through candlelight and, yet again, the right temperature of lightbulb, as per page 42. There is nothing worse than an overlit dining room. You are trying to encourage warmth and intimacy, free flowing, unguarded conversation, maybe some mild flirting, and it is impossible to do this if the lighting is better suited to an office, a dental surgery or a morgue. Your guests will feel slightly on edge and have no inclination to linger – not because you're not charming and the food isn't delicious, but because an overlit room makes people want to run away (I think it's partly about feeling like you're going to be interrogated).

So first of all, mind your lighting, and remember that in the absence of buying new lamps or lightbulbs, you can't go wrong with a ton of candles. Make sure they fit snugly in their candlesticks – I used to wrap candle bases in kitchen foil to make them fit properly; these days I use the sticky stuff below – and don't have them so tall that people can't see anyone sitting across from them. You can buy candle shavers if yours are too wide for the base of the candleholder. Either light them early or, less wastefully, buy the shorter ones that are perfect for this purpose. Candles make everyone look attractive, instil an immediate sense of relaxation and well-being, and create a lovely atmosphere the moment you light them. Never use scented candles around food, for obvious reasons of hideous scent clash.

So whether you're in a giant dining room with a dining table, or in your kitchen with your trusty kitchen table, or sitting cross-legged at your coffee table, here are my thoughts on entertaining. It's a word I can't bear – so much stiffer and more formal than the way any of us live, with its suggestion of formality and awkward, slightly constipated small talk. Let's call it having friends over instead.

HOW TO HAVE A DINNER PARTY IF YOU FEAR COOKING

The first thing that needs saying is that it isn't always about the food. Some of my most fun evenings have involved nothing fancier than some M&S dips, a load of crisps and one of those family-sized bars of Dairy Milk. Some others have involved frankly horrible food, notably a whole meal that was basically raw, including the chicken (gruesome). The hosts, terrible cooks but amazing hosts – because the two can happily co-exist – gave up, ordered takeaway, and we all had such a good time that 'dinner' ended at about 1am (on a school night!). The moral of the story is that good company always trumps food, and that being a good host can turn apparent disaster into a triumph. Of course, great food is the cherry on the cake, and although I no longer drink alcohol (see page 92), rivers of wine are never a bad idea. But mostly it's the guests, or rather the combination of you and the guests.

It's also about setting the scene, which we've just covered above. You want people to think, 'I am happy to be here and I'm glad I came,' when they walk into the kitchen or dining room, and one good way of making them feel that way is a nicely dressed table (we'll get into this in a moment), flattering lighting, lots of drinks and the offer of something to nibble on. You want an immediately low-key celebratory atmosphere. I'm also a fan of a well-curated playlist in the background – it immediately sets the scene and the vibe of the evening, from gently seductive to intensely chilled to glamorous to holiday-like to something a bit buzzier. Some of my favourite tracks are at the end of this chapter.

Raw chicken and emergency takeaways aside, I'm not suggesting you just get in some houmous and call it dinner. You need to feed the people you've asked round properly. There is nothing worse than going to someone's house and leaving feeling so under-fed that you have to stop for chips on the way home, although those chips do always taste extra delicious. If you like cooking and are good at it, you don't need me to tell you what to make.

If you like cooking less, or if the idea of cooking for more than two people fills you with dread, find one recipe that appeals to you and practise it until you feel really proud of yourself for making something so utterly delicious. This is your signature dish. Just make that. Yes, every time. Yes, for ever. There is nothing wrong with being known – being legendary! – for your amazing lasagne or roast chicken or phō. And then, in time, over the years, you might add a few more things to your repertoire. Or not. It doesn't matter, provided the thing you can make is properly great.

When I first got married, the only thing I could reliably cook for large numbers was a Nigel Slater recipe for tarragon chicken, so I just made that again and again, with really buttery mash and a well-dressed salad, and ice cream for pudding. I still think it's pretty much a perfect meal. Anyway: the more I made it, the easier 'hosting' became, to the point where I could make dinner for eight or ten or twelve standing on my head. I learned to cook eventually, but everybody who ate it loved that chicken, and if it ain't broke . . .

Incidentally, there is a recipe by Julius Roberts called Epic Tarragon Chicken available online. It is easy and it is, indeed, epic – what in my house is called a platelicker, meaning a dish that would make you abandon every last iota of propriety because it is so crazily

THE KITCHEN: PART 3

good to eat. If you're looking for somewhere to start and aren't vegetarian, I would consider learning that recipe, and upping the number of chickens if you have more than four people to feed. You are not ever going to get any complaints. (By the way, a curious thing about feeding large numbers of people is that the more numerous you are, the less food gets eaten. You'd think you'd have to quadruple, or whatever, the recipe, but this isn't so unless the people in question are hog-like family or very close friends. Family and intimates eat as they ordinarily would and don't feel shy about asking for thirds. But if the people don't know each other well, they tend to eat less, a) because they are so busy talking, and b) because most people subconsciously don't want to really properly stuff their face in front of strangers.)

I never do starters – I think they belong in restaurants, plus I don't like being overly beholden to the stove or to fussing around plating things up when I have people round. Instead, I do hearty snacks to have with drinks. They serve the same purpose but are much less effort, plus they absorb some of the alcohol, which is never a bad idea because you don't want anyone to feel actively drunk just as they sit down to eat (also, quite boring for everybody else to have one person sitting slurring and repeating themselves). The goodness of hearty snacks is that you don't have to cook unless you want to – you can buy them ready-made and then zhuzz them up a bit, if you like, with dipping or other sauces, fresh herbs or drizzles of things.

I'm thinking good crisps, good olives, frozen mini-samosas with a yogurt dipping sauce (plain yogurt with a pinch of salt, a little grated garlic and some chopped coriander in it), toasted thin slices of baguette with things on top, a cheese plate (or a whole perfectly ripe cheese with a load of crackers), charcuterie – you get the idea. Nuts. Pretzels. Pakoras. Shards of aged Parmesan drizzled with hot honey from a jar. A special shoutout here to Rahms ready-made mini-croustades, from supermarkets or online, which are a perfect receptacle for marginally fancier things like dressed crab, or egg salad and fake caviar and snipped chives, or dressed prawns, or labneh and shop dukkah, or mushroomy things, whipped feta or whipped ricotta with toppings – whatever you like: anything that isn't soggy and that would be nice on toast is nice in one of these. I'm not going to recommend that you run out and buy tubs of sandwich filler, but I'm also not saying that if you are in a panic and it's an emergency, they wouldn't do the job.

So that's the starter out of the way. We know about the main: you're going to make the one thing you know you can make as an unconfident cook. Then you need some sides and some salad (see page 54).

Just buy in pudding, like a normal European person. This can be as fancy as you like from a pâtisserie, or it could just be a really good fruit tart, or it could be lots of different flavours of ice cream and some delicious biscuits, like me in 1992. Job done. I also like going quite lo-fi with coffee and sometimes I do joke petits fours by buying a load of miniature confectionery, the sorts of things I'd get for trick or treaters at Halloween – those big bags of mini Mars bars, mini Flakes, mini Crunchies, and so on, plus some Haribo, some Dolly Mixtures for prettiness, etc. I put these on my smartest platter, which happens to be silver, and serve them with coffee. There are never any left over.

Whether you are a mini- or a maximalist, setting the table properly for dinner makes all the difference. Here again, it's a question of creating a welcoming visual sense of abundance and generosity. Now, I could write a lot about tablescaping, the painstaking art of laying a seriously aesthetic table. It is something I find very enjoyable when I have the time to do it properly . . . which is pretty much never. I also own so much wildly mismatched crockery that the idea of buying expensive new bits so that they fit into a particular theme feels like I'd be approaching hoarder territory.

But I do lay a good table, if I say so myself. Here's what I do – it's tablescaping for lazy (or merely busy) people.

- Make life easier for yourself and serve everything family-style. All this means is that you are eating as you would if you were at home (which you are), eating *en famille* (which you also sort of are, since good friends often feel like family members). So no fussy individual portions: everything goes on platters and dishes, and everyone helps themselves. Aside from anything else, this is a much more modern way of serving food than e.g. individual ramekins. It feels generous, relaxed and friendly, and it *looks* generous, relaxed and friendly, since a whole vegetable tart to help yourself to is always going to be more visually appealing than one measly slice. It is also much more conducive to people who don't know each other well striking up conversations – 'Can you pass the green beans?' 'Shall I give you some potatoes?' and so on. If someone doesn't like something, they can just not take any, which is also much more relaxing than someone telling the cook that actually they don't love beetroot.

So that's the first thing. Obviously not fastidiously plating up twelve individual servings is also much less work than just putting everything on the table, so it's a win for the cook, too.

- What you use to serve your food is up to you, and depends on what you have and on the look you like. I don't like matchy-matchy anything, but if you do, go ahead and do that – it will look beautiful and chic. You cannot go wrong with white plates or dishes.

- I tend to pull out a mix of platters, most of them second-hand, and I also use smaller shallow bowls if I'm hosting a lot of people because it's annoying to only have one bowl of something that needs to be passed up and down the table. Better, I think, to give people what they need close to where they're sitting. So I might do three or four smaller bowls of vegetables rather than one giant platter, three small jugs of sauce/condiment rather than one big one, and so on. This is important if the sauce is hot – it has less chance of cooling down if people don't have to wait for the lone jug to travel down the table to them.

But also: it just looks really nice. You are effectively decorating – making the table look populated and lively – using the food you're serving for dinner, which is another win. It's always worth picturing your menu on the table, when you do decide what to cook: a mix of vibrant colours and textures is not only much nicer to eat but also dramatically more appetizing than, for example, a uniform spread of beige or cream-coloured food. Speaking of texture: I like to vary that too in the serving dishes I use – the rough with the smooth, as it were, rough ceramics and proper china, but that's just a personal preference. As for cooking pots on the table: I'm all for it, provided the cooking pots are attractive – your treasured Le Creuset equivalent, yes, your knackered pan with the melted handle, no. For something like a big lasagne, the roasting tin it cooked in is lovely.

- The other thing – as with any decorating – is to vary the height of things. In an ideal world you'd want some things to be tall and some others to be shorter because it is more appealing and much more interesting to the eye. As in room decoration (see page 133), a thing happens when everything is the same height: your eye goes, 'Oh yes, I know what this is, boring.' If you have things of different heights, your eye goes, 'Oh! There's loads to look at. I am interested. What's that over there?' If you also have all sorts of colours and textures, the eye is basically dancing a jig of excitement.

- This doesn't mean you have to deploy an array of footed bowls, though if you have a cake or fruit stand, pile it high – I tend to do this with tomatoes on the vine, or loaves of bread, or with a pile of flatbreads loosely wrapped in a clean tea towel to keep them warm, or with the more photogenic fruit in winter. You can also vary the height of things by simply placing them on any wooden chopping boards you might have about your person, or even, slightly more precariously, by using upturned bowls as stands.

- Of course this all assumes you're eating at a largeish table that can accommodate whatever it is you're serving. If your table is small, or if your guests are crammed around it, you'll have to make use of counter surfaces, which is fine because it also looks friendly and relaxed. If your table is the right size but no more and your room

THE KITCHEN: PART 3

is large, you could deploy another, smaller table somewhere else in the room – I have an old IKEA trestle table that I keep especially for this purpose. It comes out every Christmas, either to double the size of the dining table or to act as a sort of buffet area.

- In among all this, if there is space and I've not asked so many people to dinner that we're all squashed round the table, knees rubbing, I like using fruits and vegetables as extra decoration. I've mentioned bowls of lemons and loaves of bread – handsome ones with a crust, not ready-sliced in plastic. When I don't put them on a cake stand, I sometimes put them straight on the table. You could also put them on a board, with a bread knife, or slice the bread and put it in a couple of pretty baskets (see below). In the autumn, a couple of small pumpkins and a few smaller gourds look beautiful strewn down the table, as do bunches of red grapes. In the winter, pomegranates and clementines look lovely, like a Dutch still life. In the summer, bowls of lemons aside, I would maybe do a tumble of vine tomatoes in my footed bowl. You get the idea. The cook and writer Skye McAlpine is the queen of doing this and I recommend her books very highly, not just for the stupendous and often very easy recipes, but for her impeccable styling ideas.

- I also always have flowers – tiny little sprigs in bud vases, tealight holders or jam jars. You just need a garden, or just one bunch of supermarket flowers. In the absence of flowers, I do herbs, and in the absence of herbs, a sprig of something evergreen from the garden or the walk home. If all else fails, buy some fresh rosemary and thyme from the supermarket and use that. There's always something that fits the bill, even in winter. Keep the vases small and short, because you need to be able to see the people sitting opposite you. Lavish flower arrangements are great, but not where you're eating.

- Make sure that everyone has easy access to pinch pots of salt and cracked black pepper, chilli flakes, toasted sesame seeds, relish, pickle, hot sauce, soy, tahini sauce, or whatever else specifically goes with the food you've made. With European and Middle Eastern food, I often have my nicest-looking bottle of extra virgin olive oil on the table too.

- I've mentioned Dutch still lives. To really accentuate that vibe, you need candles, as mentioned above.

MORE TABLESCAPING TIPS

- Tablecloths are ridiculously expensive given that they're just a length of hemmed fabric. I love a good tablecloth, but come on – especially as they are absolutely guaranteed to get stained and marked the moment people start eating. I buy lengths of fabric instead, and I have to tell you, I don't even hem them. I do snip off any stray bits of thread, but that's the extent of my involvement. Mind you, if you have a sewing machine then hemming doesn't take long. But I just unroll.

- On the staining: if I do use one of my two really nice, really expensive tablecloths, I sometimes (depending on the excitability of the guests, to be honest) lay a cheap paper one on top, bistro style. You can buy rolls of these online. You still get to see the sides of the handsome tablecloth, but you can relax a bit more about people splodging red wine and candle wax all over it.

- You can also use cotton or linen bedsheets.

- On the rare occasions when I use a proper, shop-bought tablecloth, it will have come from the places listed below.

- I do think proper linen napkins are a good addition when you're having people over. They're just so much nicer than paper ones. I recently read this terrible thing about kitchen roll – that it was 'kitchen toilet paper' and ever since I've thought twice about tearing bits off and using them as napkins in super-casual situations. I'm reconsidering the whole kitchen roll experience, to be honest. We still sometimes use it when it's just two of us, but yeesh, the toilet roll thing lingers in the head. It's like when my sister told me that strawberries reminded her of noses with huge gross pores – it took me years to get over it. Anyway: linen napkins elevate both the formal and the informal dining experience, so do consider them.

- I have two sets of placemats, both woven jute (robust) with a coloured border. That seems a sane number of placemats to own without veering off disastrously into obsessive territory. They go with everything. Placemats are a very good and easy way of looking like you've made an effort.

- If there are eight of us or fewer, I use our everyday drinking glasses, which are called La Rochère Perigord Short Goblet Glasses and which I like because they are affordable, sturdy and nice in the hand but also because, being short-stemmed, they work for water *and* wine *and* cocktails. One glass to serve them all! If there are more of us (I only have eight of those glasses), I use normal wine glasses and separate water glasses – again, a mixture of what I have.

HOW TO HAVE A DRINKS PARTY

I once read some tips of Jilly Cooper's about having a drinks party. You'll be able to find it online (it was originally in *The Times*, and has been requoted many a time), but here are her two most outstanding bits of party advice:

- 'If you want to chat up a chap, say, "Gosh, you're gorgeous!" or just, "Do you want to come upstairs?" Men are rarely complimented, so they'll be very flattered.'

— On how to get rid of the people who won't leave: 'I tend to ask my PA to go around telling everyone that "Jilly is tired" and it's time to go home now. It's worth hiring a PA for the night, just for that part.'

Yes, it is. She's also very against bowl food, as am I — nobody has enough arms.

Here are some tips of my own. The guests are far more important than anything else excepting the food (no food = people get too drunk too quickly and you have to deploy your PA too early. Also who wants to drink without eating? It's a party, not a stag weekend).

1. There are good downloadable, customizable invitation templates all over the place including on Etsy, on Canva, and if you're doing it by text, on an excellent app called HiNote.

2. Make the room look as nice as possible, obviously, but no one cares that much about elaborate décor or theme provided there's a joyful atmosphere, enough to eat and drink, and flattering lighting. The main thing is to have fun and/or interesting people who don't all know each other. It's nice to all know each other, but it can make for quite a flat atmosphere — 'Oh look, there's so-and-so again'. You always want a bit of NEW BLOOD, ideally.

3. Have a mixture of ages. I'm very pro older children and teenagers at parties (drinks parties I mean, not parties that go on until 3am). They add energy. If you're going to have children at yours, have supplies of appropriate soft drinks and child-friendly food — meaning pizza — and maybe a dedicated room where they can watch YouTube or play video games once they get bored with the adults.

4. Don't ever turn on the overhead lights. This is a rule of life anyway, as you know, but it is particularly pertinent at parties. Flattering lighting everywhere creates atmosphere

THE KITCHEN: PART 3

start listing a great big litany of woes whenever someone politely says, 'How are you?' You can cut their lamentations short by butting in and saying, 'But you look amazing, though! Look at you! Gorgeous!' Appealing to a person's vanity usually forces them to stop moaning. Parties are really not the place for moaning, regardless of how much you feel you have to moan about.

14. Always make a beeline for anyone standing on their own, and tell your close friends to do the same. This is especially important if someone arrives and clearly doesn't know anyone, and everyone else is already chatting and laughing in gaggles. This guest needs you! Go and talk to them the moment you spot them, then introduce them to people they might like.

15. Food: unless your friends are all aggressively carnivorous, it's a great deal easier (and cheaper) to just make all the food vegetarian. That way everyone can eat everything. If you have vegans, make a platter of vegan canapés and point them to it. There are hundreds of recipes for vegan canapés online.

16. In the absence of children or any other kind of waiting staff, lay the food out on handsome platters on a table near a big pile of cocktail napkins (and small plates if you have enough of them) and get everyone to help themselves. Don't make the canapés bigger than two bites for a drinks party. You want to go chomp-chomp and be done.

17. If the party is more impromptu, a jumbo pack of the trusty frozen mini-samosas I've mentioned above will go a long way. They're hot, they're crispy, they're filling and you can make coriander chutney to go with them – it takes two minutes and the recipe is below.

18. Never underestimate people's appetite for the humble crisp.

19. I sometimes write what the food is in chalk pens on a window, like a canapé menu. That way you can make it clear that something is vegetarian or vegan or both or neither.

Here are a couple of recipes:

Spiced apple shrub

Recipe by kind permission of Jane Lovett from her invaluable book *The Get-Ahead Christmas Cook* (Headline), which I could not recommend more wholeheartedly (along with all her other books). I love Jane Lovett's recipes. They are delicious, easy and never, ever go wrong.

This always reminds me of mulled wine, even though it's alcohol-free. However, should you wish, the addition of a little whisky or brandy makes a lovely, comforting winter drink (a hot toddy) if served warm. It's also good served warm without the alcohol. Don't be alarmed by the black pepper or its quantity; being a spice, it adds some heat and a wonderful flavour. As apples don't produce much on the juice front, you may like to double up this quantity.

6 eating apples, unpeeled, quartered, cored and chopped quite small
2 star anise
15g coarsely ground black pepper
20g green cardamom pods, bashed using a pestle and mortar to split open the outer shells
500ml cider vinegar
100g granulated sugar

Put the apples, spices and cider vinegar into a saucepan and gently heat together on a low heat. Don't let it boil. Decant the mixture into a Kilner-style jar, a container with a lid, or a bowl. When cold, cover and leave at (cool) room temperature for 7 days.
On day 7, strain the shrub through a damp muslin-lined (or similar) sieve into a small saucepan, then gather up the muslin

and gently squeeze out the last of the liquid over the sieve. Add the sugar and warm on a low heat, stirring occasionally, for a few minutes, just until the sugar has dissolved. Don't let it boil.

Pour into a sterilized bottle, leaving behind any sediment, and when cold, close with the lid or a cork. Shake before use. Dilute to taste and enjoy, or store the bottle somewhere cool for up to 2 months (store in the fridge once opened). It will last considerably longer if stored in the fridge.

Coriander chutney

1 large bunch of coriander
A couple of sprigs of mint, optional
juice of 1 lemon, or to taste
2 green chillies, deseeded and finely chopped
1 teaspoon salt
1 teaspoon ground turmeric
4 teaspoons, or to taste, brown sugar
about 3 tablespoons plain yogurt, or as needed for desired consistency

Trim off half the stems of your bunch of coriander. Whizz everything together in a blender. Add a couple of tablespoons of water if it's too thick.

You can play around with this – plain peanuts or cashews are nice added in too, as are toasted cumin seeds.

A few good playlists

There are hundreds – thousands – of these available online. My recommendation is to think of a bar or hotel (or club, or restaurant) whose vibe you like, anywhere in the world – they will almost certainly have put some of their playlists on Spotify. Here are a few mixes I like. Each of them is about 3 hours long, so I'm truncating them for reasons of space. If you'd like the full lists, look up 'Home' and then the title of the mixes below on Spotify.

Slightly sexy and louche:
- Sade, *No Ordinary Love*
- Rhye, *Open*
- The xx, *Intro*
- Massive Attack, *Teardrop*
- Maxwell, *Ascension (Don't Ever Wonder)*
- Frank Ocean, *Thinkin Bout You*
- Morcheeba, *The Sea*
- D'Angelo, *Brown Sugar*
- H.E.R. ft. Daniel Caesar, *Best Part*
- Tom Misch, *Movie*

Retro and more upbeat with dancing possibilities:
- Earth, Wind & Fire, *September*
- Stevie Wonder, *Signed, Sealed, Delivered I'm Yours*
- Hall & Oates, *You Make My Dreams (Come True)*
- Chic, *Good Times*
- Blondie, *Heart of Glass*
- ABBA, *Dancing Queen*
- Bill Withers, *Lovely Day*
- Fleetwood Mac, *Don't Stop*
- Marvin Gaye, *Got to Give It Up, Pt. 1*
- Queen, *Another One Bites the Dust*

Breezy and more summery, with bossa nova beats:
- Stan Getz & João Gilberto, *The Girl from Ipanema (feat. Astrud Gilberto & Antônio Carlos Jobim)*
- Antônio Carlos Jobim, *Wave*
- João Gilberto, *Chega de Saudade*
- Sérgio Mendes & Brasil '66, *Mas Que Nada*
- Astrud Gilberto, *Samba de Verão (So Nice)*
- Stan Getz & João Gilberto, *Corcovado (Quiet Nights of Quiet Stars)*
- Antônio Carlos Jobim, *Água de Beber*
- Luiz Bonfá, *Manhã de Carnaval (from* Black Orpheus*)*

- Stan Getz & João Gilberto, *Desafinado*
- João Gilberto, *O Pato*

More traditionally mellow and jazzy:
- Miles Davis, *So What (Kind of Blue)*
- Bill Evans Trio, *Waltz for Debby*
- Chet Baker, *My Funny Valentine (Instrumental or Vocal)*
- Stan Getz & Kenny Barron, *Skylark*
- Coleman Hawkins, *Body and Soul*
- Duke Ellington & John Coltrane, *In a Sentimental Mood*
- Dave Brubeck Quartet, *Strange Meadow Lark*
- Paul Desmond, *Audrey*
- Oscar Peterson Trio, *Georgia on My Mind*
- Ahmad Jamal Trio, *Poinciana*

A few tips on arranging flowers for parties or otherwise

- If you have absolutely no idea what you're doing but want your flowers to look impactful, buy or pick a mass of the same thing in the same colour. This is foolproof and always looks good. It also works with all-greenery.

- All flowers, whether from the garden, from a shop or through the post, benefit from a long cool drink and a rest before you put them into a vase. When you get them home, do not unwrap them from their cone of paper. The cone will help their heads stay upright while they rest and rehydrate, which makes a real difference with the more delicate blooms and with heavy-headed things like tulips.

- Trim the stems by a centimetre or two, at a 45 degree angle. You're doing this because a stem that's cut straight across can create a seal when it hits the bottom of the vase, meaning it won't be able to drink properly. Do it cleanly with something really sharp – you don't want any raggedy bits, which will disintegrate and make your water bacterial and murky. Then plunge the whole bunch into a saucepan or a bucket of cold water. Put this pan or bucket in the coolest space in your house/garage and leave it there for at least a couple of hours. Overnight is even better.

- Once your flowers have had a rest, put them into their vase. If your vase is not see-through, add a couple of big glugs of cheap malt vinegar. If your vase is clear, go for white vinegar or the juice of a lemon instead. The acidic additions discourage bacteria, i.e. stop your stems going mushy and prolong the life of the arrangement (by days!).

- No leaves whatsoever in the water. They rot, turn the water green and make your flowers die an early death. You want only clean, perfectly stripped stems below the water line.

- Change the water in the vase every day. If you have an artfully constructed hand-tied bunch from the florist and don't want the stems to loosen and spill when you take them out of the vase, the easiest way of changing the water is to put the whole vase under the tap, push the flowers gently to one side to make a space, and run clean water into that space until the old water spills out and is fully replaced by fresh.

- Some flowers are shorter-lived than others. In a mixed bunch that's a few days old, always remove any that have conked out prematurely. Otherwise they'll sit there decomposing and sullying your nice clean water, which will shorten the life of the other flowers.

- Don't put flowers anywhere too warm, like in direct sunlight or near a radiator or a fireplace. The cooler, the better. If you're having a party, keep the flowers in the cool place until needed. Sometimes if it's not frosty I put flower arrangements in the porch overnight and bring them in again in the morning. This little holiday into fresh air makes them last much longer.

THE KITCHEN: PART 3

- If you have lilies, always remove their anthers (the orange bits that stain your hands and clothes). If the anther is left there and ripens, it will fertilize the flower. The flower will then think 'job done' and die.

- Delicate flowers and any that are drooping are helped by being seared. Boil a kettle, get a mug, and dunk the bottom couple of centimetres of the stems in the water. If they're really thin and soft, 5 seconds will do it. If they're really thick and woody, like lilac, it's more like 30. You're doing this because searing the stem ends increases the surface area of xylem, xylem being the flower's water transport system.

- If you're standing in the florist, remember you don't have to spend a fortune on buying only spectacular blooms. If you were picking from a garden, you'd be picking foliage (green leafy things), some sort of relatively unshowy background flower, maybe something frothy to fill in the gaps, and only a few really spectacular flowers, which would then stick out to great effect. Buy using the same principle in the florist's.

- Even the world's most beautiful arrangement looks awful in the wrong vase. You need to have the proportions right to really show the flowers off. The rule is one-third vase to two-thirds flowers.

- If your flowers look all wrong, it's almost always because the vase is too tall and narrow. You want the flowers to splay, not stand there stiffly looking like people who come to a party, huddle together for safety and won't take off their coats. Exhale, you want to say to the people/flowers. Don't stand there bunched up tightly and looking awkward. RELAX.

- Flowers look dreadful – tragic, actually – when only their heads and a couple of inches of stem peer across the top of the vase (people do this a lot. SHORTER VASE, I want to say. The focus should be wholly on the flowers, not the receptacle, and the flowers should look at ease and like they can breathe).

- But you also don't want the flowers to splay too much. This is what happens if the vase is too short and/or if the mouth of the vase is too wide for the amount of stems. In which case the flowers spread out so much that there's an empty, sad-looking space in the middle of the bunch. Try another vase, or improvise with jugs, mugs, empty food jars (those tall chickpea glass jars are very good) and anything else you have about you. A vase doesn't have to be a vase.

- You know those annoying and hard-to-shift calcified water marks that you get on vases and that scrubbing won't get rid of? Denture tablets sort it.

- My favourite vase is simple clear glass and measures 19 x 19cm. Everything looks amazing in it. Mine is from Willow Crossley, but these proportions are widely available elsewhere.

YOU CAN PARTY SOBER, TOO: ON HOW (AND WHY) I STOPPED DRINKING

I stopped drinking either five or six years ago (I can't actually remember, except that it was summer) and I thought I'd tell you how it happened, in case it's useful for someone.

I should also say that I was never an alcoholic, which is a much more challenging scenario. But nor was I a person who always felt 100% pleased about their weekly units. I averted my eyes from newspaper headlines about what too much alcohol did to you.

Now – if you *do* feel happy with your consumption, don't read this bit – it'll just annoy you pointlessly. Some people can drink two glasses of wine and go home, and that's great. I was always more 'Shall we open another bottle?'

THE KITCHEN: PART 3

Here are the three things that made me reconsider my relationship with alcohol. It was three thoughts, really.

Thought 1: I read a viral piece which I am 95% sure was about the pornification of real-life sex with specific reference to violence, and the effect it was having on girls and young women. Somewhere in the piece, the author said words to the effect of: think back to yourself as a really little girl, hopping about loving conkers and dogs, or ballet, or Lego, or whatever. You at your sweetest, your most cheerful and curious, excited about the world, including about being a grown-up one day.

You can summon up your own version of that little girl pretty easily. Depending on the happiness or otherwise of your childhood, you may have to go quite far back. But she's right there. We don't kill off our childhood selves. We can't – they're the essence of us.

The question the piece asked (as I recall it, and obviously these are my words, not the author's) was: that little girl, that version of you at your most bushy-tailed – do you honour her and all her hopes and dreams? If the two of you met today, if you sat her down and told her all about her future and all the things that would happen to her in her life, would she still be happy and excited? And if you were very blunt and explicit about the less nice things and she was scared and started to cry, would you at least be able to reassure her that you would always take care of her, never knowingly endanger her, and that you had her back?

This piece stuck in my head for months. I knew I'd sometimes thrown that little girl (me!) to the wolves – unsafe places, unsafe people, stupid risks, bad situations, you know the drill. Eventually – it took ages because I was always trying to push away the obvious conclusion, because I liked wine – I had to admit that there was one common denominator: every single wolf-throwing, going back decades, had involved alcohol.

Thought 2: So then I thought (quite defensively, because, as I say, I liked wine, plus note the cynical tone that always creeps in when people feel threatened) 'yeah, woo-woo inner-child cobblers, whatever – but what about all the good things that have happened to me as a consequence of drinking? Eh? What about those?'

Really fun drunken evenings with people you love don't count – they are to do with loving the company of those people and the alcohol component is secondary. I tried to think of an actual *outcome* that was great – something really wonderful that happened as a direct result of drinking and that made me wake up in the morning going, 'Wow, that's fantastic'.

My list was blank.

Thought 3 – because by this point thoughts 1 and 2 were occupying quite a lot of space in my head – was that I started drinking alcohol in my late teens (Southern Comfort, lemonade and lime, to hide the disgusting taste) because I was insecure and felt Not Enough without it. Alcohol not only made nights out more fun, and other people more fun, but it made *me* more fun. Funnier, wittier, sharper, more outrageous, more confident, thus – surely, no? – more attractive. Less a boring outlying asteroid, more the Sun itself, at least in my own head.

All teenagers feel they are Not Enough, but by this point I was a woman in my fifties, and actually, thanks to a great deal of therapy, I knew that I was enough and had been for some time. So then I thought, 'Maybe I won't have a drink for the rest of the week.'

As I say, that was five or six years ago. I am perfectly open to having a drink. There is alcohol in the house for when people come round. I like choosing wine for when we have people over, I like pouring wine for them, and I like people drinking around me. I find it convivial and jolly. I don't look at those people and shake my head sadly, or judge them in any way (unless they start crashing into furniture, at which point I might do eyebrows). Inasmuch as I think about drinking at all, it's 'maybe on my birthday,' or 'next Christmas, I expect'. Maybe tomorrow, even: never say never. But the birthday or the Christmas or the party come and go, and here I still am.

THE KITCHEN: PART 3

RECOMMENDATIONS

- **Sticky stuff for candles**: **Stick-Um** candle adhesive (from Amazon, among others).
- **Candle shavers**: Widely available online.
- **Pretty baskets**: Even the most basic online retailer now offers a very good selection. If you're after something fancier, try **Maison Bengal**, maisonbengal.co.uk, **The Basket Room**, thebasketroom.com, **Ibbi**, ibbidirect.co.uk, and **Lola & Mawu**, lolaandmawu.com.
- **Tablecloths**: **Zara Home** is brilliant for affordable tablecloths, and much else besides. For heavy linen I use **Linen Tales**, linentales.com, who are in Lithuania, or **Etsy**.

FOUNDATION 5
ON PAINT AND COLOUR

At the time of writing, grey paint has been officially pronounced dead, and despite my great dislike of these sorts of arbitrary pronouncements, grey is the only colour I actively dislike. Why would anyone paint a room the colour of sorrow and bad weather when they could paint it the colour of warm light on a beautiful morning? Nevertheless, I accept that grey can look fantastically elegant, that many truly beautiful interiors have plenty of grey in them, and that grey is much more 'grown up' than my personal favourite, which is pink. If you like grey, go for it. Don't let anyone tell you that it's passé. Fashions come and go, but colours are eternally colours. This applies not only to grey but to all of them – all of that 'colour of the year' malarkey is nonsense. Not only does any so-called colour of the year contain built-in obsolescence – by the very nature of the thing, another colour will come along next year – but also the principle is absurd. Colours are colours. Just use the ones you love.

HOW TO CHOOSE COLOURS

Colour makes people nervous. I'm the other way round: white stresses me out. Or rather, the wrong whites do. The chief offender is the pure brilliant white that is so beloved of builders, renovators who flip buildings for a quick sale, and the people who design new builds. It is glacially cold, with some blue in it, just to give the full operating-theatre effect (pair that with overly white lighting and you have the perfect recipe for the least joyful, least welcoming room imaginable).

The idea is that white is inoffensive, makes rooms seem bigger, that anyone can imagine themselves living with white walls, and that if you don't like it, it's a lot easier to picture a white room painted black than a black room painted white. (Please don't paint a room black. It has its adherents, but black sucks out all the light and all the air. It literally takes up space. It feels so oppressive. No one skips around feeling chipper in a black room. What a very dark room does have in its favour is that it can look jewel-like and it can be an amazing backdrop for art, especially but not exclusively serious art in ornate frames – it sort of adds gravitas. It's also good with elaborate mirrors and a ton of house plants. I think dark rooms can work well in new builds, which tend not to have many features so focusing on a spectacular, rich colour can give the eye the impression that there's more going on than there actually is. But I'd still always go forest green, navy blue, darkest red, or a very dark, bitter-chocolate brown, rather than black.)

That bog-standard, inexpensive, very bright white from the DIY store always seems like a good choice when you don't yet know what to do paint-wise: it's unobjectionable, and you tell yourself it'll do just fine while you unpack, arrange the furniture and get a feel for the space. This is all absolutely true. But it presupposes that painting the walls is a breeze, and that really *isn't* true. Painting walls is a faff – especially when you've finally got the room looking like you want it to look: this is a really annoying time to be dismantling it all again so you can repaint the walls in the colour you'll finally decide on when you get round to it. So what I would always do is go for a warm white, everywhere. Literally every paint brand does a whole ton of them – whites with a tiny bit of green, of pink, of yellow, of brown, of grey, of blue (not warm! beware!), and so on. If you want something absolutely neutral, as in neither warm not cool, Schoolhouse White from Farrow & Ball is a classic for a reason. I prefer Pointing, which has a warmer undertone, but really I like most warm whites, all the way to the ones that look like clotted cream: they are immediately cosifying. You want a white that bears absolutely no resemblance to the dentist's surgery, or indeed the operating theatre. Do that, and white looks stunningly beautiful.

Incidentally, white is also a perfect backdrop if your objects are colourful. Not only does it make their vivid colour look intentional and modern, but the combination of bright objects *and* bright furnishings *and* a brightly painted room can sometimes look quite whacky, a bit too 'fun', the interiors equivalent of 'I'm mad, me.' Of course that may be exactly the super-playful look you're going for, in which case please ignore me. But I am assuming that you want to give your possessions their best chance to shine. The problem with colour on colour on colour (plus perhaps pattern on pattern on pattern) is that everything sort of recedes into an impression of one over-bright, jumbled-up mess. If you want the eye to be drawn to specific pieces, and to create an impression of relative calm rather than something closer to chaos, then white walls are your friend.

BEING SCARED OF COLOUR

One of the reasons for colour nervousness is that people think they don't know what they like. The problem is compounded by the fact that anyone would get confused, what with the 75 squillion paint colours on offer and the microscopic nuances between them. But actually, of course you know what you like! You know what colours you do and don't respond to. And, crucially, you can get dressed. A really useful thing to do if you're confused about paint colours is to go and look at your wardrobe, by which I mean the items you really love wearing and that make you feel great, not your work wardrobe. Is it mostly a sea of neutrals? Is it mostly a riot of colour? In which case, which neutrals? Which colours? Bright, clear colours, or smudgier, softer shades? Make a note: they're your favourites.

Or perhaps your wardrobe is a mixture of both? Mine is. I am naturally drawn to colours, but I quite like head-to-toe camel sometimes.

This is because in head-to-toe camel, I feel I don't have to think about anything: I chuck it on, I like the way it looks, and off I go. Would I want to spend my life in camel? No. But it has its uses.

What this tells me in terms of decorating my house is that too much camel (or beige, or navy, or black, or cream, or grey if you must) wouldn't be my cup of tea, but that touches of it might be a nice idea, because in the right situation I find the colour calming and anchoring when I wear it – restful, almost. Which is exactly how these neutral colours work in a domestic context, too. They give your eye a rest from the colours elsewhere (by the way, talking of anchoring, every room, no matter how romantic and airy, benefits from having something black in it. It's the equivalent of wearing biker boots with a pretty dress: it stops things from looking winsome or overly cutesy).

The reverse is also true: if you're drawn to neutrals, a splash of unexpected colour somewhere in the room wakes your eyes up and adds vitality to an otherwise overly sober room, which can sometimes read as a tiny bit on the dull side. 'A splash' can be something big, like an item of furniture, but it can also mean a cushion, or a kettle, or an ornament. Consider making it red. If you don't know about 'unexpected red theory', it is the idea that adding a pop of red to a room where it doesn't obviously belong (hence the 'unexpected') immediately elevates that room's aesthetic and completely transforms it in one fell swoop. Weirdly – or not: it's to do with friction – this is absolutely true. The phrase 'unexpected red theory' was born on TikTok, but the principle has existed for a long time among interior designers. Unexpected red makes a room come alive. The red thing can be anything at all, from a small object to a large armchair – all it needs to do is be red and 'not go'. Try it, because it absolutely works. (You could of course use any colour you liked, but I do think red is the most effective.)

But we're still in the wardrobe. I've clocked the neutrals, so now I'm looking at the other colours in my wardrobe and thinking about how they make me feel. There's a lot of pink: the bougainvillea-pink dress, for instance, makes me feel like a party

FOUNDATION 5: ON PAINT AND COLOUR

on a hot night in high summer on holiday. Is this something I want for my house? No: it's too high-energy, too frou-frou and too season-specific; I want a sludgier pink that's more subdued and that doesn't give me a hangover. The letterbox-red track pants I'm never out of at the moment? I love that bright red; I find it happy, positive and energizing. But I always wear the track pants broken up with white plus a neutral; I would certainly never wear top-to-toe red every day, because I'm not in a Chris de Burgh song. Mental note: yes to red, but not great big blocks of it: I like it best with other colours.

What about this lovely pea-green jacket? It reminds me of spring, I find it peaceful to look at, it feels an optimistic sort of shade: it's a yes. Could I do a whole green room? Yes, actually, provided the green was both fresh and warm (if this is you, the green that's been in various places in my house for the past ten years is Invisible Green by Edward Bulmer. I couldn't recommend it more – it is to me the perfect interiors green). And if not a whole green room, then certainly objects, fabrics and maybe the odd paint trim.

So now I'm getting somewhere. There are lots of colours in my wardrobe, but I've identified the three I like best – in this instance pink, red and green, plus some useful neutrals. I've thought about how they make me feel and I can imagine how they could make me feel if they were on the wall. Now I just need to translate the results into paint.

Why have I only picked three colours? Because I don't initially want too many colours in my room, because sometimes they turn a room into soup.

ROOM SOUP

If you have white or not-quite-white walls, you don't need to think about room soup at all, because all colours go with white: go for it. But if you have many, many objects, sofas, cushions, books and so on and so forth all in different colours, it may be time to winnow things down a bit.

As previously noted, I love colour and I love pattern. My house is filled to the rafters with both. But you know how when you're a little child wearing a plastic apron with sleeves, learning that red + blue makes purple, blue + yellow makes green and so on, you at some point get an overwhelming urge to mix up ALL the colours in a big squishy scribble and see what you get, and how the answer is a disappointing murky grey-brown? I think the same thing sometimes happens with too many colours in one room. Everything disappears into an unsatisfying soup in which individual items become harder and harder to make out.

HOW TO STOP COLOURS TURNING INTO SOUP

If you have a ton of things in a ton of colours, here's what works for me.

1. Pick two or three to start off with. I'll go with three – the pink, red and green from my wardrobe.
2. Repeat them throughout the room, and include, if you like, any of the related colours in between. My three colours are really only two colours, because red is simply a more intense version of pink. That means pale pink, hot pink, bright red, dark cherry red and so on all count as one colour. So do any greens from pistachio to apple green to something darker and more foresty.
3. I like to designate a specific neutral at this point. In my case it's always brownish, meaning anything from the colour of a single-shot latte to actual coffee beans, because remember we are operating all along the scale of a colour.
4. (I'm giving you punchy examples that are easy to visualize, but of course your colours could be much subtler – it works whatever you pick.)

FOUNDATION 5: ON PAINT AND COLOUR

5. I'm going to stick to these three (really two) colours + my browny neutrals when I initially decorate the room. So I might have browny-pink walls and a moss green sofa. I could add a brownish (neutral) rug with a punchier pink in the pattern, and maybe some small bits of green (any green) in there too. I could have neutral curtains, say a cinnamon-coloured heavy linen (same family as the brown, ergo neutral), or patterned ones (I would go for a red and white ticking stripe).
6. The bones of my room would now be in place. It would look very bare, because it would have nothing else in it. But the initial combinations of colours would be harmonious to my personal eye, and I would feel happy and comfortable among them.
7. I would now go through my many multicoloured possessions and try them out in the room. I'd add some red, green and pink (and go all up and down their colour scales), but with a light hand. This is very personal, but I don't like anything that looks so deliberate that it almost feels themed. So I might have, for instance, one green lamp base with a pinkish shade, one green candlestick and a red armchair, but stop there.
8. I would make lavish use of anything along my neutral scale, from café-au-lait to brown-brown.
9. Everyone's taste is different, but for me the room might well look too carefully thought out and colour-coordinated (I appreciate that both these things are many people's idea of perfection). I would need to rough it up a bit by adding unexpected elements colour-wise: a splash of yellow, or something blue, or something completely unrelated to the rest of the room.
10. I would now have a colourful room, but not room soup.

TWO IMPORTANT THINGS TO KNOW ABOUT PAINT

Thing 1: I'll say it again because it's important: the thing to know here is that for decorating purposes, all the iterations of a colour count as one. For instance: you can go from the palest pink to the darkest red – they're all on one spectrum, so for our purposes they all count as red. You can go from pistachio green to something mossier, and then to a strong bottle or forest green. You can go from a rich, warm creamy colour all the way to dark brown, or from the palest lilac to a dark violet, and so on. They're in the same family, whether they are siblings or distant cousins. As above, my pink, red and green and really just red and green.

What this sliding scale means is that any colours along the scale go together: you don't even have to think about it. A pale pink room leading to a dirty pink room leading to a browny-pink room will always look like you know what you're doing. Ditto cream to nicotine to toffee, and so on. If you want rooms that work together but are all different, this is the headache-free way to go about it. If you want the rooms to feel particularly seamless as you travel through them, don't jump directly from e.g. cream to toffee: it's clunky. Try cream to the colour of a pale camel coat to a cinnamon shade and *then* the toffee. Or, to put it more simply and for example purposes only: if you want things to feel harmonious and considered, don't have a white room leading off a black room. Go black, then dark grey, then lighter grey, then dove grey, then white.

This isn't to say you can't have a blue room with a red trim leading off a yellow room – you absolutely can, and you'd be a person after my own heart. But in all cases, you need to know this one other thing about paint:

Thing 2: There is only one other thing to remember, which is to do with the intensity – the density or opacity – of the shade. It's a

FOUNDATION 5: ON PAINT AND COLOUR

bit like tights: you wouldn't wear 10 denier on one leg and 80 on the other, because it would be visually jarring in a not good way.

Tights aside, the best way I can explain this is to say, think of paints – not emulsion but actual paints that you paint pictures with. We all know that watercolour paint is not the same as oil paint: you get completely different effects. Watercolours are, well, watery: pretty and delicate. Oil paints are thick, full-on and densely pigmented. You wouldn't start painting in watercolour and think, 'What this picture needs is a good old dollop of oil paint,' and if you were painting an oil portrait you wouldn't think, 'I know, I'll do the eyes in watercolour.' The two simply wouldn't work together and you'd ruin your pictures, because watercolours are wispy and ephemeral and oil paints are thick and intense.[1]

Or if you were cooking something very gentle and delicate, you wouldn't then squeeze half the contents of a bottle of chilli sauce into your creation: it would obliterate all the subtlety and completely defeat the point (actually I would do exactly this, but that's my problem). It is the same with wall paint. I can have pistachio green and a more foresty green in the same space, but the pistachio needs to have the same depth – the same richness and opacity – as the darker greens. It can't be the watercolour version. It can't look *thin* and have something *dense* next to it. So if you like rich, jewelled colours, don't suddenly lob in a wishy-washy baby-blue room. If you like a wash of gentle pastel colours, don't suddenly throw in an intense orange. It won't make for an interesting contrast – it will only look madly dissonant, not in terms of the colours but in terms of the opacity. One shade is not remotely intense and the other one is: one is watercolours, one is oils. They don't ever work together. Which isn't to say that you couldn't have orange, to be clear – just that the orange would need to be very light and wispy to go with your pastels: the diluted colour of a big glass of fizzy Vitamin C rather than the colour of Doritos.

---

1. So are some people – terrible combination.

WHY I LOVE PINK

I don't mean Barbie pink, though I wouldn't necessarily discount it out of hand, either. I *love* pink. I've never not had at least one pink room in any house I've lived in. I still mourn a fantastic, fairly punchy (but *beautiful*) shade called Kinky Pink by an extinct company called John Oliver, who had a tiny shop in Notting Hill in the olden days. It was in every kitchen I ever had for two decades, and people used to knock on the door to ask what it was. Happily, though, the wonderful specialists Papers and Paints in Fulham in London (papersandpaints.co.uk) have the John Oliver paint swatches and can match any of the colours.

When I say pink, I don't mean millennial pink, or that sort of Fie-sir-I-am-but-a-maid pink, or those grey-pinks that veer into lilac. I mean classic, timeless pink-pink, from pig pink to raspberry. The reason I love it, apart from obviously finding it deeply pleasing to the eye – more than pleasing: uplifting, comforting, joy-bringing, *lovely* – is how intensely flattering it is in an interiors context.

It makes everyone look their best. Pictures and art and flowers look glorious against it. Lamplight bounces off it and glows. On a gloomy day, it makes the chilliest room feel loved. On a sunny day, it's essence of summer. Dark, poky room? Pink turns it into a jewel box. Room so big it never feels properly lived in? The answer is pink, which brings warmth and life. Pink makes a room feel so convivial that nobody ever wants to leave.

Crucially, pink is hugely flattering to people's complexions at any time of day, and doubly so by candlelight. It literally makes people look more attractive. What more could you want from a wall colour?

I am an expert at pinks. There are hundreds of pink paints on the market, and the sad truth is that the vast majority aren't very nice – something that is much truer of pinks, oddly, than it is of, say, blues or yellows. I spend a lot of my time saying (or thinking), 'That pink is awful.' Blue, in fact, is usually the issue with pink: some pinks with blue in them undo all the goodness and can look wintry – which is not the idea – and even faintly nauseating. Sometimes they remind me a bit of cold meats. So here are my favourite life-enhancing warm pinks, from the pale and lovely to the more assertive. I know each of them personally. If you're looking online, you will already know that online colour reproduction is not always brilliant, but I promise you these are all wonderful in real life.

I've given you various levels of punchiness. They are not high-street paints, for the very good reason that those paints are made with, basically, plastic, meaning they are flat and one-dimensional. These pinks are made from natural pigments, meaning the colour has depth and changes slightly depending on how the light moves around the room. This is why poncy paint brands are worth it: the paint looks like a living thing.

Always get a sample pot and paint as big an area as you can – pinning up a little card isn't going to give you any kind of sense of what the colour will look like once it's up properly. And note that some of these brands allow you to specify a percentage of the colour, i.e. to knock it back if you feel it's too much. But to me these colours are all perfect as they are.

- Sulking Room Pink, by Farrow & Ball
- Templeton Pink, by Farrow & Ball
- Madeleines, by Francesca's Paints
- Parsonage Pink, by Papers & Paints
- Rose Pompadour, by Papers & Paints
- Park Walk Pink, by Papers & Paints
- Kitty, by Edward Bulmer
- Mason Pink, by Edward Bulmer, which is the colour of my sitting room
- Rose, by Edward Bulmer
- Jonquil, by Edward Bulmer – this is the colour of my hallway and office
- Cuisse de Nymphe Émue, by Edward Bulmer
- Carmine, by Little Greene

– Julie's Dream, by Little Greene
– Leather, by Little Greene
– Tuberose, by Bauwerk (limewash[2])
– Rosehip, by Bauwerk (limewash)
– Crab-apple, by Bauwerk (limewash)

---

2. Limewash is a gorgeous earthy paint finish that looks a bit like raw plaster, but coloured. It requires an absorbent wall, which most walls are not if they have been previously painted with normal, modern paint. But fear not! Bauwerk supply preparatory products that will enable you to use their limewash anyway. I won't lie: it's a bit of a faff – but a beautiful finish.

THE SITTING ROOM

Where the living is easy

In the mid-nineties my then husband and I bought a lovely tall, thin house in Stoke Newington. We were moving from a house in nearby Holloway, a converted matchbox factory that had no outdoor space and a dangerously steep and winding metal staircase to get up or downstairs. Neither of these was the best idea with one toddler charging about and a baby on the way.

The house in Holloway was a really good example of the need to buy a house for your actual life, rather than a house for your fantasy life (a principle that also applies to decorating it). We were relatively young – only one of our friends also had children – and saw ourselves as the sort of people who could plausibly live in a groovy, warehousy space, even if the bedroom rattled when the overground went past. And even if buying the matchbox factory (despite what 'factory' implies, it only had 1.5 bedrooms – they only made teeny little matches in it, after all) took every last penny of our money, so that we couldn't afford to paint more than two rooms, or change the murky grey, once-cream carpet in the bedroom, or the ugly cabinets in the user-unfriendly kitchen. Or, I've just remembered, the bank of mirrored wardrobes opposite the bed. The house had at one point belonged to a pop star. The perceived glamour of this, I am sorry to say – the pop star himself, if not his sex mirrors – played a persuasive part in us applying for a mortgage that we couldn't afford.

It became painfully clear very quickly that we'd wildly overreached, so that was that. I wasn't sad – it was also very clear that the house did not remotely work as a family home with young children in it. When we put it up for sale, a television presenter, well-known at the time, came to view it with his then wife. When I showed them the guest loo, there was a massive poo in it, all by itself with no loo paper. This poo belonged to the toddler, who had cleverly taken himself off to the bathroom without asking for assistance on this particular occasion, alas. Unfortunately for all involved, the size of the poo made it look very adult (it's weird how babies sometimes do that), as though my husband or I just did poos without wiping, let alone flushing. The TV presenter's wife shrieked 'Ugh!' when she saw it, as well she might, and gave me a really disgusted and accusatory look. I started to explain about potty-training but was very aware that, blushing and stammering in my embarrassment, I sounded like I was not only lying but blaming an innocent child for my own faecal chaos. There was no second viewing.

The lovely new house in Stoke Newington, by virtue of its extreme narrowness, only provided enough living space if we turned the sunny, first-floor sitting room into our bedroom, which we did. (I don't know why we kept buying unsuitable houses but we were young and silly and cared more about looks than practicality.) The previous owners had slept in the basement, but that was too far away from the children. It was also a dark, uncheerful, slightly damp space that we thought we could use as a sort of tiny sitting room instead (tiny because half of it was a giant boiler cupboard, a washing machine, a drying rack and some fitted wardrobes). But it was depressing down there. So we lived in the kitchen of that house.

The new baby spent his time contentedly in a Moses' basket on legs next to the kitchen table, which is a very handy place for a newborn baby to be based – I repeated the kitchen cot idea in a different house when my next child came along. Who wants to be charging up and down the stairs all day when you could just station yourself and the baby near the bottle sterilizer, the kettle and the mugs? Also kitchen cots get babies used to sleeping through noise, and make them very well socialized, what with people coming in and out all the time. And then when you finally go to bed after the last feed, you just take them up with you. I'm very pro a two-cot household.

Anyway, back to Stoke Newington: as I say, we never used the basement so-called sitting room, because it was so gloomy and cramped – the entire space was taken up by two giant sofas that were ludicrously too big for it – and also because of the mushroom smell. I could do something with the room now, but at the time I was too knackered and sleep-deprived.

My point is that people need sitting rooms. As a new mother of two, I needed to nip to a comfortable sofa in an attractive room in between childcare, normal work and housework. I needed twenty-minute naps that didn't involve my actual bed, because getting into your actual bed in the middle of the day is a whole other thing to an efficient, baby-coordinated catnap, and really unconducive to getting up again and getting on with the day. Your body is outraged, because it thinks, 'Hey, whoa, I thought we were going to bed? We're so tired. Why are we up again?' meaning that you get up feeling discombobulated rather than refreshed.

Sitting rooms are really important. Everyone needs a room to flop and unwind in. I learned my lesson: in every subsequent house I have consciously made my sitting room so comfortable that it lends itself perfectly to naps: a space where you can happily hunker down with a book and a cup of tea before dozing off.

SQUISH

The sitting room is about physical comfort. It's about flopping down on to something soft and going 'aah'. It's about putting your feet up, both literally and figuratively. It is where you watch TV, where you have a snooze, where you lie about with a hot drink doing nothing in particular – and where you play with children or grandchildren, entertain, throw parties, celebrate life events. If you have small children, it can also be the place where, once they're in bed, you remember why you like each other.

For me, this room is about squish. It's about the most comfortable sofas, ottomans, rugs and good lighting. It's about setting a particular kind of mood: relaxation, obviously, but I also feel very strongly that sitting rooms are where you tell your story (see page 23). They are both absolutely private, a place where you can lie around in your pants should the fancy take you, and also absolutely public, a place where visitors come and hang out before dinner, and come back to afterwards when they get tired of the hard kitchen chairs. The items in the room need to be interesting, aesthetically pleasing and specific to you. So, if you're worried about other people judging your taste (see page 66 for help in alleviating that worry), the sitting room is the room where that fear can become most real.

Let's get rid of that fear once and for all. Here is everything useful I would tell you if we were in my sitting room.

The first and arguably the most important thing is: layering. All rooms need layers, but I feel it is particularly important in a sitting room, where you spend so much time and where visitors sit. A room without layers feels flat, one-dimensional and a bit thin, no matter how lovely the things in it are. Layers add dimension, richness and depth. Think of them as a cake: a three-tiered confection is more exciting than a slab of something that hasn't quite risen. Here is what I mean:

- **Layer 1:** this is your big furniture plus rugs and curtains – all the items with the biggest surface area.
- **Layer 2:** this is your lighting, art, mirrors, bookshelves, little side tables and so on – things that take up a fair amount of real estate but not as much as your sofa or coffee table.
- **Layer 3:** this is all your smaller bits, so decorative objects, cushions, throws, flowers, candles, book stacks, bowls, baskets, framed photographs, smaller art pieces that aren't on the wall, etc.

Making sure that you've considered all three layers, regardless of what your decorating style is, is what makes a room come alive. Layering also applies when it comes to styling surfaces. There is more about this on page 133.

SITTING DOWN

How to buy a sofa

- Obvious but so easily forgotten in the heat of sofa enthusiasm: measure your space properly, with a tape measure rather than by eye or in footsteps. Even the most beautiful sofa in the world looks terrible crammed into a space that is even a little bit too small for it. Equally, a too-small sofa looks comical and unmoored in a larger space.

- Allow room for a side table. Every sofa needs a side table, it's like bacon and eggs. A side table with a lamp on it immediately turns the sofa into a cosy little zone. Also you don't want people awkwardly perching their drinks on the sofa's arms. If you're going to have a floor lamp on the other side, allow for that too when you're measuring.

- Remember that you're measuring for depth as well as length. The sofa may fit the space lengthwise, but you need to make sure it's not going to jut out too far into the room if space is limited, or if it's a space that people need to walk past all the time. Nobody wants to squeeze past a sofa every five minutes.

- Annoying but true: as with mattresses, you get what you pay for. In particular, a hardwood frame is always going to cost more than a metal or particleboard one, but it will also mean that your sofa has a much longer life. Yours should come with a guarantee; look elsewhere if it's under fifteen years.

- You want your sofa cushions to be at least partially feather (more expensive) – all-foam or all-fibre (cheaper) aren't quite as comfortable and tend to go flat over time. Mind you, all-feather needs constant plumping. Half and half is a happy compromise.

- Always check vintage first: if you're lucky, you can find real bargains at auction and on online auction sites. People get rid of the most amazing sofas all the time (and also rip out perfectly lovely kitchens, such a pointless waste). Any sofa can be reupholstered – though it is not cheap to get this done professionally – so don't let that trouble you. I only say this in case you're one of those baffling people who look at property particulars and say, 'Ooh no, I hate the colour.' Which I'm sure you aren't, but I am amazed that these people exist. PAINT! I want to say to them. IT'S ONLY PAINT! Ditto upholstery.

- I would hesitate about buying a sofa without having sat on it, and then lounged on it for a good old while. Comfort is everything, and an awful lot of sofas, both new and vintage, look much better than they feel to sit on for any length of time. You can identify your dream sofa online and read all the reviews, but it really is best to then make your way to the nearest showroom and park your bottom on it. Not just your bottom: as with testing out mattresses, you need to stretch out on it. Are you going to use the sofa for napping? Adopt the napping position, not just for thirty seconds but for a good, leisurely five minutes. How do you sit – normally, or do you prefer to tuck your legs under you? If it's the latter, take off your shoes and sit like that for a bit. How's your back? Don't go for maximum squish, tempting as it is, if you fare better with a bit more lumbar support. Do you lie stretched out with your feet on your partner? Try that too. You need to pretend that the showroom/shop floor is in your house and really get into it. No perching timidly because you're worried about looking eccentric. Sofas are major purchases.

- Don't just go on colour or vibe – have a proper think about fabric. It needs to work with your real life, as opposed to the fantasy life in which you maintain your sofa in a state of eternal pristine-ness. If you have three small children and two large dogs, you can maaaaaybe still have velvet, but make sure it's been treated against the worst of staining (the relevant fabrics are called 'smart' fabrics and are much more durable than regular fabrics because they're made out of synthetics; Scotchgard helps a bit too, though only up to a point).

- What you probably can't have is anything terribly delicate. Mud aside, one of my dogs likes digging himself a nest on sofas with his claws, which makes any coverings at all challenging – I have throws and sheepskins on his favourite, which more or less does the trick. I like the look of them (just as well), but I'd be annoyed if the throws, etc. were completely obscuring exquisite upholstery that I'd set my heart on.

- Removable, washable covers are a godsend, not least because you can change the look of your sofa – a pale linen in summer, say, and something heavier and cosier in winter. They also prevent getting sofa boredom, although I rather like sofa boredom – think of it more as a trusty, reliable, faithful old pal and the boredom turns into love. Make sure any removable covers can go in the washing machine – going off to the dry cleaners every two seconds rather defeats the point, in my view. Also, always wash at 30 degrees and hang them out to dry: I've yet to meet removable covers that didn't love to shrink a little bit in the dryer.

- Always, always get swatches. You need to feel the fabric with your hands, and also online colour reproduction is not a true indicator of what the colour is like in the flesh.

- Be aware of the Martindale rub test figure, if there is a figure provided. This determines how much an upholstery fabric can get rubbed before showing signs of distress. If you have an energetic household, you'll want a high score, which translates as 20,000 rubs or more. If you are a very seemly person who never sprawls, never makes a mess and always sits nicely, you can go for something much lower.

- A word in praise of leather sofas. I don't mean giant fake Chesterfields in stiff, shiny leather with a Union Jack flag cushion propped in one corner, like in a faux gastropub in the late 1990s. I mean squashy sofas in soft, buttery, conker-coloured (my personal preference) leather. One, these are timeless. Two, I love the way they look and how comfortable they are. Three, I also love the fact that nothing can harm them. Not armies of children, not pets, not spills – nothing. They just wipe clean.[3] Four, they also look better and better as they age. Vintage is your best friend here: they will come ready broken-in if the leather was a bit stiff in the first place, and they will have developed a lovely patina of the kind that money can't buy. PS it's important to moisturize leather occasionally with a leather product to keep it supple.

- Check the leg height. Some sofas come ridiculously low as standard, and you have to order normal-length legs specifically. I don't mind rolling off a sofa on to the floor, but older people can find these low-level sofas challenging to get in and out of. If you have elderly people about, it's a good idea to have at least one very structured, stiffish chair about for them to be comfortable in. If you're tall, you might need to order tall legs if you don't want to sit with your knees underneath your chin (unflattering).

- Don't buy into trends. I don't ever advocate buying into trends unless it's something small like a bag charm or a flavour of instant noodle. A really top-notch sofa should last pretty much a lifetime (and its price will reflect its life expectancy). But even

3. This is also why leather trousers/leggings are brilliant when you're looking after small children, and for the messier gardening/animal jobs.

if your budget is modest, sofas aren't things you should need to replace every few years. My eldest son has the IKEA sofa we had when he was a toddler in his house in London – it's been recovered in corduroy and has new legs in a more contemporary shape, but other than that it's still going strong thirty years later. Nothing dates a sofa faster than a covering that was fashionable five years ago. If you happen to absolutely die of love for said covering and know you will never tire of it, then great – go for it. If you like it now because it's everywhere and you keep seeing it and everyone seems really into it, ask yourself how you'll feel about that x years down the line, when everyone has moved on. I say 'x years,' but trends move much faster than that these days, which is why it is always so important to trust your gut and go with what you love, whatever you're buying – sofas or otherwise.

- I would always recommend buying a classic sofa in a classic shape with classic, relatively neutral upholstery. You can use throws and cushions to make it feel of the moment, if that matters to you, safe in the knowledge that underneath the cool accessories is a true, solid, reliable workhorse.

THE JOY OF ARMCHAIRS

Sofas are for sharing, but there is a particular delight in sitting on something that is designed purely for solo occupancy – for making one person as comfortable as it is possible for them to be. It is like a mini-kingdom (for your arse).

They are also constructed in a different way to sofas. A sofa needs to bear several people in mind and is therefore necessarily more one-size-fits-all, but an armchair is designed solely with the comfort of one person in mind. This can translate into better, more ergonomic and better-contoured support for your back, deeper cushions, more lumbar support, and of course your own armrests. There is nothing like an armchair (and a decent light) for reading in: you are cocooned in your own world. Unlike sofas, armchairs are also great at breaking up a space without taking up bulk and dominating the room.

An armchair demarcates an area beautifully by making it immediately crystal-clear what the area is for. I love the personal territory aspect of them. If you live with several other people, 'dad's armchair' is like a little island in a busy household.

Being lighter than a sofa, an armchair is also more manoeuvrable: you can spontaneously turn it to face whatever you want it to face without doing your back in. It is brilliant at filling an awkward or unused corner, turning a dead zone into something that is both useful, comfortable and aesthetically pleasing.

Needless to say, armchairs also provide the opportunity to inject whatever you want to inject, be it pattern/colour/energy/calm, into a space. They're particularly good if you want to go bold but are concerned about the boldness being too much when applied to an entire sofa. Armchairs can feel very personal much more easily than larger items of furniture. No wonder people get so attached to them. Armchairs are your own personal haven. Buy them as carefully as you would a sofa – the same advice applies when trying them out.

THE JOY OF OTTOMANS

I think technically a footstool is for trotters up and an ottoman is intended as additional seating, but the words seem to be used interchangeably. I like them as a coffee table, piled with the papers, a lovely tray and a plate of crumpets, though they're really handy as extra seating too. Ottomans are a really versatile piece of furniture. They're nice to look at – the good ones remind me a bit of sturdy pets – and they're so *useful*. Some of them have hinged lids, meaning extra storage. Being squishy and maybe patterned/textured, they can also make a room feel more inviting.

They're not often cheap, ottomans, and the ones that are cheap*er* are often let down by their legs, though you can fix that. Leg

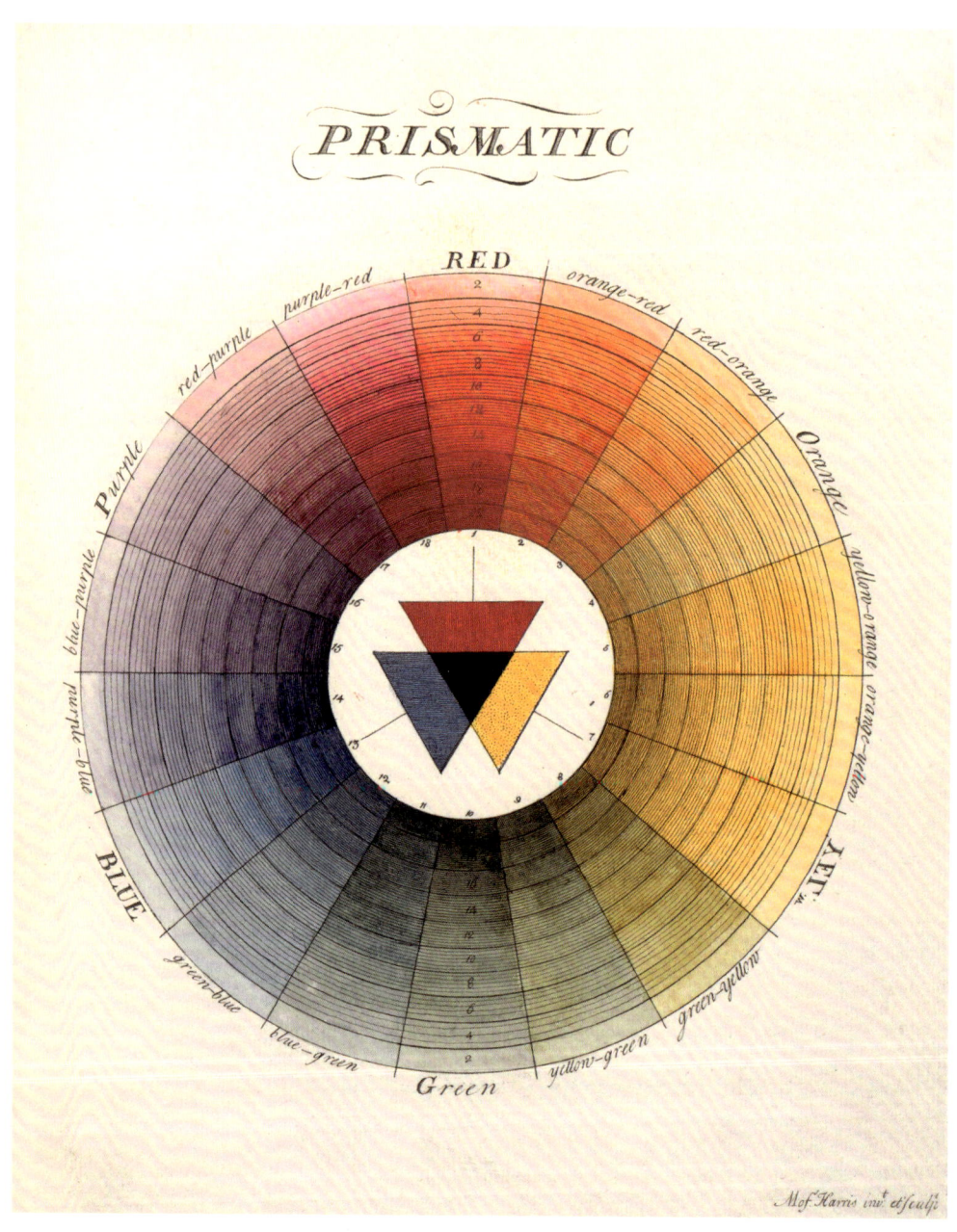

Prismatic Colour Wheel (1766)

fittings seem to be broadly universal, meaning you can swap bad legs for good legs, though please measure first for safety. Legs make such a difference (also true of inexpensive sofas). Vintage aside, the obvious solution to the expense of otts is to upcycle an old one if you're handy with a staple gun.

YOUR ROOM NEEDS A GOOD BACKDROP

Let's start with the walls. For most of us, that means paint (see the foundation on page 97). It can also of course mean wallpaper, but wallpaper is such a vast subject that I'm going to leave you to it. Whenever I fancy wallpaper, I go down such deep rabbit holes that they basically become one gigantic, planet-sized warren. The only thing I would say about wallpaper is, commit to it. Remember what I was just saying about things needing to look intentional? Wallpaper is heaven, except when it feels like a shy experiment. Shy experiments aren't convincing. They just feel hesitant, which is not the vibe anyone wants for their home. What I'm saying is, do all four walls. My only other thought about wallpaper is that if you like and display art, whether it's photos of the children or serious paintings, some very beautiful large-scale wallpapers can compete for attention in a headache-inducing way.

THE MEANING OF ART

Once you've decided on your walls, you can then start thinking about what to put on them, meaning art. (I feel that my most loved things belong in the sitting room, but the below is applicable to any room in the house, including the hallway: you know what you'd like to display where.) What do we mean when we say art? What *is* art? Short answer: art is anything you want it to be. If you like it, up it goes.

Longer answer: Paintings you like. Prints you like. Posters you like. I am a HUGE believer in posters. No, they don't look studenty – not if they're properly framed. Children's drawings. Photographs (I don't mean professional portraits, though go for it if that's your bag – I mean professionally printed frames from your camera roll). So far, so obvious.

But also, any kind of memento – I whack up anything I'd keep in a scrapbook, if I still kept a physical scrapbook (I use mymind.com for an online one). I get everything that is meaningful to me framed, and without wanting to blow my own trumpet, these things look amazing hung collectively or individually on a wall (or in little clusters of three or five). Over the years they have included:

– Restaurant menu(s) from a significant night(s).
– Branded restaurant paper napkins and drinks mats.
– The room service tab from a hotel stay.
– Letters I cherish.
– Pressed flowers.
– Scraps of fabric, e.g. the last remaining fragment of my son's blanky.
– Little notes from when the children were learning to write.
– Later notes from when the children were e.g. obsessed with Pokémon.
– Birthday cards.
– Valentine cards.
– Postcards of art I've loved in museums.
– Touristy postcards of touristy things from places I've had fun in.
– Cartoons I've torn out of newspapers or magazines, or found online and printed.
– Particularly handsome wallpaper samples.
– Illustrations, e.g. botanical, cut out from mildewed books from car boots.
– Printed-out non-intimate emails that give good news.
– Various children's certificates, e.g. GCSE, swimming proficiency, grade 1 ballet.

THE SITTING ROOM

- Theatre tickets.
- Opera programmes.
- Festival tickets, lanyards, wristbands.
- Train tickets from special journeys.
- Doodles.
- Orders of service.
- The sleeves of beloved vinyl records.
- Printed-out text conversations that were memorable and/or funny.
- The first and only cryptic crossword you ever completed.
- A particularly apt paragraph from old paper school reports.
- Group photographs that I am attached to but wouldn't put up anywhere else, of e.g. the netball team in 1981.

And so on. Literally anything you like the idea of. If your item is small and you'd like it blown up, online printing services are brilliant (see below). Now, obviously you can jumble all these things up together or keep to a stricter colour palette – a narrow one or a wide one: it's entirely up to you and to the look you like for your home. As for the hanging, you can do it by eye, you can do it by perfect symmetrical measuring, you can make the spaces between the art equidistant – or not. You can go for any effect you like, from impeccably curated to looser and more bohemian.

But that's not all! You can also have *anything* three-dimensional mounted and box-framed. You know how you keep things for sentimental reasons but often don't actually have anywhere to put them, and so they end up in a shoe box in the loft? Frame the more significant ones. Remember you don't even have to put all of these on the wall – some of them also work upright on a shelf (very good for breaking up acres of books) or lying down on a surface like a coffee table. A few ideas:

- This one is for a wall: souvenirs from a whole trip, smartly framed into a giant collage – the whole caboodle, from boarding passes to room keys to menus, museum ticket stubs,

beer mats, photos, *l'addition* and everything else you grabbed as a memento. A good framer can help you with layout, or you can use an online graphic design platform like Canva to play around with the placement of things – they have tons of templates.
- Nice shells.
- Nice pebbles (both of these tend to get lost on a table or shelf. But not in a frame!)
- The completely random, out-of-character small item you inexplicably felt compelled to buy at the charity shop but have no home for anywhere, e.g. a vintage bead necklace you'd never wear, or a small pottery animal.
- The broken, glued-back plate you love but don't dare use any more.
- Nice vintage items of clothing, from a football shirt to the silk scarf that's too beautiful and too fragile to wear, to your great-grandmother's full-length evening gloves, or her swimming cap, or your grandpa's tank top.
- A friend has the stub of her last-ever cigarette box-framed. It has her lipstick on the filter and it looks fantastic.
- Beloved old toys that are beyond playing with – a Lego figure, maybe, or a bath toy that saw particularly long service.
- Something broken or incomplete that you don't want to throw away.

Now, really good framing or boxing doesn't come cheap. This doesn't actually terribly matter in a space that people are only ever passing through: here you can easily get away with the best ready-made frames you can afford. I think paying for proper framing makes an enormous difference when the item is going to be in a place where you sit and stare at it: it can elevate the humblest poster (one of my favourites cost £3.50 from an exhibition at the Barbican about the dancer Michael Clark). The trick is to find a framer you can have conversations with and whose taste you like. A merely competent framer will fob you off with a bog-standard thin oak frame, and while that is perfectly okay – I had bog-standard thin oak frames for decades of my life – finding a fantastic and imaginative framer really does open up a world of possibilities. I found mine by taking a picture to a whole load of different framers and saying, 'I'm not sure what would look best with this.' Eventually I came across someone whose eyes lit up as she produced a variety of frames in different styles to suit a variety of tastes – the point is that every single one looked amazing. We now know each other so well that I would trust her to frame anything with my eyes closed. I have a lot of things on a lot of walls and finding this framer completely changed my home-decorating life.

FRAMING TIPS

1. Think outside the box. You can put a minimal thing in an ornate frame or vice versa.

2. You can put a tiny thing in a much larger frame – it draws more attention to it and makes it feel more substantial.

3. In which case you'll need a mount, this being an area of card or paper that fills up the rest of the space, with your item in the middle.

4. Though it doesn't even have to be the middle: setting the item off-centre can also be really effective, again because it looks considered, which adds weight to the arrangement and makes it look grander than it is.

5. Be inventive when it comes to mounts. They don't have to be plain white, cream, grey or black. They can be any colour you like.

6. They also don't have to be made out of card – try wrapping paper, old wallpaper samples, or fabric.

7. They don't have to surround the image, either: they can also work as the background to it, with the picture sitting on top.

8. Play with texture. The clean lines of a black and white photograph look less interesting in an equally clean-lined skinny black frame than in something less expected – a thick, faintly rustic wooden frame, for example. Equally, something old-looking can sometimes best be shown off in a modern, minimal frame. Contrast always keeps things interesting.

9. Think about where the frame is going to go. It doesn't have to be somewhere obvious, like the hall wall or on the wall in your sitting room. It could be leaning on the ledge above the kitchen door, or live on the front of a boring cupboard, or be a pleasing surprise in an unexpected corner. I really like framed things on very full bookshelves – not sitting on the actual shelf (though that works too) but actually hung from it.

10. If you like a mixture of frames, vintage is your friend.

11. High-street framers I like are on page 139.

12. Very important: so many people hang their pictures too high. They should be at eye level, so you can see them.

Another thing I would say is that there's a lot of very generic affordable art around, or at least generic-seeming to me, which doesn't mean it isn't great if *you* like it. I'm thinking of prints of, say, a glass, with NEGRONI written underneath, or of a forkful of spaghetti and PASTA in big letters. Recently I saw a huge poster that just said TIMES LIKE THESE, which made me properly hoot. What does it even mean? Times like what?

Or there's the whole photographs of the Amalfi coast in the 1960s genre. Or prints of big shapes. I like big shapes, but why would you have a generic print of big shapes on your wall when you could have something that is meaningful to you? (Again, if the merest sniff of a big shape makes your heart beat faster, then ignore me and go right ahead.)

People buy indifferent art to put on their walls because so many people don't trust their own taste. Meaningless phrases or big shapes,

THE SITTING ROOM

like walls painted all the colours of boredom (Ennui, Fatigue, Lassitude, Malaise) don't semaphore great taste – but that's okay because they don't have to. Their only job is to say, 'Look! This is absolutely fine! I do not have actively *bad* taste.' The very fact that someone decided that PASTA would make a great print – that someone *curated*, if you please, a selection of PASTA-like prints – makes people think that it must have at least some merit, and that it is therefore a safe buy.

But nobody wanders about thinking, 'What this room really needs is a large print saying PASTA.' What happens is that they don't trust themselves to put up something they truly love, in case – well, in case what? In case other people. In case a visitor says they don't like it. In case someone makes fun of it. In case someone says, 'Ew, what's that weird print?'

I will say this again because it is a thing to always remember. The only person who lives in your house is you, or you and your family, and you are the supreme rulers of your castle. Do you like something? In it goes. Do you feel indifferent about something? Leave it in the shop. More money is wasted on items where the person goes, 'Oh God, I don't know, I suppose this one will do,' than over the spontaneous buying of little things that make your heart sing.

It is not your job to decorate hesitantly using someone else's template, unless theirs is a template you die of love for (and that you feel confident would work in your own space, not necessarily a given). It is your job to surround yourself with things that make you feel happy. And if someone does say something about the weird print, or the eccentric whatever, so what? You live there and they don't. Also, if anyone is rude enough to remark negatively about something you have chosen to display, I would think twice about offering them cake.

The best places to buy art for your walls are junk shops and auctions, but I appreciate that not everyone has the time to waft around looking. Sometimes there's a big gap on your wall that you just want to fill asap. There are some of the online places where I look below. I don't differentiate between paintings, posters and prints because I like and buy all three.

But first, I look in my house. I *love* shopping my own house – it is unbelievably satisfying and also free. Things get moved around, reframed, fished out from the loft, nicked from another room. This works best if you are quite old (probably), were completely bemused by the mass embracing of Marie Kondo soullessness, have amassed a lot of bric-a-brac over the years, and/or have the space to store it.

But even if none of that applies, looking at what you already have with a fresh eye – rather than the eye that takes everything for granted because it's so used to certain things being in a certain place – can yield rich pickings. The junk-shop painting that's always struck you as a bit gloomy becomes un-gloomy and merely atmospheric if you move it somewhere where daylight shines on it.

PLATES AS ART

Don't forget about plates, though maybe not at person-height in a narrow hallway. I *love* a plate on a wall, or ideally a cluster of several plates. Obviously a plain white IKEA one wouldn't look as impactful as something more decorative, but anything coloured or patterned usually looks fantastic, whether it is a hand-made, hand-painted treasure or something more mass-produced. If the latter, working with a group of plates is better than putting up a single one: single things demand your full focus, and it's better if the item in question is fully deserving of it. A group, on the other hand, can give the impression that the component parts are more special than they actually are. Odd numbers are more effective than even; this is true of décor throughout the house. Car boot sales are a rich source of fantastic old plates, as is eBay.

I have a load of cabbageware plates on the wall to the side of the cooker in the kitchen, collected very cheaply over the years from various junk and charity shops. In another room I have a cluster of five Astier de Villatte plates, all presents (well, presents I asked for) over several Christmases. If your tastes are more minimal, plates still look amazing – home in on texture rather than colour or pattern, which is the best rule for minimal interiors across the board.

The best way to hang plates is by using those round, flat, bright yellow adhesive things that don't seem to have a brand name but say 'The Original "Invisible" Disc Plate Hanger' on them. They are cheap and unbelievably efficient – they grip like the most ferocious superglue but the glue washes off easily with warm water if you later decide you want to eat off a particular plate instead. They come in various sizes, the largest of which can hold up to 2kg. I have never had one come off in decades of use. Please obey the instructions on the card they come stapled to and don't try to hurry the process up – they need to sit on the back of the plate overnight to work their magic.

LIGHTING

We've already talked about lighting in my foundation on page 41, but in the sitting room in particular, lighting is also about the right lampshade. The warmer the colour of the shade, the warmer the ambience in the room, so for example a mint green shade with a cool white bulb is never going to feel anywhere near as soft and hunkery as a dim, golden bulb inside a parchmenty, yellowy, pinky, reddy or browny shade. If you fancy a cooler-coloured shade – greens and blues – it will still look warm provided you have the right bulb, and cosier still if the shade is lined in a soft neutral colour, or in gold, which throws out a lovely diffused light. Generally a fabric shade will soften light further, more so than a standard card one, though there are exceptions: anything parchment-looking is great at emitting soft light.

My sitting room is awash with table lamps, because they and their yellow bulbs provide an abundance of ambient light – and the more ambient light, the cosier the room.

Then there is this other fundamental truth: the more little lamps you have, the richer the feel of the room. I mean literally rich, as in wealthy. Little glowing lights bring opulence and an almost decadent sense of extreme ease and comfort. In an ideal world, they all need to be at different heights. I don't mean one tiny and one massive – I just mean each very slightly different in height from the next. I have eight of these lamps plus one reading light in my sitting room alone, which does look slightly extreme written down, but which works beautifully in real life. No overhead lighting at all, not that I'd ever use it: ceiling lights are an absolute buzzkill. With this number of lamps, smart sockets are obviously a good idea – I can turn things on and off automatically using my phone. Prior to the invention of smart sockets, it took twenty minutes to turn off all the lights in the house. I'm not even joking. But it was still worth it!

THE MAGIC OF ROUND THINGS

So we've got our walls sorted. We've done something about the lighting. We have bought a lovely sofa, and possibly a lovely ottoman. Now we need round things.

Whatever the room, most items in it – tables, chairs, sofas, in this instance – are made up of straight lines and angles. So is the room itself. So are rugs, pictures, fireplaces, mantelpieces, window frames, paintings, shelves, mirrors, lampshades, televisions. So are books, storage units, cupboards, side and coffee tables – it's a very long list. And so are many of the smaller decorative items we strew around.

None of this is a problem, unless you look around the room and think, 'Hm, everything in this room is nice, I wonder why it never feels cosy.'

You may never think that, of course. If you want something that feels very formal and smart, there's probably no issue (also poor you, you're really in the wrong book). But if the object of the exercise is to make a space feel welcoming, then all those straight lines are not helpful. You are a soft, curved human, surrounded by hard angles. It's not relaxing. That's why you don't feel cosy. You need round things. Round things have magical, interiors-dilemma-solving properties.

Think of straight lines as tailoring. You wouldn't (I imagine) sit at home wearing top-to-toe tailoring plus office shoes plus a briefcase – if you were heading off to work you would seek to soften the ensemble, maybe with a silk scarf, maybe with a less structured handbag rather than a briefcase, maybe with a more playful, less uptight shoe. For the purpose of comparison, in a room context those accessories are the round things.

The round things can be anything – a round rather than a rectangular mirror, a curvy vase rather than a long thin sharp-edged one, an occasional table that is circular, a non-spiky plant with rounded leaves, a round basket. Basically, round shapes feel friendly, and hard lines do not. Try it: find a surface that isn't quite doing it for you, and swap out something linear for something curved. Repeat as many times as you like, though always keeping a mixture of shapes. See? It always works. It's partly to do with contrast – which, yet again, keeps the eye alert and engaged rather than bored – and partly because circles feel warm and convivial in a way that an excess of straight lines does not.

A NOTE ON TEXTURE

As you'll have gathered by now, texture always matters because it adds dimension and depth to the room. This is always important, but never more so than if your taste runs minimalist. For illustrative purposes only – it's an extreme example – imagine a plain white room with white furniture in it. We've sorted out the light and it is beautiful. We've sorted out the shapes, and they are beautiful too. But our room still looks flat, try as we might to make it not look so. Our room looks one-dimensional.

Why? Texture, or the lack of it. There is nothing for our eye to grip on to. Nothing sticks, so it glides past everything, yawning.

Now picture the same white room. There's a lavishly tufty white rug on the floor. The sofa is cream linen. The lampshades are cotton fabric. There's a pale wooden console with lots of candlesticks on it – still all white. Some are rough ceramic, some are nubbly papier-mâché, some are smooth bone china. There's a white metal armchair with a sheepskin throw on the seat. There's a white beaded chandelier hanging above the coffee table, which is made of clear glass. The curtains are wafty white gauze. The room looks amazing. Why? Because we have paint, wool, wood, linen, cotton, ceramic, papier-mâché, china, fabric, metal, fur, beads, gauze and glass in it. Yes, everything is white, or shades of white – but it's a feast for the senses. There is tons to look at. Our eye is delighted. It glides over nothing, but rather takes everything in. What a lovely room, it thinks to itself – correctly.

Now let's apply this principle to something less drastic than an all-white room. If you love neutrals, texture is just as important. You need contrasting textures to keep things interesting. Just as you wouldn't wear head-to-toe vinyl (I mean, it's a look) or denim – denim hat, denim shirt, denim trousers, denim belt, denim shoes, denim bag, denim coat, etc. – so head-to-toe taupe, let's say, in very similar textures, is never going to look especially interesting. But, as with the white room, if your taupes a) go up and down the colour scale and play around with it, so that you have everything from taupe-taupe to almost-brown, and b) play around with texture as above, you have a fantastic room even before you've started accessorizing it with art and objects in – maybe – a couple of other colours. An example: I am extremely covetous of my mother's taupe sofas, which are upholstered in inviting, tactile microsuede. She has a perfect eye, which helps, but is a minimalist to her core. Her modern, Italian sofas are taupe and angular, all clean straight lines – not, on paper, what I would go for in my own home – but the reason I covet them is that they are really fat. The upholstery is immaculate, but it is lavish. The cushions are deep and inviting. The texture is tactile and moreish. You sink into these sofas and never want to get up again. The lines of them look borderline severe, but the texture and upholstery mean they're actually as friendly as a puppy. My mother knows what she's doing – none of this is an accident – and the result is perfection:

neat, chic, linear, minimal, but warm and comfortable. It's a beautiful look.

Texture is still important if you have a maximalist room, because similar textures read as very samey: imagine the nightmare of an all-velvet room, for example, or all-chintz. You'd feel suffocated and claustrophobic, or like you were going for a tarot reading at a seaside fair in 1958. In a more maximal interior, you want each object to shine because if they all start melding into one, the only impression anyone's going to get is 'mess'. Demarcate your objects by putting something matte next to something shiny, something vintage next to something modern, something smooth next to something more rugged.

THE FURNITURE PLACEMENT IN THE ROOM

The traditional way of furnishing a sitting room is to have all the furniture around the edges and a big empty space in the middle, perhaps made less empty with a coffee table that is rarely large enough. (Coffee tables that are too small look really, really terrible and throw out the proportions of the room, making it look like a normal-sized person wearing a doll-sized hat. Always go as big as you can in the space available. This is also true of area rugs, i.e. rugs that demarcate a specific area, like under the sofas and coffee table. Always make sure your rug is large enough for all the feet of the furniture to be sitting on it. A too-small rug, no matter how beautiful, looks ridiculous. If your rug is comically tiny, put another one alongside it – they need to complement each other, but they don't need to be identical twins.)

I don't think this way of laying out furniture is optimal. Few of us have such an abundance of sitting-room acreage that we can afford that wasted expanse of space in the middle. Also, it's not convivial. If the room is big, people are sitting miles away from each other, all around the edge of it. If the room is small, the arrangement is a really bad use of space. So do consider bringing your furniture in a bit and away from the walls. It immediately feels friendlier, apart from anything else. If you look at photographs of those vast, grand drawing rooms, you will see that they always, always use items of furniture to zone out the space, and never, ever have said furniture pressed up against the walls. Sofas, incidental tables, side tables, ottomans – among others – are free-floating, miles away from the walls, creating a series of cosy-seeming places to sit and talk. If your furniture is light, as in, if it doesn't weigh very much, consider placing something heavier behind it – a console table behind a sofa, say, to stop it skidding halfway across the room when someone flumps down on to it. If you don't have the space to do this, even the narrowest shelf, just a few inches deep, fixed to the wall behind the sofa will make a huge difference. Put things on it, obviously!

THE OBJECTS IN THE ROOM

It should be clear by now that when it comes to choosing objects for your sitting room, you should be guided by the things that speak to your heart, that tell your story and that make you feel at home.

But there are ways of displaying things – even things that, objectively, some people might find unattractive or peculiar – that will make them look both good and intentional. 'Intentional' is very important. You can't have things sitting about apologetically and sort of cowering. Timidity is the enemy of a pleasing aesthetic. Objects aren't shy baby deer. Our hypothetical papier-mâché pig from page 26 can't be peering sadly out of a dark corner, covered in dust. You have to have, or pretend to have, confidence. That, and a decent backdrop (which we've covered already).

THE SITTING ROOM

HOW TO STYLE ANY SURFACE IN A HARMONIOUS AND VISUALLY SATISFYING WAY

- Whether you're packing things in or going for something ordered and restrained, as we have seen you want a mixture of textures, a mixture of sizes, a mixture of shapes and a mixture of heights.

- Don't have lonely objects unless they are very large. A candlestick looks silly on its own on a large surface but handsome and substantial if you give it a friend or two.

- Group smaller things in odd numbers.

- If the surface you're styling has a back, meaning if the back of it is up against a wall, then layer that surface like mad. Layers give dimension, as we have seen. If you have everything displayed in one straight line, you've made your surface (and its objects) flat and one-dimensional. A 1-D surface is never going to look either interesting or visually satisfying.

- Put something at the back of the surface – a propped-up picture, for example – and then something smaller in front of that, slightly off-centre – let's say a bowl or vase – and then something in front of that, again not perfectly lined up, which could be a candlestick. Repeat all along the surface until your eye is satisfied by the composition. The surface will now look rich and visually complex.

- If the smaller things are not especially attractive but are useful/ necessary things, e.g. your bedside table might feature AirPods, ibuprofen, a biro, earplugs, a chewy for the dog, your phone and some hand cream, put them into a basket or on a tray. Devote the rest of the space to more photogenic things – a lamp, some books, a bottle of scent, a water jug, or whatever. Do the same thing on a hall table or shelf, where this sort of random arrangement also seems to congregate, and with things like reading glasses and remote controls (which also stand less of a chance of getting lost if they are corralled).

- A living thing is always a good idea – a plant, some flowers, a branch of something interesting from the park or garden. They bring energy and light to whatever they're sitting on. They don't have to be large or lavish. I'm always going on about the wonder of £1 supermarket daffodils on my Substack – instant beauty and cheer on any surface and in any room.

- If you are styling a coffee table, remember that ideally it needs to look appealing both when you're sitting down and when you're standing up.

- You don't need new things to fill any of these surfaces if you think they're looking a bit sparse. Simple stacks of books and magazines look amazing on a coffee table (very upper-middle-class country house) – just break up the straight lines by perching round things like a little bowl or cordless lamp on top, or in the gaps, every now and then.

WHY YOUR NICE THINGS LOOK INSIGNIFICANT

This is another common problem, in the sitting room as elsewhere. The answer is: because they're too small, probably. Most people's are. I was recently explaining about too-small objects to a friend who has recently moved house and who was complaining about things looking wrong in her sitting room. Her reaction was, 'Oh my God, how did I not know this?', which made me think I should share it in case it's useful. If you know you know, but if you don't it changes everything.

My friend's issue was this: she has some really nice objects, as in purely decorative items that sit about in various rooms bringing pleasure whenever the eye alights on them. This is their only job – to bring joy through beauty, to remind her of a happy memory, to make her feel contented whenever she looks at them, and to feel pleased about her shopping choices.

But, my friend said, none of this really happens. The eye does not alight. Joy does not come. The objects are lovely – a small painting, some enviable ceramics, a shell and some candlesticks, among other things – but instead of looking glorious and meaningful, 'They just look really random and unspecial. I can't understand why.'

I can. Well, I can now, x number of houses later. It's because the objects in question are *too small*. To put it a different way, they don't have enough visual weight.

You know when you have a surface – a coffee table, shelf, console, bedside table, dresser or whatever; it can be anything at all – that doesn't look quite right despite having nice things on it? Nine times out of ten it's to do with the smallness of the things. Same thing if you've ever said, 'Thank you – I always feel it's rather lost,' when someone compliments you on something in your house (usually because they've only just noticed it even though you've had it for nine million years).

The objects aren't too small in themselves, obviously – a candlestick is always going to be candlestick-sized, a bud vase is by definition mini – but they are too small *for the surface they're on*, and this robs them of their presence and by extension of their visual appeal. Being too small, they become lost, and all your good work sourcing them and loving them is lost alongside.

We all have small things, obviously. Small things are great. Nobody lives in The House of Giant Objects. But there's a right and a wrong way of displaying them, and a very easy fix. We need to make them bigger and more noticeable, by which I mean we need to give them more visual weight.

On my coffee table I have, among other larger things, three eggs made of stone, a little apple cast in bronze, a small ashtray stolen from Mirabelle restaurant in the late 1990s after a particularly fun night, a big box of matches for lighting the fire, and a little bud vase. If I put any of these things down directly on to the coffee table, they would look both absurd and absolutely lost. The little stone eggs would roll around like losers. The bronze apple would be alone and forsaken. The ashtray would be marooned. The matchbox would look random and the bud vase tiny and unmoored.

All these items need to be raised and corralled to give them their full weight and impact. So the three eggs made of stone live in a little bowl. The bronze apple and the ashtray sit at the foot of a small table lamp; all three have been elevated by being placed on a short stack of novels. The box of matches is in a rattan tray, along with some tealights, the bud vase with a paper flower in it, two candlesticks and a couple of spare candles. Everything is visible and everything is shown off to its best advantage. In between these items are a small vase of flowers, magazines and various coffee table books.

I have another coffee table in the house, this one in a former barn, so a huge space this time – and the bigger the space, the more the need for chunk if you don't want things to look weirdly doll-sized. This table has stacked hardback novels and coffee table books on it rather than paperbacks, a huge bowl on it filled with narcissi at the time of writing – this isn't the place for one weensy terracotta pot, charming as they are. The candlesticks sit on a large vintage brass tray to give them weight – they would look spindly and lonely without this anchoring base. And so on. On the walls here, the smaller pictures are hung in groups to give them heft, rather than hung on the wall with loads of space around them, where they would look disproportionately minute, and therefore lost.

GOLDEN RULES:

- Give small things more visual weight by either raising, grouping or corralling them.
- Group your small things in bowls or on trays, and they immediately look significant.
- Giving them a book plinth immediately elevates them (literally).

- Bowls are good for two or three things (see note on odd numbers below).

- Trays are fantastic for corralling larger things. Grouping them makes them look considered and substantial, and more to the point makes you really *see and appreciate* them.

- Remember to vary the heights of your tray or plinth composition. Things also look flat and insignificant if they're all the same height. You want tall things in there as well as shorter ones. The one draws the eye to the other.

- You don't want even numbers when you're creating a little vignette of this kind. Or of any kind. The eye likes symmetry, so if something is in pairs, the eye quickly glides over the display thinking, 'Ah yes, all is as it should be.' But odd numbers stop it in its tracks and forces it to take a closer look – which is what you want when you're displaying something. You can do threes or fives, or sevens if you have a lot of something.

Some favourite coffee table books

I am very against 'coffee table' books that are mindless – generic pictures and inane captions. I need books that I properly love, with timeless content that I want to revisit often and words that are useful and teach me things. Here are some of my faves. They're all interspersed with paperbacks and novels and candles and paper flowers, at the moment. I also like coffee table books on the kitchen table, where I can properly read them.

- *The House of a Lifetime: A Collector's Journey in Tangier*, by Umberto Pasti and Ngoc Minh Ngo (Rizzoli). Every page is a dream because Pasti is a genius and a visionary, both indoors and when it comes to making a garden.
- *A Wandering Eye*, by Miguel Flores-Vianna (Vendome Press). He is a famous interiors photographer and has made several

exquisitely beautiful books, but this one is a collection of pictures he took on his phone. They're like paintings and make you look at normal things with a fresh eye.
- *On Flowers*, by Amy Merrick (Artisan). Deeply aesthetically pleasing but, crucially, also full of useful information.
- *Flora Britannica*, by Richard Mabey (Chatto & Windus). Info-packed and scholarly. Also, shameful confession, I really love the green of the cloth jacket underneath the paper one.
- *Coming Home*, by Barbara De Vries (Rizzoli). I love Dutch interiors and this book is marvellous – undone and unstuffy and completely charming.
- *Kabinett and Kammer*, by Sean Scherer (Vendome Press). He is an American designer, collector and proprietor of a shop that is a sort of cabinet of curiosities. This was his first book and it is extremely pleasing to leaf through. I don't know why American interiors are so American, but they are, aren't they? Even the atypical kind like these. There's always a very specific sort of orderliness to them. Lovely, though.
- *Outside In*, by Sean A. Pritchard (Mitchell Beazley). A wonderful garden and flower book. It is heaven from start to finish and jam-packed with useful tips and advice.
- *Raucous Invention: The Joy of Making*, by Mark Hearld (Thames & Hudson). I'm a huge fan of Mark Hearld, an artist who can seemingly turn his hand to everything – collages, prints, textile design, wallpaper, sculpture. Everything is informed by a love of the natural world and of British folklore.
- *Sofia Coppola Archive*, by Sofia Coppola (Mack). I can't tell you how beautiful, inspiring, fascinating and sort of *nourishing* this book is. I look at it at least twice a week. It's basically a collection of everything that's ever caught her attention and found its way into her work – snatches of things, collages, personal photographs, random bits and bobs, annotated scripts, images and stills from the shoots of various films, etc., etc. AND the text is wonderful.

RECOMMENDATIONS

- **Good ottomans**: Look at **Rowan & Wren**, rowandandwren.co.uk, who have lovely ones and good sitting-room furniture generally. Also **Arlo & Jacob**, **Soho Home**, **Dunelm**, **Weaver Green**, Sophie Robinson's range for **DHS**, Nina Campbell's range for **Next**, **Swoon**, **Birdie Fortescue**. At the luxe end, **The Tolstoy Edit**, the tolstoyedit.com, and **Susan Deliss**, susandeliss.com, both have divinely gorgeous options. **The House Upstairs**, thehouseupstairs.co.uk, is somewhere in the middle, beautifully made and also excellent for sofas.
- **Nice frames for photographs**: **Zara Home** and **Addison Ross**, addisonross.com
- **High-street frames for art**: I would strongly urge you to find a local framer so that you can touch and feel the materials yourself, but reputable and budget-friendly companies include **frames.co.uk**, **my-picture.co.uk**, **theframedpicturecompany.co.uk**, and **easyframe.co.uk** for digital photo printing. **The Printspace**, the printspace.co.uk, specializes in handmade fine art framing with sustainable materials.

Buying art online, a list to get you started:
- **Collagerie**, collagerie.com, has a fantastic, curated collection of limited edition prints from interesting artists. **Etalage**, etalage.co.uk, source and sell antique fine art prints, vintage oil paintings and decorative pictures. **Partnership Editions**, partnershipeditions.com, commission and sell prints and original artworks from emerging artists. **Wilson Stephen and Jones**, wsjgallery.com, is a brilliant online gallery curated by people with impeccable taste. **Plakatcph**, plakatcph.com, sell interesting posters from Denmark. **Mason & Painter**, masonandpainter.com, for charming vintage paintings and affordable originals. **Pallant House Gallery Bookshop**, pallantbookshop.com, have affordable etchings, woodcuts, screen prints, lithographs and wonderful old exhibition posters

and prints. **Tinsmiths**, tinsmiths.co.uk, have nature-leaning prints from contemporary artists and glorious, inexpensive letterpress posters printed especially for them. **Glassette**, glassette.com, which is recommended generally as an early port of call for all decorative objects, has an excellent art selection, from original works to prints.

– **The Mainstone Press**, the mainstonepress.com, have limited edition prints from artists like Eric Ravilious and John Minton. **Abbott and Holder**, abbottandholder.co.uk, have a vast repository of paintings and drawings, many affordable, some less so. The physical shop is opposite the British Museum (they are helpful and charming people) but it's all online too. Sign up to their list and you'll be emailed new stock. They also have a framing service. And museum shops are such a rich source of posters – **The Royal Academy** does absolutely massive ones called Epic Posters that are a great way to fill a wall in one fell swoop.

– **John Lewis make the best rug grip**, and that is just a fact.

FOUNDATION 6

NO STUFF, OR ALL THE STUFF?

I like big stuff, I cannot lie

Sometimes I want to wear something very plain and minimal – no fuss, neutral colours and a kind of implied efficiency. Sometimes I want to dress more elaborately. And it's fine, because my wardrobe contains both options.

But you can't really do that with interiors. Furnishing and decorating your house is expensive, even if you're doing it on the cheap. You have to be reasonably consistent in your look, not veer too wildly in another direction, and I think that many of us are sometimes curious about what it would be like to live inside a completely different aesthetic.

Personally, I like rooms that make you feel like you're in a nice-looking nest and are welcome to take a nap at any time. Rooms that make you feel like you should sit up straight (on the hard sofa) are not for me. I dislike even the suggestion of grey. I like garden flowers much more than fifty white tulips all cut to exactly the same height, and higgledy piles of books more than anything that could be called 'sculptural' or 'curated'. The idea of making a house look 'like a hotel' is puzzling to me – I spend a significant amount of time trying to find hotels that look like someone's house.

There was a recent trend on interiors TikTok called 'Intentional Clutter', which is Gen Z for 'spaces decorated by people who love stuff'. It coincided with the annual reprise of a more fashion-based trend called Frazzled Englishwoman. This one reappears every autumn/winter and essentially means 'artless, slightly flushed woman, very much a stranger to the mirror selfie, messy hair, charmingly dishevelled, possibly idiosyncratically dressed, trying to get from A to B in the drizzle on her bike'.

The patron saint of Frazzled Englishwoman is of course the great Helena Bonham Carter, but *generic* Frazzled Englishwoman is a descendant of Barbara Pym's quintessentially English heroines, except that she has sex, vigorously and uncomplicatedly, like a really cheerful labrador. Afterwards she's absolutely *famished*. (She is specifically English – her French counterpart wouldn't eat at all, her Italian counterpart might wander off naked for a little coffee and a bite of peach, but Frazzled Englishwoman puts on her fleecy dressing gown, nips downstairs and makes herself a fried-egg sandwich. Then she gets back into bed and sleeps like a log for a solid eight hours.)

Put the two concepts together – the clutter and the frazzle – and you get quite close to something approaching real life, which is a first. How often is that a trend? More, it's a trend that young people can play at but not actually access, because they're not old enough to be convincing in the roles. So it's a trend for the middle-aged! For us!

Combining Frazzled Englishwoman and Intentional Clutter makes perfect sense, because the true Frazzled Englishwoman always lives in a cluttered house. True, she would never admit to her clutter being intentional, because that would mean admitting to carefully curating it, and her whole thing is that it just sort of *happened*. But chances are that it absolutely was curated, at length, give or take lanyards and old bills stuffed in among the things on the dresser. It's careless-seeming, vaguely bohemian, but fully intentional all the same.

As you will have gathered by now, I adore clutter – the lack of it gives me a lonely, desolate feeling – but the clutter has to be highly aesthetically pleasing to me. The easiest way of achieving this is not to buy anything hideous unless it makes you laugh, in which case it should take pride of place (also this saves your room from death by Ghastly Good Taste, as on page 68). Clutter, done well, is beautiful.

But none of that means I don't sometimes daydream about

FOUNDATION 6: NO STUFF, OR ALL THE STUFF?

the serene, austere beauty of a more minimal interior. I appreciate and admire their lofty and cerebral restraint – 'I don't need mismatched *trinkets*. I don't need *photos of the children* everywhere,' I say to myself. I go to The Modern House's online magazine and coo over the pictures (this is an estate agency specializing in outstanding modern homes). I try to imagine myself in the pristine spaces, wearing a Toast dress and sipping white tea from a rough-hewn artisanal mug. As I click through the pictures, it takes me about thirty seconds to start uttering my eternal cry, 'But where's your stuff? WHERE IS YOUR STUFF?' Clever storage, obviously, but as previously noted, I don't love the idea of hiding away the business of daily life. Aside from seeming madly anal (to me! no disrespect intended to anyone un-anal who loves minimalism and has walls of cupboards), it also seems slightly fraudulent, like claiming you are the one bear who doesn't shit in the woods.

Being someone who derives an enormous amount of pleasure from looking at beloved, meaningful *things*, in truth I am suspicious of people who live in houses without them. Everything is too concealed. The only thing on show is (immaculate) surface and emotionally meaningless *objets*. I appreciate it aesthetically, but I don't entirely trust it. It's furtive. Put it this way: the bloke who turns out to be the serial killer rarely has a jolly kitchen with mismatched mugs and dog hair on the rug (although how extra-creepy when he does).

There are minimal interiors that I practically worship. The problem is that they are all the exceptional interiors of people with an exceptional eye, more often than not interiors dealers or professional interior decorators. Most people attempting something similar do not have exceptional eyes – or exceptional houses – and so their spaces just look flat and anodyne. Going the other way – adding colour and gaiety – is much easier to get right.

Many of us are two people when it comes to interiors. Maximalism and clutter is exuberant and joyful, and who doesn't want that? Minimalism is appealing because it suggests order, serenity, and by extension control – also quite appealing. The play of light on empty surfaces is calming, even soothing. Everything is beautiful and sits beautifully in its place.

But it isn't cosy, the colours are sludgy, it all goes to pot the moment you have trainers cluttering up the hallway, and maintaining ordered perfection to that extent requires either extraordinary self-discipline or staff (one of the ironies of monk-like minimalism is that it is beloved by the extravagantly rich, who like to imagine that they are simple folk with very few needs). In the absence of staff, guess who keeps everything looking perfect? Laurence Llewellyn-Bowen posits that minimalism is misogynistic because its lack of softness, embellishment and comfort 'removes the woman from the space', an idea that's been kicking about in my head ever since I read it.

As previously noted, my mother has excellent taste. Seeing Maralunga sofas, Carimate chairs, Castiglioni lamps, etc., etc., is deeply nostalgic for me, in the same way that a hostess trolley might be for someone else. A friend once asked me whether my parents' house was, like hers, full of china figurines of shepherdesses and dogs. No: we had contemporary furniture and raw plaster walls before they were a thing. So perhaps it's no great surprise that my own house is the polar opposite of the ones I grew up in. It has a ton of stuff in it – stuff that is attractive and sits nicely together, at least to my eye, but stuff.

Having had design classics up the wazoo, I don't mind china dogs or the odd bit of brown furniture. I like colour *and* pattern *and* texture, even though two out of three of those is usually considered enough. But during one of the lockdowns, I suddenly wondered what the house would look like if I adhered rigorously to a narrow colour palette of black, cream and that nice conkery brown that I love, with the odd bit of green thrown in. I wasn't going to repaint the walls, but I rearranged my many objects, swapped out all the colours in the house for neutrals – which I already had because, as I say, I am two people – and deployed a few cream-coloured throws. I did things like 'curate' my hardbacks so the cloth spines were all in the same

FOUNDATION 6: NO STUFF, OR ALL THE STUFF?

family of colours (I stupidly threw away a lot of lovely book jackets), arranged objects in clusters of similar shades, different textures and varying heights and removed all but the subtlest, tiniest pattern.

Long story short: I killed the house. All the life and heart went out of it. The rooms felt calm, but it's not like they'd felt agitated before. Now they felt morgue-like. The uniformity and blandness of everything depressed me: it was like eating stodge instead of spice. My things were perfectly nice, but they were so visually similar – being one of only three colours – that I stopped looking at them properly. I stopped even seeing them. Everything felt like it was the colours of cheese. I can totally see how cheese colours are many, many people's idea of heaven, but they are not for me in that sort of concentration. I lasted two weeks before putting everything back exactly as it was.

A PRACTICAL NOTE ON CLUTTER

There's gorgeous clutter, where the eye delights in every single object, and there's 'Oh my God, is she a hoarder?' We are aiming for the former. Clutter happens when you have a lot of beloved objects (which is good) and they are strewn around willy-nilly (less good) and right next to each other. We have seen how to avoid this above: by corralling things and being thoughtful about how and where you display them.

If you do all this and your room or surface still looks like a hot mess, you need to add some negative space. What negative space basically means is: leave empty gaps sometimes, to give the eye a rest. Negative space is a visual pause, and the more stuff you have, the more necessary it becomes if we are to avoid a sense of blurs-into-one overwhelm. You need the occasional focal point in a room, and you need to give it space to breathe. If you had a magnificent chandelier, let's say, you wouldn't then add loads of smaller pendant lights all across your ceiling. Or if you had one oil painting that you particularly loved, you wouldn't ram a load of posters up against it: you'd let it occupy its space. That's all negative space is: making room for a particular object to shine, so that you can't miss how lovely it is. For more on decluttering, see page 198.

A NOTE ON MIXING DIFFERENT DECORATIVE STYLES

'I love it, but it doesn't go.' Maybe, maybe not. But before you dismiss the thing you love and that speaks to your heart, remember there is no rule that says that everything in a room has to match. In fact, there are plenty of rules saying the exact opposite. Robert Kime, the late, great antique dealer and interior decorator of rare genius (including to the King, in fact), said, 'I love things that don't match, and I want my rooms to be lived in, not looked at.' He also said, 'An amalgam of styles plunges a place into life. It gives the room a voice.'

(He was full of good advice, which I can't keep quoting endlessly, but here's one more from his obituary in *The Times*: 'If you only buy from smart antiques shops, your house will look like a smart antiques shop. If you put a great tapestry together with a farmhouse table that has a bowl of cowslips on it, you will probably see the cowslips first. The eye doesn't know how expensive the tapestry is.' This doesn't only apply to antiques shops, obviously: it is just as true that if you buy everything from one particular store, your house will just look like that particular store. I appreciate that this is sometimes the point, but I am not personally at all keen on houses that look like hotels or members' clubs. Those hotels are necessarily designed to appeal to the lowest common denominator, which is why most are masterpieces of bland anonymity even at the de luxe end: there's nothing to dislike and there's nothing to *feel*. Anyway: Kime's point is that a beautiful thing is a beautiful thing, whether it is a cowslip or a priceless tapestry, and feeling that one is too smart to be combined with the other is wrong-headed.)

FOUNDATION 6: NO STUFF, OR ALL THE STUFF?

I subscribe to a school of thought that thinks that if I love something, then it will go with the other things I love, and I have always decorated my houses accordingly. However, I am very confident about what I like, hate anything looking contrived or matchy-matchy, and like for houses to evolve organically – which, obviously, means accumulating stuff over the decades and trusting that it will all meld together into an aesthetically pleasing whole. But I appreciate that matchy-matchy is very much a look, that not everyone shares my aversion to symmetry, and that anyway not everyone is as confident/foolhardy in their taste as I am. If that's you, and you want to mix different styles without creating a visual mess, here's a foolproof tip: restrict your colour palette.

Say you collect jugs. A riot of colourful jugs, some modern, some vintage, some antique, is my idea of heaven. But if the very idea of this unholy, lightly chaotic hodge-podge of styles brings you out in hives, then only collect (for example) white and cream jugs. The Georgian one will sit happily and harmoniously next to the one from H&M Home, because they will be unified by their shared colour palette. I am using jugs as an example – you can apply the principle to anything from art to furniture. Provided the items in question have a common language – in this instance, colour – then they will communicate successfully 99% of the time. Another example: say you like cushions (me too). A cushion with a bold seventies print will sit happily next to a vintage kelim one, a chintzy one *and* your latest high-street find if they all belong to a similar colour family – if they're all in earthy shades, say, or blues, or greens, or whatever – because they will all look related. Those same cushions in a riot of different colours might have more difficulty creating a harmonious whole. If you're ever in any doubt when decorating a room, this is a good rule to follow, except it's not a rule because you can break it whenever you like. But it's a nice one to start with if you feel hesitant. Remember that, as per page 104 in the paint foundation chapter, a colour isn't a fixed colour, but all the varying shades within that family. So green isn't only moss green, but all the other greens too.

Having said that, I encourage you to get bolder over time. Mixing styles and periods without fear results in wonderfully satisfying, nourishing, layered, complex interiors. And by putting, say, an IKEA table next to an antique chair, you address matters of texture (page 129) and friction (page 67) without even being aware that you're doing it.

THE LOO

Privacy please

You know that famous quote from Virginia Woolf – 'a woman must have money and a room of her own if she is to write fiction'? I used to think about it in the guest loo of the house I lived in at the time. The 'money' in Woolf's quote meant 'a private income', and I didn't have that. And the only room of my own was this loo: the one place where I could grab five minutes' peace, which was also the title of my children's favourite picture book at the time. In it, poor, highly relatable Mrs Large, an elephant person, tries in vain to grab some time for herself by having a bath – just one measly little bath – away from her family. She's made herself a cup of tea, she's put her bath cap on, the bath is run, she's good to go. But the children keep visiting with their various requests, and in the end they all get in with her.

My children knew the downstairs loo – as opposed to our shared bathroom – was not a place I liked being visited in (often, through the door, I could hear an indignant small voice shouting 'SHE'S NOT ANSWERING!' to another indignant small person), and so sometimes I just used to go and sit in it for a breather. Once the indignant small child/children had stomped back to their Lego and Cartoon Network, it was quiet. So blissfully quiet. It was peaceful. So blissfully peaceful. It was incredibly small and badly lit, but whatever: it was a sanctuary, a tiny respite from family life. Which I loved! And still love! But you know how it is. Sometimes you just need to be by yourself for two minutes, no matter how much you love the person or persons you're escaping from.

I've subsequently stopped going to loos on peace-seeking missions (I also used to do it on dates with bores, or as a mini-break from really deathly dinner parties), and these days I do have a room of my own. But I still have very fond feelings for guest loos, and for box rooms, and for sheds, and for any kind of room that people go and sit in when they just need a break. My stepfather used to disappear to the guest loo with the newspapers, for hours; someone else I knew did the crossword in theirs; I have over the years spent many a happy half an hour reading in the loo, despite owning an armchair. Loos can be very special rooms, especially if you don't actually even need the loo in the first place.

This seems a good, if unimaginative, place to tell you about scenting rooms. We'll just get the unlovely obvious out of the way: no air freshener is better than an open window, in this particular room or elsewhere. Air freshener of any description makes me gag, personally – I don't care if it's cheap or posh, I just don't like it. I also think that those horrendous plug-in air fresheners and room sprays are really just one up from vaginal deodorant. No one's vagina needs noxious chemical deodorizing, because the body keeps the area clean all by itself, and also soap exists. What those 'intimate' deodorants (I even hate the vocab) are to do with is the paranoid fear of being found 'dirty', and that fear only exists because of patriarchy, frankly. Any man who is familiar with women's bodies knows – and appreciates – that women's bodies smell of women's bodies, not of chemical Tropical Orchid or mimsy vanilla. On a side note, I have observed that men who are tremendous shaggers actively like bodily fluids, e.g. the smell of sweat, more than people who are more sexually restrained.

Anyway: same thing with house deodorizers. Your house doesn't smell bad, so why would you want it to permanently smell of anything other than itself? If you've burned the toast, open a window. If you

Candlelight is never not flattering

Plain but not boring: the joy of texture

The taste of home

have many pets, wash the upholstery regularly. If someone's rolled in fox poo, wash them in dog shampoo (you can use ketchup in an emergency, weirdly – it absolutely works and it is worth keeping a bottle in the glove compartment, along with a spade in the boot if you have a terrier who is prone to darting down burrows or setts). As with vaginas, I hate the idea that people are so insecure about how their house smells that they buy products to artificially make it smell of something else.

Everyone's house *does* have a smell – you will remember this from when you were little and went on playdates (I say playdates – my generation tended to just run about outside being feral and come back in when it got too dark. People romanticize this over much, in my view – it must have been idyllic in the countryside, but in cities it also meant you got flashed a lot and were constantly having to swerve pervs). I loved the new smells of people's houses when I was a child, and I still love them now. They're so interesting, and they become friendly once they are familiar. They're never easy to describe, unless they're something obvious like the smell of spring onions or cumin seeds, but they're a whole mood. So please don't deodorize your house's own scent into oblivion. It's your house, not an armpit.

Still, I appreciate that not all loos have windows to open, more's the pity (a design oversight: dear builders, please put windows in toilets), so if you feel the need to scent the room, always go for something as natural-smelling as possible: an essential oils concoction sprinkled on to hand towels; two or three bars of wrapped, highly fragranced hand soap stacked on the sink, the radiator or the back of the cistern (these work brilliantly in a tiny room – they scent the air deliciously but don't shout about NEEDING TO MASK ODOURS); nicely fragranced pumpy soap and hand cream; those sticks you stick in a bottle of scented liquid. I have put these last because I don't love the way they look and the scent of them is often overwhelmingly – even nauseatingly – strong, especially in a small room. If you have one that you really like, consider decanting it into a tiny bottle and only using two or three of the sticks (which you can also cut in half). The rest can go in a bigger room.

HOME

A FEW FAVOURITES

Aesop hand soap. Yes, it's expensive, yes, it's become shorthand for a certain kind of person in a certain sort of house, yes, everything about it from the bottle to the fragrances is a cliché. But the scents remain unimprovable, the expense is perhaps mitigated by the fact that, unlike the kitchen pumpy soap, this one won't get used that frequently, and the glass bottle is beautiful. I love Aesop. They get it exactly right in terms of the heft of their scents, unlike many perfume houses whose handwash is overwhelmingly strong, scenting your hands far too insistently and for far too long.

Should this somehow have passed you by, they also make the original, much-imitated Post-Poo Drops, which are exactly as they sound. They are an all-natural, all-delicious smelling little bottle, a few drops from which will make the loo smell innocent and fragrant post-flush, as if you'd opened the window and lived in a giant garden filled with scented botanicals. (Very good present, the Post-Poo Drops.)

You can obviously just buy an Aesop-level of handsome pumpy glass bottle and decant anything you like into it, or refill your used Aesop with something else. I like the following brands:

Expensive
– C. Atherley (geranium, sublime)
– Commune
– Grown Alchemist
– Malin + Goetz
– Verden
– Buly 1803
– Susanne Kauffman

Less expensive
– Ortigia
– Neom
– Savon de Marseille in a bottle
– Goodwash

THE LOO

- Dr Bronner
- Neal's Yard
- Kiehl's

Cheap
- You can't beat a scented bar of soap. My favourites, including Aleppo soap and savon de Marseille, both made from olive oil, divine-smelling and lovely to use, are all from French Soaps, frenchsoaps.co.uk, who also sell the best natural household cleaning products.

Elsewhere in the house, keep scented candles away from anywhere that is even vaguely food-related – they clash horribly, and a scented candle in the kitchen can easily put you off your dinner, because it's all you can smell. For the same reason, I would never have them in a dining room or other eating area. If the eating and living areas were conjoined, i.e. all one big open-plan room, I would always blow a scented candle out a good hour before dinner. People over-burn scented candles anyway: if it's of decent quality (desirable: their smoke is not super-duper to breathe in at the best of times), then burning one until the top of the wax has completely and evenly melted should be enough. The idea is that the scent then lingers. No need to have the candle lit for hours!

I prefer a subtle and evocative scent to anything punchier, especially if we're talking about a situation where people are wearing fragrance themselves. Things can get quite headachey otherwise. I would also always opt for something green/fresh/woody rather than for anything overly sweet or cake-like, for the same reason of avoiding headaches.

Love scented candles as I do, I sometimes prefer using incense or pot pourri. Well, I say pot pourri – I only really like one, but I like it so much that I've used it in every single house I've lived in for the past thirty years. It is by Santa Maria Novella (they only do one) and it is just called Pot Pourri. It smells of Tuscan hillside in the baking heat, because it's basically made out of Tuscan hillside: an all-natural, no-artificial-anything mixture of herbs, leaves and roots. You need a tiny, tiny bit for a whole room – like, a couple of pinches. Used this way, it's hauntingly lovely – you catch a sniff of it every now and then – but it is the opposite of 'my house smells bad, so have this instead'. I say this about the pinches because after a while you stop being able to smell it yourself (rather like a favourite perfume) and it's tempting to go and top up your little saucers or tealight holders or whatever you've decanted it into. Don't – until at least six months later. If I really were showing you around my house, I would say, 'Come and sniff this right now,' and you would go, 'Oh my God, what is that?' assuming you hadn't said it the moment you came in through the front door. It really is that good.

Always buy a wooden loo seat if you can afford it, and spend as much as you can. I can't tell you how often I or a partner have had to deal with wobbly plastic loo seats that got loose and veered off whenever anyone sat on them – years' worth of retightening/buying new bolts/buying new plastic loo seats, all of which turned out to be a totally false economy. The problem stopped the moment I bought an eye-wateringly expensive (for a loo seat) really heavy and solid wooden version, and I've never looked back. I started with one and gradually upgraded all the loo seats in the house. That was at least ten years ago and not a single one has ever had to be tightened or adjusted in any way. They just sit there being reliably sturdy. Mine are from a company called Tosca & Willoughby, looseats.com.

The loo is also a good place for one really nice hand towel, of the kind that won't bobble or get prematurely frayed (well, two – one in the wash and one in situ), and for some excellent reading matter.

A short list of the best loo books

You don't want anything with a narrative, unless people really are going to sit in the loo for a couple of hours on end (which I would consider peculiar or concerning in a guest). Anthologies and funny books are best. There are new loo books published every Christmas, but here are some stalwart favourites:

THE LOO

- *Clean and Decent: The Fascinating History of the Bathroom and the Water-Closet*, by Lawrence Wright (Penguin Classics).
- *What If? Serious Answers to Absurd Hypothetical Questions*, by Randall Monroe (John Murray). This answers questions like the number of New Yorkers a rampaging T. Rex might eat in a day. Monroe founded the legendary web comic xkcd.com.
- *Christmas Crackers*, by John Julius Norwich (Penguin). Literally heaven. Every Christmas, the author used to send his friends a little compilation of funny, interesting, moving, odd or informative snippets he'd come across the previous year. These eventually got collected as the first *Christmas Crackers*, and further volumes followed. The original is available second-hand, or see also *The Ultimate Christmas Crackers*, a compendium of all of them (John Murray). Ignore the 'Christmas' bit – it's not relevant to the contents.
- *Eliot's Book of Bookish Lists*, by Henry Eliot (Particular Books) – *the* most brilliant selection.
- *Brilliant Maps: An Atlas for Curious Minds*, by Ian Wright (Granta) – endlessly interesting.
- *Cracking Cryptic Crosswords*, by Colin Dexter (Offox Press). Dexter, the inventor of Inspector Morse, provides clear and simple instructions about how to start solving cryptics. It's a short, slim paperback, and everything is in small manageable chunks. I have been reading this book for ten years and can now maybe do two clues of a whole puzzle – but it's my brain, not the book. The book is brilliant.
- *Letters of Note: Correspondence Deserving of a Wider Audience*, by Shaun Usher (Canongate). This is really too good for the loo – some of the letters will blow your mind, some of them will move you to tears, some of them will make you laugh to the point of wanting to pee (hurrah! you're already in the right place!). The original is just the most wonderful compendium imaginable. I would consider putting a second copy in your bathroom. Or by your bed. Or in any guest bedroom. It is perfect.

– I really admire the art of diary-keeping, and I admire my favourites – they include Kenneth Tynan, Samuel Pepys, Helen Garner, Kenneth Williams, David Sedaris – too much to think of them as loo books. Diaries are perfect for loos, though, because obviously the entries are usually briefish. I'd go for a compendium instead, such as *The Penguin Book of Diaries* (selected by the great Ronald Blythe).

– *Molvania, A Land Untouched by Modern Dentistry*, by Santo Cilauro, Rob Sitch and Tom Gleisner (Overlook). The best spoof travel guide ever written, and properly, honkingly funny (out of print but easily findable).

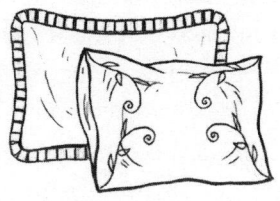

THE BEDROOM

Wahey and also zzzzz

There is one thing I feel is especially important to aim for in bedrooms, and it is this: no tech during the week. I'm not claiming I always manage to stick to this, but I'm getting better at it. Tech completely kills bedrooms' vibe. This is fine if you think of yours as just a functional place to sleep in the way some people think of food as being merely fuel (who are they??), but I want to encourage you to think of your bedroom as the haven, the sanctuary, the oasis of peace that a bedroom should be. I want you to feel absolutely relaxed and unstressed in it, to lie in bed feeling happy and contented, and it is so much harder to do this if there is a phone, a tablet or a laptop anywhere near you. Not only will your calm be interrupted by the pings of texts and chats and emails and people wanting things, but you will absent-mindedly waste hours of your time going online for no particularly good reason. You might even, if you're anything like me, occasionally find yourself buying random crap that you absolutely don't need at 10pm at night.

Bedrooms are for recharging, and you can't recharge if everything you look at makes you (or your wallet) feel depleted. Think of tech in the bedroom as a toxic friend, one of those vampiric ones who always wants something, never gives anything back, and makes you feel drained just from spending time in their company. You're supposed to be *relaxed* in there, not thrumming with various low-level anxieties brought on by social media, the endlessly grim news cycle, your recent doomscroll or the guilt induced by impulsive purchases.

There also is a lot to be said for not being permanently available either to other people or to the algorithm. Nothing disastrous is going to happen if you leave your phone on the kitchen table overnight (also, if you're constantly on at your children to get off their phones, it's a good idea to model this yourself sometimes, if only to show that you are actually *able* to be detached from yours).

I am old enough to remember when mobile (dumb) phones first arrived, and to remember how utterly scandalized I felt at the idea of my private time being something that could now be invaded by anyone, at any time of the day or night. I am these days as addicted to my phone as anybody else, but deep down I still feel that way – like, 'Leave me alone for two fricking seconds, could you? I am busy,' even (in fact, especially) if I am busy doing nothing. Or sleeping.

The reason I'm saying 'during the week' is that I am trying not to be hypocritical, because I really like lying in bed reading things on my iPad on a weekend morning. These things are almost exclusively Substack newsletters about cooking and gardening, or I might spend a happy half-hour looking at the dog videos that TikTok correctly thinks I'd like. But I try to be really strict with myself during the week. Sans phone, if there's anything rattling about my head as I fall asleep, it is the plot of the novel I was just reading, which is very different from being kept awake and jangling by a hundred different snippets or images of news/gossip/whatever agitating thing I've accidentally let into my brain before closing my eyes. If you sleep with somebody, I also think there is something tragic about both of you lying there in the dark, physically together but completely disengaged from each other, faces lit by the glow of your respective screens. It's the sort of thing you'd put in an apocalyptic novel to indicate the coming of the End Times. You're in bed with (one hopes) someone you love: have a chat, have a snog, have sex, lie there in companionable silence – anything, really, that isn't demoralizing evidence of you both finding each other less interesting than whatever random nonsense is on your screens.

Let's start with the room itself. The first thing is that your bedroom is a place of intimacy. It needs to have *the potential* to feel sexy. I'm not saying make an outright boudoir, both for the reasons outlined below and also because with so many people working from home, bedrooms are sometimes part-office. They're also a family space if you have youngish children or grandchildren who like to come and visit. Some of my happiest memories of my children's childhood are of us all piled up into my bed, with biscuits, watching children's Saturday morning TV, which was a thing back in the olden days.

But despite children, pets, home offices or anything else, the *potential* for sexiness needs to be there. The bedroom needs to be as inviting as possible, whether that's to you as a solo person or to you as part of a couple. I would say that it's extra important if you are an Old Married Couple – hopping into bed with someone once is one thing, and nobody's really going to be paying attention to the décor, but Old Married Couple conjugals really benefit from as agreeable, and even seductive, an environment as possible. Mood is real. It has a real and measurable effect. Bedrooms should feel like the place where you can park the fact that you bickered over dinner or had a micro-row about what show to watch on telly. They should be serene enough to make you feel serene too. When I say 'seductive' I don't mean red silk walls and sex toys on a plinth, ranked in order of size, though you do you. I mean whatever is seductive to you as a person – whatever suggests intimacy. For me, as ever, a lot of that is to do with lighting: for obvious reasons, it needs to be as flattering and scene-setting as possible. Note that bedrooms need two kinds of lighting: the sexy kind, as in golden-toned dim lighting, and the reading kind, as in unsexy white light that lets you read in bed with your specs on and your pyjamas buttoned right to the top. I have very minimal reading floor lamps, as thin and unobtrusive as possible, and my standard port of call is always IKEA. They are neither ugly nor beautiful, but they are inexpensive, effective and recede if you match them roughly to the colour of the walls. A skinny white light against a pale wall can become almost invisible if there are prettier things near it to distract the eye. A black light against a contrasting white wall would demand all your attention.

Speaking of wall colours: go for whatever is most soothing to you. For me the bedroom is a good place for shades that are too soporific for the rest of the house. What I like in here is a kind of sumptuous plainness, so white, but very rich white, accentuated by more sumptuously plain things, like wooden objects with a really fantastic patina, dull brass, the more tactile fabrics, yellowish lighting, heavy curtains, an old mirror, beeswax candles, lots of books. It feels opulent in a very restrained way, due to the relative lack of pattern and the very restricted palette. And it works for me: the proof is that even writing this paragraph is making me feel like going off for a quick nap. My tastes are of course personal: go for whatever induces the same feeling of quiet contentment in you. To me, a really successful bedroom should make you feel the opposite of energized. It should make you feel serene and mellow.

We also need to factor in furniture. If you have fitted wardrobes, paint them the same colour as the wall, so they recede: fitted wardrobes are great, but they are not all anybody wants to be looking at. When I lived in London I had colourful patterned wallpaper in my bedroom, which looked lovely until I turned my head to the left. The patterned wallpaper threw the bank of plain white fitted wardrobes into sharp relief, so that they were unavoidable and un-ignorable. I'd have been far better off saving the wallpaper for elsewhere and matching the walls to the wardrobes to make them go away.

Here in the country where houses are roomier, we have antique, mismatched chests of drawers as bedside tables, one each. Not only is this very useful clothes storage-wise, but it also provides you with a wide surface to play with, meaning you can have a sizeable bedside lamp, should you want one, a big old pile of books, a radio, an analog alarm clock (no tech!), a carafe of water, a notebook, your jewellery box, and whatever else you'd like on there. For years my bedside tables used to be Alvar Aalto stools, which looked cool but could only accommodate one Anglepoise and one glass of water. Go as big as you can with bedside tables, and don't think 'bedside tables' means 'a pair of matching bedside tables that are sold as bedside tables': stools, chests of drawers, beautiful chairs, old trunks, side tables, small coffee tables, floating shelves, cubbyholes, bookcases, console tables, drinks trolleys, windowsills, even a stack of books or magazines all provide excellent and aesthetically pleasing alternatives.

I find the presence of books helps create a calm, cocoon-like atmosphere that is seductive to me, plus, as Anthony Powell wrote, 'Books do furnish a room' (it's the title of the tenth novel in his *A Dance to the Music of Time* sequence). That tip – about books making a room feel lived-in and inviting – applies to every room, not just the bedroom. My bedroom books are exclusively comfort reads, because they're what I like in a somnolent state. There is a list of my favourites at the end of this chapter.

If you are a heterosexual couple, I think we need to bear in mind that a 'traditionally' 'feminine' room is not necessarily especially inviting to the man part of the unit unless he is merely an occasional visitor, in which case he will probably find it charming/amusing. Less so if you live together and his own presence and interests have been completely eradicated. I'm not saying you have to recreate a bachelor pad or have games consoles/a poster of Jeremy Clarkson/black sheets and the scent of an ill-judged aftershave polluting the air, but equally anything overly frou-frou is not going to be conducive to creating a room that he, the man, wants to spend more time in than he has to. Which would be sad, since it's supposed to be a sanctuary for both of you.

In general, when it comes to houses, I think it is completely fair for one person to be the interiors boss and have the majority say in decorating – but I do think it's sensible to make accommodations for both parties in bedrooms. Despite my love of pink, for instance, I would not have a pink bedroom; despite my love of flowers, I would not have flowery bedding unless the pattern were very stylized; despite my love of prettiness, I go more gender-neutral when it comes to bedrooms. For a start, it's more relaxing: this is the one room where I like to have less, rather than more, to look at. My own bedroom is much less colourful than the rest of the house. The art is muted. The colours of the furniture and objects are sludgier, chalkier and more obviously soothing, with lots of texture on the bed to add a bit of interest. (The problem with beds is that they are so big, and if you go too neutral you can end up feeling like there's a huge blocky island of white cotton in the middle of the room, taking up and dominating most of the space. I happen to love white cotton bedding, but you can see the issue whatever the bedding colour. It's just this huge lumpen rectangle, squatting there like it's an invader. If your bedding is plain, and even if it isn't, I would make a point of adding different fabrics both to the room and to the bed itself, using the texture advice on page 129 – so silk and velvet as well as cotton, and so on, just to break things up a bit.)

If you possibly can, invest in blackout curtains or blinds. These are life-changing if you have ever been a light sleeper. Blackout fabric is even arguably sexy, because it makes the room feel like you are two little furry creatures snuggled up deep underground. I think blackout curtains make some primitive part of the human brain feel safe, perhaps because they make rooms feel like caves. It's also a hundred times easier to fall asleep in a properly dark room, and to sleep longer: if it weren't for the blackout curtains, our dogs would want breakfast well before 5am, when it starts getting light, for the whole summer. As did my children when they were small, before we got them blackout blinds.

Now, to the bed. I am obsessed with bed (I have my best ideas in it) and I am obsessed with sleep (eight hours a night or I'm out of whack). I find the idea that sleep is a waste of time, or that it is in some way impressive in a macho way to function on very little sleep, to be absolutely deranged. It is the emptiest of boasts. Sleep is everything. Storing up days, weeks or months' worth of fatigue has terrible repercussions on your body, your brain, your emotions, your mental well-being, your daily interactions – on your whole life. We

THE BEDROOM

can't always all get as much sleep as we deserve, but bragging about being up and about in this really suboptimal state is just weird. When I am sleep-deprived, I make a point of going to bed comically early the following night to catch up on myself. I am also a great believer in catnaps and siestas, though these have to last twenty minutes or under otherwise you wake up groggy.

I am also incredibly fussy about my bed, and about all the beds I come across. I am the princess in *The Princess and the Pea*. All the very detailed information I'm about to bombard you with is the result of years of studying beds in minute detail, resulting in some very categorical conclusions.

A pillow isn't just a pillow, a duvet isn't just a duvet, and a mattress isn't just a mattress. Two of these three items are your most important bedroom purchases, so I'm going to take them individually.

PILLOWS

Central to a good night's sleep. Too hard and you wake up with a stiff neck, aching shoulders and a spine that feels misaligned, too soft and you wake up feeling much the same way, though for different reasons. The wrong pillow can, over time, completely mess up your neck, shoulders and back, as well as your actual nightly rest. Only you know what feels comfortable to you, so the only advice I can reasonably give you is: always, always try the pillow out before buying it. I know it's tempting to buy bedding online, but unless you get lucky by fluke, you're unlikely to hit the jackpot.

This would be a shame because the pillow jackpot is a very real thing. You think your pillows are completely fine until one day, whether at someone's house or in a hotel or a holiday let (less likely: they are often bad pillow central), you suddenly wake up one morning going, 'Woah, that was an incredibly good sleep.' It's the pillow! Well, and the mattress, obviously, but first things first.

Your sleeping position, your weight and your firmness preference are all relevant here. If you sleep on your side, you can throw your neck and spine alignment out of whack if the pillow is too high (tall) or too low (flat). If you sleep on your back, you want to make sure your pillow doesn't thrust your neck too far forward, because you'll wake up with neck and shoulder ache if it does. If you sleep on your front, your pillow needs to be relatively flat to prevent your spine from arching backwards.

Very broadly speaking, a front sleeper does better with a soft, quite thin pillow, a back sleeper benefits from something medium-firm because it will hold their head at the correct angle, and a side sleeper might want to go firm-firm for the same reason. But you never actually know what feels perfect for you until you lie on it – not just for a few seconds, but for a good length of time. Most shops make this difficult by not providing an actual bed with a mattress you can lie on to sample pillows, but we must all do our best and improvise. I have spent many an hour in John Lewis laying my head against about a dozen different display pillows. In my experience, in the absence of a mattress you can go and lie on with your potential new pillow, the best thing to do is buy the pillow that you find most comfortable, take it back to the car, put it on the back seats and lie across it there for at least ten minutes. Have a little nap if feasible. Take it back and swap it if you are not divinely comfortable. A good pillow should make you go 'Wow, I love this pillow.'

Also: it is unusual for two people sharing a bed to have identical pillow needs. They would have to have the same body type, the same sleeping position and the same personal preferences when it came to what they considered a dreamy pillow. Everyone should try out their own pillows.

We also need to talk about fillings.

- Natural – duck or goose – down pillows are what we imagine when we say 'cloudlike'. They are super soft and fluffy. They are the most expensive, but they last a long time if you look after them properly. They do have a tendency to go flat after a couple of years, but you can't have everything. Solo goosedown is the ultimate, Hungarian for preference (I wonder why Hungarian geese are fluffier than other geese).

- Natural feather – still goose or duck – are soft, but not quite as cloudlike. Down is fluffy, feathers are feathers: flatter, with quills that sometimes poke through.
- Feather and down is, obviously, a mix of the two.
- Synthetic down is made of synthetic fibres that mimic the softness of real down. They're cheaper, a better bet than real down if you have allergies, and usually machine washable. The better ones come very close to being cloudlike.
- Memory foam is made from either solid or shredded foam. They're very firm and often ergonomically designed. I personally don't love the idea of sleeping on what is effectively plastic from petrochemicals, but some people swear by memory foam because it really moulds itself to you and thereby relieves tension and pressure.
- Latex is completely natural – you can get organic latex pillows – and comes from rubber trees. It has natural anti-fungal, anti-bacterial and anti-dust-mite properties. It can come as a wodge (harder, obviously) or in little clusters (softer). It is breathable and stays cool in the summer. Latex pillows are quite springy but do not mould themselves to your head and neck in the same way as memory foam. Note, some people are allergic to latex.
- Kapok is also natural and can also be organic. It feels close to synthetic down fluffiness-wise, except it's not synthetic. It is sometimes mixed with other materials.
- Hybrid pillows are a mix of some of all of these.
- Wool pillows are natural, can be organic and are breathable, so are great at regulating temperature. They tend to flatten over time.

- Buckwheat pillows exist and are a nice idea, but they are incredibly noisy – they rustle and echo inside your ear whenever you move your head.

- I don't know what the pillow law says, but I wash both 100% goose down (mine are from John Lewis) and synthetic pillows in the washing machine. I also dry them in the dryer, and they are perfectly happy and emerge re-fluffed. But check the label when buying pillows, because anything requiring specialist cleaning is a pain in the backside, and air-drying is all very well but not in the British climate (which I know is on the turn, but still).

DUVETS

A mediocre duvet isn't going to do you any physical harm, unlike a bad pillow or a shoddy mattress (we'll come to those in a moment), but it's still important in terms of temperature, cosiness, breathability and a good night's sleep. I don't like feeling weighed down by my bedding unless the boiler's died again and it's minus double figures – those weighted blankets are my idea of hell – and I can't stand feeling too hot. I would always rather be slightly too cold and grab an extra blanket. So I'm never going to have a good night's sleep under the heavy duvet that is someone else's idea of bliss. Again, two people sharing a bed may have completely different duvet needs. If that's you, be Scandinavian about it and have two singles instead of a double. Some brands offer wider than normal single duvets so you don't have to worry about being insufficiently enveloped (the worst). If you don't mind the bed being a slightly odd shape when you make it, you could always go for two queensize duvets.

- I would always go for a duvet that is bigger than the bed size. It feels much more luxurious, especially if you sleep with a duvet hogger. So a double on a queensize bed, a kingsize on a double bed, a superking on a kingsize bed and an emperor on a superking bed, though that last one might be over-egging it unless you like wrapping yourself up like a caterpillar in a cocoon.

- Togs ('thermal overall grade') tell you how warm the duvet is going to be: the higher the rating, the warmer. You can easily get custom pairings if one of you likes it cooler and the other one warmer.

- Materials: pretty much the same as with pillows, above. Unless you're worried about allergies, I would opt for a natural and breathable filling because I think it's nice for your skin to be able to breathe. My own preference is for super-expensive, super-fluffy Hungarian goosedown. Having said that, the guest duvets in my house are synthetic, for reasons of cost and washability, and are pretty amazing too: there isn't actually that much in it in terms of how they feel to sleep under unless you are really finickity (join my club).

- I don't think you need to lie on a display mattress to test out a duvet, and I think they're safe to buy online, though physically weighing them up in person is always going to be preferable.

- Whichever material you pick, try to buy a duvet that comes housed in a cotton cover, for breathability. I use only all-cotton or all-linen bedding for the same reason. I wouldn't wear synthetics next to my skin all day, every day in life, and I don't sleep on or under them for the same reason.

MATTRESSES

This is the big one, the most important purchase in the bedroom. I am obsessed with my bed, so I would argue that it is actually the most important purchase in the entire house, which is why I am going into the matter in such nerdy, techy depth here. A good mattress is life-changing, and that's all there is to it. I really mean it: it changes your life. A good night's sleep – a really *idyllic* night's sleep – completely alters how you view the world, how you cope with its stresses and how you feel about every single day that you spend on God's green earth. As we all know, we spend about a third of our lives sleeping. You have to honour that third. Sleep is when we revive and when our bodies repair themselves. Save on other things and get the best mattress you can afford. You will never regret it.

Everything you ever wanted to know about buying a mattress

The absolutely first thing to say is, NEVER BUY A MATTRESS WITHOUT TRYING IT IN PERSON. You can read and absorb every single thing I'm about to tell you, but mattresses are exactly like falling in love. It's all very well having a list of requisites to tick off, but sometimes they all fall by the wayside when you meet The One. When you know, you know, with people and mattresses (and dogs, actually).

There are four things to consider before you start.

YOUR SLEEPING POSITION

Side sleepers are usually happy on a softer or medium mattress, because these allow your shoulder and hip to sink in a bit. You want this because it promotes the correct spinal alignment and also cushions pressure points.

Back sleepers are usually happy on medium to medium-firm mattresses. These support the natural curve of the spine without letting the hips sink in too much.

Front sleepers are usually happier on a firmer mattress, which prevents the spine from arching unnaturally. It is really hard to alter your sleeping position on purpose, but sleeping on your stomach isn't brilliant due to potential neck and back strain.

Wrigglers: If you don't have a consistent sleeping position and move around a lot, look for a medium-firm mattress made out of a material that responds quickly to body movement, e.g. latex or pocket springs (much more on this below). These make it easy to wriggle. Some other sorts of mattresses make it less easy because they are so dense or moulded to you that movement takes an effort, which is a weird feeling and affects the quality of your sleep.

YOUR WEIGHT

This is an important factor that is often overlooked – and then people wonder why their expensive mattress is already dipping and uncomfortable a mere six months in, or why it is so unpleasantly hard and unfriendly even though you like things firm. The mattress needs to support you and whoever else you're sleeping with. It simply can't do this if it's not up to it – or if you're too light for it. If you weigh 95kg and above, you need a firmer, more supportive mattress to prevent sinking. If you are 65kg and under, you're likely to find a firmer mattress too hard. Go for something softer, safe in the knowledge that it won't dip within months.

YOUR BUDGET

Mattresses range wildly in price. Decide how much you're willing to spend. Under £500 will get you a basic open coil or thinner foam mattress. Quality and longevity may be limited. £500–£1,000 will get you entry-level pocket sprung, decent memory foam, or basic hybrid options. These variations are all explained below. £1,000–£2,000 will get you quality pocket sprung mattresses, often with natural fibre filling, or better-quality memory foam/latex, or well-constructed hybrids. If you can afford it, this is a good price range to aim for in terms of the quality/value ratio. £2000+ takes you into premium territory – handmade mattresses with high spring counts, generous natural fillings (like wool, cotton and horsehair), high-density foams, or pure latex.

The next thing to bear in mind is temperature regulation. If you tend to get hot at night, avoid materials that trap body heat, like traditional memory foam. Look for options that give better airflow, like pocket springs, latex, or the newer gel-infused foams. Natural fillings tend to breathe well and would always be my personal preference.

WRIGGLY PARTNERS

This is called Motion Transfer in the trade, which I consider myself an honorary member of. If you sleep with someone who moves a lot and feel like you're being tossed about every time they change position, you need to consider how well your mattress absorbs movement. Memory foam and pocket springs are generally excellent at isolating wrigglers, meaning you're less likely to be disturbed. Open coil mattresses tend to be much less good at this.

Allergies: If you suffer from allergies, then obviously shop for hypoallergenic mattresses. Latex (a natural material, as we saw in Pillows, above) is naturally resistant to dust mites and mould, though obviously it's not much cop if you have a latex allergy. Many synthetic foams are inherently hypoallergenic – meaning that dust mites don't care for them – and some mattress covers are also treated to prevent allergen build-up. The question here is more whether you have sensitive skin that isn't allergic as such but doesn't thrive in close proximity to man-made materials.

Mattress types

- **Innerspring mattresses** use a core system of metal springs for support.

- **Open coil (or continuous coil)** means that the springs are interconnected in a single framework, i.e. all the springs move as one. These are the most affordable option, are widely available and are relatively lightweight. On the minus side, they provide less support, they have high motion transfer (i.e. you'll feel your partner move about), they are less durable, and they can eventually become noisy/squeaky.

- **Pocket sprung:** This means that each spring is housed in a separate fabric pocket. The springs therefore all move independently of each other within their individual cells. What you get here is very good support tailored to body weight distribution, minimal motion transfer (movement) and good airflow/breathability. These mattresses are durable, come in a wide range of firmness levels and are available at lots of price points depending on spring count and fillings. On the minus side, they can be heavy (relevant because you need to turn your mattress to keep it in good nick) and they are more expensive than open coil.

- **Memory foam:** These are made from viscoelastic polyurethane foam that softens with body heat and therefore contours closely to your shape. If you have a lot of aches and pains, they provide excellent pressure relief; they are terrific at isolating wriggling, and you feel cocooned by the foam. They never squeak.

   However: they retain heat (though newer foams often have cooling gels or open-cell structures), can feel slow to respond when changing position, can smell absolutely horrible when you first unbox them, and they can feel hard to move about on, leading to a sort of micro-claustrophobia.

- **Latex:** These can be made from natural latex (from rubber tree sap), synthetic latex, or a blend. They are highly durable, responsive to movement and have a jolly, bouncy feel. They are as good as memory foam in terms of pressure relief (for aches and pains), they have good temperature regulation, being more breathable than memory foam, they are naturally hypoallergenic and resistant to dust mites/mould. But: they'll cost ya (especially 100% natural latex), they are very heavy, and some people find the bounciness more annoying than jolly.

- **Hybrid mattresses:** As the name suggests, these combine different layers, typically a pocket spring support core with 'comfort layers' of memory foam, latex, or gel foam on top. The idea is to offer the best of both worlds – the support and bounce of springs with the pressure relief of foam or latex. Depending on the materials in the layers, they can offer pretty good motion isolation, too. But they can be expensive, are potentially less durable than pure latex or high-end pocket sprung (the layers will degrade first), are often heavy, and many are single-sided (meaning they can't be flipped, only rotated).

- **Beds in boxes:** These are the ones that come vacuum-packed, rolled up and boxed. Most of them are memory foam, latex, or hybrid. They're convenient (they get delivered neatly in their box) and often come with long trial periods. They take a while to unfurl/expand after unboxing (also good luck re-boxing them if you change your mind), and they have a distinctive, let's say, smell when you first unpack them.

Still with us? There's more! As you can imagine, I am very fun in mattress shops.

Materials

If I'm going to spend a third of my life lying on a particular surface, I want to know what – if anything – it's doing for, or to, my health. All mattresses sold legally in the UK must meet stringent fire safety regulations, which influences the materials and treatments used, so that's nice. But synthetic, man-made materials are primarily derived from petrochemicals. The more common ones include polyurethane foam, aka polyfoam, which is very commonly used to provide comfort and support. Then you have memory foam, aka viscoelastic PU foam, which is a type of polyurethane foam that reacts to heat and pressure, meaning it contours closely to the body. Also gel foam, which is memory foam or polyfoam infused with gel beads to improve heat dissipation compared to traditional memory foam.

Other synthetics include synthetic latex (SBR – styrene-butadiene rubber), which is man-made latex designed to mimic the feel of natural latex. It's cheaper but less durable or breathable. Polyester is used extensively in mattress covers and as a fibre filling layer, and adhesives (glue) are used to bond different layers together.

Does any of this actually matter, or am I just a middle-class cliché? Yes and yes, in my view. Some things to bear in mind:

VOCs: Polyurethane foams, including memory foam, can release Volatile Organic Compounds (VOCs) when new. This is what's behind the 'new mattress smell' (polite version) you get from those box mattresses. VOCs are gases released from certain solids or liquids, and examples include benzene, formaldehyde and toluene. High concentrations of these can cause short-term effects like headaches, dizziness, nausea, eye/nose/throat irritation, and can worsen respiratory conditions like asthma. Most of these gas releases occur in the first few days/weeks and levels fall quickly if you leave the windows open.

Always look for certifications like CertiPUR-EU, which ensure the foam is made without certain harmful chemicals and has low VOC emissions. Oeko-Tex Standard 100 certification, which is more usually applied to fabrics but can cover entire products, also tests for harmful substances.

Chemical flame retardants: UK fire regulations are among the strictest in the world, meaning that mattresses often require fire-retardant treatments, especially those containing synthetic foams. In the past concerns were raised about some of these potentially leaching out and accumulating in the body, with links to issues like endocrine disruption and developmental concerns. Those have been banned or phased out, hooray – but the newer chemical flame retardants, being newer, don't come with a ton of long-term health data. You might prefer to minimize your chemical exposure. Or not – we're all stuffed full of microplastics already, tragically.

Glue: Adhesives used to laminate the layers can also contribute to VOC emissions. Water-based adhesives are generally considered to have lower VOCs than solvent-based ones.

Are you thinking, 'Yeah, I don't love any of that, actually'? You have alternatives.

NATURAL MATERIALS

These are derived from plant or animal sources. Bear in mind that although materials like wool have some natural resistance, natural fibres can potentially harbour dust mites more easily than synthetics, so use a dust-mite-proof mattress cover. On the plus side, materials like wool, cotton, hemp and latex allow for better air circulation than many synthetic foams. Wool is particularly good at wicking away moisture (it's also naturally fire-resistant, cleverly).

Where sourced responsibly, natural materials can be more renewable and biodegradable than petrochemical-based synthetics, but bear in mind that 'natural' doesn't always mean 'chemical-free'. Cleaning, bleaching and processing fibres can involve chemicals, and conventionally grown cotton uses significant amounts of pesticides and herbicides. If that bothers you, read the labels. GOLS (Global Organic Latex Standard) ensures latex is 95%+ organic raw material and meets strict processing standards. GOTS (Global Organic Textile Standard) ensures the organic status of textiles like cotton and wool by harvesting through environmentally and socially responsible manufacturing. Oeko-Tex Standard 100, as above, tests for residual harmful substances. For materials like wool and horsehair, look for brands that are clear about ethical and sustainable sourcing practices.

- **Natural latex:** Processed sap from the rubber tree. A small percentage of the population has a latex allergy, which can cause reactions ranging from skin irritation to anaphylaxis. If you have a known latex allergy, avoid natural latex mattresses, obviously.

- **Cotton:** Plant fibre used in covers (often organic) and sometimes as a filling layer. Breathable, though can flatten over time.

- **Wool:** Animal fibre used as a 'comfort layer' or within the cover. Known for excellent temperature regulation (i.e. insulates when cold, breathes when warm), is moisture-wicking and has natural fire resistance.

- **Coir fibre:** Fibre from coconut husks, often used as a firm, breathable support layer or insulator pad over springs.

- **Hemp/flax:** Plant fibres known for durability and breathability, sometimes used in filling layers.

- **Horsehair/mohair/cashmere/silk:** Luxury animal fibres used in high-end mattresses for resilience, comfort and moisture management.

BUYING TIPS

- **You must try before you buy:** Spend at least 10–15 minutes lying on a mattress in your usual sleeping position in-store. Don't just sit on the edge or press it with your hand or park your bottom on it and bounce for three seconds. Lie down and pretend you want to go to sleep.

- **Look at trial periods:** Many brands, especially online ones, offer risk-free trial periods, sometimes of up to a year, but check the small print of the return process and any associated costs before buying. Some retailers offer an exchange rather than a full refund.

- **Check the guarantee:** Look for a guarantee of at least 5–10 years. Have a proper look at what is covered (e.g. unreasonable sagging) and what isn't (e.g. normal wear and tear).

- **Bed base compatibility:** Your existing bed base needs to be compatible with your new mattress. Slatted bases should have slats close enough together to provide adequate support (the mattress manufacturer will have their own recommendations, so check what they are), especially for foam or hybrid mattresses. If you have an existing divan base, bear in mind that a spanking and spankingly fancy new mattress won't feel optimally comfortable if the base it's on is old and knackered. I learned this the hard way. Also the 'wrong' bed base may void your guarantee.

BEDDING

Let's start with my best and most extravagant tip.

I can't remember exactly why (fiddling about for days with baubles and bits of ivy will have come into it), but I was really badly behind with everything last Christmas. The downstairs of the house was looking lovely – the tree was up and every room was festooned to the hilt, as it is every year. But the upstairs of the house looked like feral raccoons lived there.

People were turning up to stay in a few days' time and I just wasn't ready – all the guest bedrooms were a tip, everywhere needed vacuuming and dusting, and I was really behind with the laundry. I had a huge pile of things that needed ironing because they'd sat on top of the dryer and not been put away, meaning they'd creased unreasonably in protest. All the bedding for the spare rooms was either dirty or, as above, unreasonably creased even by my lowly (because I hate ironing) standards. We don't have a cleaning person and there wasn't a one-off one to be found for love or money. My partner and I both had tons of work to do before knocking off for Christmas. It became clear that something would have to give.

So we took all the bedding we own – decades' worth of bedding – to be laundered professionally. Every last sheet and pillowcase, down to the single duvet covers that used to be on my now-adult children's beds when they were little, and haven't been used for years. I can't really explain why this felt so completely decadent, but it really did, much more guilt-inducingly than anything more traditionally decadent I might have got up to in life. I felt like a spoilt Roman emperor or a banker's wife. I mean, doing your own laundry, using machines: it's not hard, it is? Until it is.

By this point it was perilously close to Christmas, but the nice woman at the dry cleaners said that she *thought* there was a chance that they *might* be able to do it in time, *maybe*, but that she couldn't by any means guarantee it. Did we still want to go ahead? Yes, I cried. Yes! I was fully committed to the project by this point, plus there was no way we were schlepping binbags full of laundry back into the house.

You can probably see where this is going. They tried their best, but they couldn't, in fact, do it in time. And now they had every item of spare bedding that we owned, and they'd closed for the holidays. In the end I went to John Lewis, who had dramatically reduced Christmas-themed bedding on sale (it was by this point the afternoon of 23 December), so I bought that. I was annoyed about it at the time, but people were so delighted and amused to find their beds covered in robins and Christmas trees and skiing dogs wearing scarves that the Christmas bedding immediately became a new family tradition.

We got the laundered bedding back in the New Year. I don't even have the words to describe how wonderful this bedding feels. It has been lightly starched! It has been immaculately ironed, even the linen duvet covers! It has been folded so neatly that the creases are like origami! (I am using the present tense because I am writing this in the spring and we still haven't got anywhere close to using all of it.) You get into bed and even though your bedding is not in the first flush of youth, the sheets and pillowcases feel like you're at Claridge's. Getting into clean sheets is always a blissful experience, but getting into professionally laundered clean sheets is *divine*. So that is my recommendation: if you can, have your sheets laundered and pressed for you every now and then, for a treat – and it really is a treat. There is simply nothing like it.

*

Bedding, rather like pillows, is more important than you'd think, because the materials used make a real difference to your comfort levels. There are also considerations when it comes to laundering, assuming you're not sending your sheets away as above.

Cotton is the most popular natural fibre, and for good reason. It is highly breathable, it is soft (especially varieties like Egyptian or Pima), it is durable, and it gets softer and softer the more you wash it. It is good for sensitive skin, available in various weaves – percale is crisp, sateen is silky – and at various price points. Organic options are available.

The downsides are that it is prone to wrinkling, can shrink if washed at too high a temperature, and the quality can vary hugely. Non-organic cotton production has environmental impacts.

- **Egyptian cotton** is a specific type of high-quality, extra-long staple cotton grown in Egypt. It is super soft, smooth, strong, durable, breathable, and it doesn't pill. It is expensive and quite a few sheets call themselves Egyptian when they actually aren't – look for certification.

- **Linen** is made from the fibres of the flax plant. It is extremely durable and gets softer and better with age. It is highly breathable and moisture-wicking – a lovely choice in summer and if you get hot in bed, though I also find it wonderfully toasty in winter. It is naturally hypoallergenic and anti-bacterial. You don't need to iron it (hooray!) and it has a relaxed, timeless, quite sexy look, provided you find creases timeless and sexy, which I do. Flax is a sustainable crop. It's expensive and it can feel a bit rough when you first sleep in it – this is sorted by washing, though. For me the joy of linen is the 'the older, the better' factor.

- **Polycotton** is a blend of polyester (synthetic) and cotton (natural) in varying proportions. It is affordable, durable, wrinkle-resistant and 'easy care', meaning it doesn't take long to dry and needs minimal ironing. It tends not to fade at all. It is less breathable than 100% cotton and it can trap heat. It's also less absorbent, can feel less soft or slightly synthetic, is prone to pilling over time, and is less eco-friendly due to the polyester aspect.

- **Microfibre** is made from very fine synthetic fibres, usually polyester. It is cheap, usually very soft, lightweight, wrinkle-resistant and durable. It dries quickly and is hypoallergenic. But it is not very breathable, meaning it can cause overheating and/or sweating. It can feel slippy and generate static, it releases plastic microfibres when you wash it (to be fair, so do an awful lot of clothes) and it doesn't absorb moisture well – a bummer if you get too hot in bed.

- **Brushed cotton/flannel:** The cosiness! This is cotton fabric that has been brushed on one or both sides to raise its fibres, sort of like backcombing hair. It is very soft, warm and almost fleecy-feeling. Incredibly comforting in winter. Despite the brushing, it retains some of normal cotton's breathability. It's not for the summer, though, and it can pill. I don't think that matters because it makes you feel like you're in *Little House on the Prairie*.

- **Silk:** A natural fibre produced by silkworms. Extremely smooth and soft (perhaps *too* smooth and soft?), hypoallergenic, naturally temperature-regulating, and gentle on skin and hair because it reduces friction. Silk pillows really do make you wake up with marginally smoother hair and a marginally smoother face, if that's a concern. Silk is very expensive, is a pain to look after – hand-washing, special detergents – and snags quite easily. It's not measured by thread count but rather by momme weight – look for something in the region of 19–22.

- **Bamboo (often presenting as viscose/rayon/lyocell):** Fabric made from processed bamboo pulp. Soft and silky, breathable, moisture-wicking, naturally hypoallergenic. Bamboo can be more sustainable than conventional cotton if it is processed responsibly (like Tencel/lyocell, which has its own special method). If it is not, processing can involve harsh chemicals (this is the case with viscose/rayon). More expensive than cotton, and not in my view as durable.

A NOTE ON THREAD COUNT

Does it matter? Sort of. It only applies to cotton, and even then you should never base your shopping choices on thread count alone. Briefly, thread count is the number of horizontal and vertical threads woven into one square inch of fabric. The higher the thread count, the finer – thinner – the yarns used. The finer the yarns, the smoother and softer the fabric.

But! This doesn't address the question of the *quality* of the fibres being used. You could have a sheet with a very high thread count, but if it was made of inferior fibres, meaning shorter and stubbier, you wouldn't have the dream bedding you were anticipating. In fact, you'd have been better off with a much lower thread count, but composed of high-quality – meaning long – fibres, like Egyptian or Pima. Also some manufacturers artificially inflate the thread count by using multi-ply threads, i.e. twisting two or three less good threads together and counting them individually. So a 600 thread count sheet using two-ply threads might feel coarser than a 300 thread count single-ply sheet. Moral of the story: don't get too hung up on it and aim for single-ply.

The weave comes into play too, because it affects how the bedding feels. Percale feels crisp and cool, and typically has a thread count between 200 and 400. Sateen (not the same as satin) feels silky and has a slight sheen, often with thread count between 300 and 600+. It's really down to personal preference – what you like the bedding to feel like against skin – rather than numbers, but here's a rough guide:

200–400: A reliable number for good quality, breathable cotton sheets. **300–500** is optimal, in my view. **400–600:** very high-quality sateen weaves using fine yarns. **600–800+:** could be amazing, could be less breathable due to excessive density, or could be fake news due to use of multi-ply yarns. If you come across this range at what seems a miraculously low price, don't be fooled. It's always better to buy from reputable brands.

Some comfort reading favourites for your bedside table – or for anywhere, any time, frankly (in no order)

- *The World of Blandings*, by P. G. Wodehouse (Everyman)
- *Happy All the Time*, by Laurie Colwin (HarperCollins) (all of Laurie Colwin's novels)
- *Crooked Heart*, *Old Baggage*, *V for Victory* and *Small Bomb at Dimperley*, by Lissa Evans (Doubleday)
- *Tales of the City*, by Armistead Maupin (HarperCollins)
- *Mapp & Lucia*, by E. F. Benson (Wordsworth)
- *Riders* and *Rivals*, by Jilly Cooper (Penguin)
- *The Camomile Lawn*, by Mary Wesley (Vintage) (all of Mary Wesley)
- *The Light Years*, by Elizabeth Jane Howard (Pan) (and all the volumes of the *Cazalet Chronicles*)
- *The Diary of a Provincial Lady*, by E. M. Delafield (Macmillan)
- *Heartburn*, by Nora Ephron (Virago)
- *Excellent Women*, by Barbara Pym (Virago) (all of Barbara Pym)
- *Cranford*, by Elizabeth Gaskell (Penguin Classics)
- *The Pursuit of Love*, by Nancy Mitford (Penguin Modern Classics)
- *The Whalebone Theatre*, by Joanna Quinn (Fig Tree)
- *Circle of Friends*, by Maeve Binchy (Arrow)
- *Miss Benson's Beetle*, by Rachel Joyce (Doubleday)
- *Brother of the More Famous Jack*, by Barbara Trapido (Viking)
- *Eligible* and *Romantic Comedy*, by Curtis Sittenfeld (Doubleday)
- *Consider Yourself Kissed*, by Jessica Stanley (Hutchinson)
- *I Capture the Castle*, by Dodie Smith (Vintage)

THE *PLAY* ROOM

Let joy back in!

'What did you do as a child that made the hours pass like minutes? Herein lies the key to your earthly pursuits.'

I'm quoting Carl Jung, a) because what he is saying is so profoundly true, and b) because it has such profound applications when it comes to both the look and the feel of our homes. The decorator and architect Ben Pentreath – the man who single-handedly revived and reinvented the country house aesthetic – made much the same observation in his magisterial 2024 book *An English Vision: Traditional Architecture and Decoration for Today*. 'My friend George Saumaurez Smith has got a great line: "You are as an adult who you were as a child",' Pentreath wrote. 'We often think we can reinvent ourselves in life, but I'm interested in exactly the same things I was at eight as I am at 53 – furniture, interiors, painting, colours, old buildings and old places.'

It's true of all of us, I think, but that eight-year-old self gets so buried by life stuff that you have to make a conscious effort to get her back. When she reappears, though, bear her in mind when it comes to paint swatches and kitchen units. Give her a say.

My child self liked writing stories, drawing, creating sitting rooms (never whole houses) for my dolls in old wooden wine crates, making scrapbooks, finding a corner to read in for hours, making collages (partly because the glue smelled of marzipan), the Arctic and its peoples (I was obsessed by igloos and to a lesser extent sealskin clothing), *Astérix*, snails (because they carried their home with them everywhere – one for my therapist), spies, detectives and anything related to espionage, playing chess, the Alps (because of Heidi), beaches (less because of the sand and water than because of the wild feeling of *standing at the edge of an entire country*), shipwrecks, pirates and Life At Sea generally, cooking, big dogs (pet wolves!), little dogs (mini-wolves!), paintings of domestic interiors, especially Dutch and Flemish ones (this was in Brussels, so there were a lot of them about), and places where the streets were made out of water (we went to Bruges all the time).

You get the idea: with the exception of snails – I still admire the house business, but I am too furious with them eating my flowers to really like them any more – these are all things I still love and think about all the time. Most of those other childhood interests turn up in my Substack newsletter: maybe not the igloos – though what are igloos if not interesting homes? – but the books, the dogs, the dolls' sitting rooms which become posts about interiors, the paintings, the digital collages.

Here's what I think about the whole business of that childhood part of you receding and receding until it's almost vanished (it seems to come back in extreme old age, which I find both intensely disturbing and mildly comforting): if you are a person who, for whatever reasons, had to shorten their childhood in order to accommodate the perplexing behaviours of adults, then you have probably almost completely lost touch with the child you once were. And the child you once were is *you*. Like, core you.

This also applies, perhaps less dramatically, if your childhood was textbook idyllic. It applies because life happens. We get knocked down, and then we learn our so-called lessons and carry on. We 'evolve' to cope. The evolution *always* involves burying more and more of that chipper, optimistic little person beneath endless coping strategies and protective layers.

And then those coping strategies and protective layers get embedded. And then we acquire more of them in adulthood, to the point where we feel they're what we're really like. But they're not. I can only write subjectively, but I felt this more and more strongly the older I got. Like, what is this? Is this me? It's not the me I remember (I think my stopping drinking was related to that feeling).

I had a very strong idea of what my 'grown-up' house would look like when I was a child. And do you know what? It looked like the house I currently live in. *What is this?* My house. *Is this me?* Yes. This would only have been partially true of the other houses I've lived in, because for a long time I was busy performing what I thought adulthood should look like. Sometimes I'd look at a room after decorating it and think, 'Ha, very grown up.' I'd feel pleased for having pulled it off. That is not at all the same as thinking, 'Wow, I love this room,' or 'I want to play in it.'

It's taken such a lot of time and effort to get here – to get to the point where my rooms make me feel straightforwardly joyful – because by middle age you are walking around literally weighed down with stuff that is not just *heavy*, but that is also blocking the view of your child self, which is so much part of who you actually are. Which means that an enormous and important part of you is missing in action. It's the part that has to do with joy. Enthusiasm. Open-heartedness. Curiosity. The sense of wonder, even of awe. *Delight*.

What is also missing in adulthood is the idea of *playing*. Not playing makes you sad, but having fun makes you feel guilty. Why, though? Feel guilt about doing something truly terrible. But pathetic low-level guilt about how you spend your free time? No. We've all been trained to feel bad if we're properly enjoying what we're doing, especially if that thing is so-called frivolous. We could have been working! We could have been reading an improving tract! We could have been out volunteering! So why are we rearranging the objects in the sitting room with a contented, slightly gormless smile on our face?

There is nothing wrong with rearranging the objects. Or with taking pleasure in watching Netflix in bed with a big sack of crisps, or having lunch with friends, or poring over paint charts, and yet these pursuits are seen as, at best, 'guilty' pleasures (ridiculous phrase), even though these sorts of snatches of enjoyment are what get most people through the day. Also, do men feel bad for going to the football or nerding out at vast length over indie music? Would anyone call those pleasures 'guilty'? Of course not, because men are allowed – even encouraged – to *play* without being made to feel that they're bunking off. It's why they have sheds, which are really playrooms, and keep their games consoles – their toys – out in the open.

Never mind man-sheds – we should all be making our whole houses our playrooms. But we don't, because so many people were fast-forwarded (or fast-forwarded themselves) into adulthood that they rushed past the pure pleasure of *really loving stuff* – of just being massively, unselfconsciously, enthusiastically into something. That is a great loss, a *grave* loss, even, and doubly so if what used to be enthusiasm was eventually replaced with cynicism. (I used to have a high tolerance of cynicism – I often mistook it for wit – but these days I *cannot bear* cynics. The person who is always questioning motives, always moaning about how shit everything is, always looking for the cloud rather than the lining; always bitching and grumbling and complaining: literally, I have to leave the room: go and give out your horrible energy far, far away from me.)

But it's never too late to get back in touch with that child-like (which is not the same as childish) version of yourself. We all need more joy. We should all be geeking out on our joy, all the time. And that joy lives inside you in the form of the child you were. Let her out! And then let her take a good look at where she lives, and decorate accordingly.

RECOMMENDATIONS

A few favourite books about interiors:
- *English Decoration*, by Ben Pentreath (Ryland, Peters & Small)
- *Perfect English Farmhouse*, *Perfect English Townhouse*, *Perfect French Country* and *Perfect English: Small and Beautiful*, all by Ros Byam Shaw (Ryland, Peters & Small)

- *New English Interiors*, by Elizabeth Metcalfe (Frances Lincoln)
- *Axel Vervoordt: Timeless Interiors*, by Axel Vervoordt (Flammarion)
- *Josef Frank – Against Design*, by Christoph Thun-Hohenstein, Hermann Czech and Sebastian Hackenschmidt (Birkhäuser)
- *David Hicks: A Life of Design*, by Ashley Hicks (Rizzoli)
- *Parish Hadley: 60 years of American Design*, by Sister Parish, Albert Hadley and Christopher Petkanas (Little, Brown)
- *The Secret Lives of Colour*, by Kassia St Clair (John Murray)
- *The House Book*, by Terence Conran (Mitchell Beazley)
- *Haute Bohemians*, by Miguel Flores-Vianna (Vendome Press)
- *A Visual Diary*, by François Halard (Rizzoli)
- *Every Room Should Sing*, by Beata Heuman (Rizzoli)

THE BATHROOM

'I am sure there are things that can't be cured by a good bath but I can't think of one.'

– Sylvia Plath, *The Bell Jar*

I fear bath tubs are on the way out and that there will come a point where they become relics, oddities, symbols of a bygone, more sybaritic and more wasteful eco-unfriendly age. Fewer and fewer people have one these days, seeming to prefer the brisk efficiency of showers – which of course take up far less space and use up far less water. They're also rather more hygienic than sitting there in your own dirty water, I suppose, though if you wash every day – which I sincerely hope we all do – then 'dirty' is somewhat melodramatic.

But they're not quite over yet. And there are few things more heavenly than soaking in hot, scented water while chatting companionably to someone perched on the loo (the *closed* loo!).

Décor-wise, an unreasonable number of bathrooms take their inspiration from nautical themes: shells, blue and white, something made out of driftwood. This is nice, and nautical bathrooms have the virtue of at least looking fresh and clean, which are both good starting points bathroom-wise.

I prefer bathrooms to feel more like normal rooms, so I decorate them accordingly. My bathroom has a jug of garden flowers in it, season allowing, lots of books (old paperbacks, not precious ones that I don't want ruined), a small pile of physical magazines by the bath (the only time I still read physical magazines), plates on the wall (better than art – plates don't mind damp or steam), and old vintage shelves on the wall for products and bits. Bathrooms are the perfect spot for a rug, perhaps one of those machine-washable ones made out of recycled plastic bottles (always use rug grip: you don't want to go flying in here of all places). In an ideal world you'd have an upholstered armchair in there, for friendly bathtime gossip, but that presupposes that you have room for one. If you can squeeze one in, though, then do: it transforms the feel of the room and its softness immediately makes it a place of conviviality and relaxation. I like junk-shop ones (brown furniture looks great in a bathroom) with slightly old-fashioned upholstery. Bathrooms are places of hard lines and can feel excessively efficient and businesslike, borderline clinical, slightly like work loos – it's nice to break up the hard lines, and that feeling, with softer items.

Armchairs aside, you can do this with bath mats and towels, of which more in a second, but also with your storage items: baskets are always going to give a warmer, more relaxed feel than stacks of clear Perspex boxes; favourite lipsticks in a pretty dish add visual interest and are easily to hand; plants that love dampness add life and colour. If you are able to be persuaded away from the old white and blue, try warmer colours on the walls. The problem with bathrooms is that you want to feel energized by them in the morning and intensely relaxed by them at night, so I wouldn't go for anything at either extreme of the colour spectrum: this is a good room for mid-shades that lean towards warm. Very white bathrooms have a certain brisk Teutonic appeal, but I always feel like I'm waiting for a colonic, and they also make me feel chilly when I come out of the bath or shower. Do also refer back to the lighting chapter if you have bathroom spotlights: the colour temperature of the bulbs is especially relevant here.

Now, you don't need me to tell you how to turn your bathroom into a spa. I've tried to turn mine into a spa countless times, only to be foiled by a lack of storage (one of my jobs is reviewing beauty products – I have dozens of samples on the go at any one time, and

I need them out where I can see them otherwise they get forgotten about, because I am old). Also, trying to turn a family bathroom into a spa is a hiding to nothing: other people will leave their unattractive stuff everywhere and you'll just end up feeling frustrated at the unrelaxing visuals of it all. It is much better to just focus on one or two manageable aspects of the spa project, namely delicious products and some sort of sense of calm. When I still drank alcohol, the latter could be achieved by candles and bath wine. These days I get the same effect from a bath book and bath tea, though bathroom candles (real or LED) are instantly relaxing. However, I like seeing what I'm doing when I'm shaving my legs, and to see to read, so I'm stuck with the overhead spotlights.

What I do like is for my bathroom experience, spa or no spa, to feel luxurious, like a treat. What this translates as is good bath products, really good towels and a lovely, cocooning bathrobe to pad about in afterwards. I like the pink-cheeked, damp-haired, squeaky-clean feeling of post-bath in childhood, and this involves being wrapped up in something toasty.

HOW TO BUY THE BEST BATHROOM TOWELS

We are after optimal softness and absorbency. That means paying attention to the fibres (again. I sound like some sort of fibre obsessive). The best bathroom towels are made from Egyptian, Pima or Supima cotton because all of these have nice, very long fibres that are super soft, feel super luxurious and are super absorbent. The next best are Turkish cotton (slightly shorter fibres), which are a really good staple purchase for everyday. Then you have normal, bog standard cotton (stubbier fibres), which is perfectly nice but which gets rougher as it ages, so that you end up with towels that feel like cheese graters. I consider this a false economy. Organic cotton tends to be more expensive and thus comprised of longer, or even extra-long, fibres. The label will tell you.

The construction of your towel makes a difference too. Terry loops are the standard – the longer and denser the loops, the softer and more absorbent the towel. Combed cotton means that the short fibres have been removed before spinning, leaving only the longer, stronger ones. Combed cotton towels are smoother, more durable and shed less. With ring-spun cotton, the fibres have been tightly twisted together, thereby creating stronger, finer yarns. These towels are softer and more durable.

Zero-twist or no-twist towels are as they sound: the loops are created with no twists, relying instead on the strength of long fibres like Egyptian or Pima. This results in the kings of towels – luxurious, chubby, extremely soft, perfectly absorbent. The downside is that they are not as durable and will shed a load of lint at first (but not subsequently).

More towel tips

- Wash them before using them for the first time. It helps with shedding.

- Vat-dyed (the label will say) towels are the most colourfast.

- White towels look amazing but show up every last rogue fleck of stray mascara. You can bleach them, but I prefer using sodium percarbonate (see below) like an old French housewife.

- When buying, check that the towels' hems look robust and are well-stitched.

- Weight and density are measured by GSM here. GSM stands for Grams per Square Metre. 300–400 GSM: lightweight and thin, dries quickly but doesn't feel plush or especially absorbent – a beach towel rather than a sexy bath one. 400–600 GSM: medium weight. This is the standard range for good quality everyday normal bath towels. 600–900 GSM: heavyweight. These are thick, plush and highly absorbent towels that feel luxurious. In my house they were historically called Mummy's Towels. Note that being heavier, they take longer to dry. Mummy's Towels really hated being left on the floor after unauthorized use by someone who was not Mummy.

SOME FURTHER BATHROOM THOUGHTS

- Do not dismiss shower curtains as being inferior to shower screens. You can get some beautiful fabric-looking ones. These, again, soften the room and alter its feel; they also introduce colour or pattern – or both – and give a more relaxed look, if that's what you're after. Hang your shower curtain right up close to the ceiling – it will make the room look grander and feel more spacious.

- A chunky, tightly woven bath mat is a wonderful thing both to land on and to look at. In my view the best, bar none, are the ones I recommend below.

- Coloured sanitary ware is on the way back, and is already installed in the interiors-forward bathrooms of interiors-forward people. This is quite funny if you are of the generation that grew up with avocado bath suites, as I am, and is indicative of the general trend – not that we believe in trends! – for warmer, quirkier, more individual interiors. Having spent about twenty years laughing meanly at the very concept of avocado bath suites, I now find myself longing for a pale pink sink or a primrose-coloured loo. I wouldn't actually curl my lip at avocado, either.

- Anything the right shape can be turned into a sink: it doesn't have to be white porcelain. If you're the sort of person who goes on holiday and buys gigantic bowls from local potters or ceramicists only to get home and find you have nowhere to put them – well, now you do. It will need to be plumbed in properly, but this is not a complicated job (if you are a plumber).

- If your bathroom feels dated – though I'm not really sure what that means: if you love it, it's not dated at all – then a quick and relatively inexpensive way of making it feel more current is to change the taps and shower heads.

- Another quick way is to regrout the tiles, if you have tiles, that is.

- I get a strange and almost visceral kick out of squirting chemicals down the lav, walking away and coming back to a pristine and gleaming toilet. But bathrooms are closed spaces where fumes linger and with, often, poor ventilation (get a dehumidifier in there, is my advice), and it is a good idea to use more natural cleaning materials in here. You can do a lot with bicarbonate of soda and white vinegar – I always thought this was a wishy-washy suggestion, like having camomile tea when you need a Valium, but it really isn't: they blitz through most grime situations in the most satisfying way. My favourite natural cleaning products are coming up.

MY FAVOURITE BATH THINGS

– Olverum bath oil
– C. Atherley No 1. Geranium Bath Oil
– Wiberg's Pine Essence
– L'Occitane Almond bath milk and body wash/shower gel
– De Mamiel Soothe bath soak
– Verden Arborealist bath oil
– Omorovicza Budapest Bath Oil
– Susanne Kauffman bath oil
– Aesop Geranium Leaf Body Scrub

THE BATHROOM

Unsexy but useful products for your bathroom cabinet

- Get a Microplane Colossal Foot File. Yes, Microplane as in kitchen graters, which is an unlovely thought. This is not a foot file for the faint-hearted and you must use it with a very light hand. It is *extremely* sharp. I would go in gently, on damp feet (i.e. having lightly patted them dry straight after a shower or bath) over a few nights. If that doesn't do it, use on dry feet, but please go easy – too much enthusiasm and you'll take off too much skin, really hurt yourself and hobble around for weeks.
- If you are prone to dry skin on the body, like if you have dry shins, a moisturizer containing 10% urea will sort you out.
- Cracked heels: you want O'Keefe's Healthy Feet cream.
- The best toenail clippers are German. They make all other nail clippers seem toothless and feeble. I don't know why, and I don't care to think about it. Always cut straight across.
- If you have skin bumps on your upper arms (keratosis pilaris), bumpy armpits or discoloration of the underarms, glycolic acid such as the keenly priced toner from The Ordinary will perform miracles in double-quick time.
- If you have rheumy eyes, Optrex Brightening Eye Drops make your eyes look like you've done something amazing with your makeup. Don't use them too often – they make the eye blood vessels contract, which obviously wouldn't be a brilliant idea on a daily basis.
- Sexual heath: Boots online doctor or similar is also the place to go if you have a vaginal (or indeed penile, what a word) issue that you don't especially want to discuss in the local chemist's – HI EVERYONE, JUST HAVING A CHAT ABOUT MY VULVA WITH THE PHARMACIST – and that can't immediately be cleared by anything you can buy over the counter. Obviously go to the doctor immediately if the issue seems weird or drastic.

- If you have thigh rub or general chafing, the solution is an anti-friction stick. They're all much of a muchness. Megababe do a good one.
- If you have excessive bra sweat, know that bra liners exist.
- Ingrown hairs: glycolic acid, as above.
- Constipation: CosmoCol, available without prescription, works significantly better and faster than anything that comes in tablet or capsule form.

RECOMMENDATIONS

- **Sodium percarbonate** for your whites, plus **all the best natural cleaning products** a person could wish for from **French Soaps**, frenchsoaps.co.uk (they also, as you might have guessed, sell outstanding soap). My favourite brands from here are **Fer À Cheval** and **La Corvette**. I also passionately love **Purdy & Figg**'s, purdyandfigg.com, all-natural, planet-friendly and delicious-smelling multi-surface cleaning range.
- In my view the nicest **bath mats** are the thick 100% cotton ones sold by **RE-found Objects**, re-foundobjects.com, among others. They are pleasingly old-fashioned-looking, come in pretty colours as well as neutral ones, are a perfect size, launder beautifully and last for ever.
- If you don't lug giant pottery basins with sink potential back from holiday, there are hundreds on **Etsy**, or various companies can provide you with one, including **London Basin Company**, londonbasincompany.com.

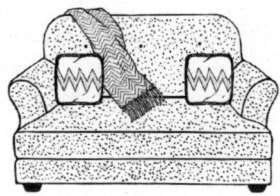

THE SPARE ROOM

One room, many uses

If you are lucky enough to have a spare room, you will know that they often need to be adaptable and serve multiple functions. They might need to be able to transform from a work space to a guest room in the space of half an hour. They might be part gym, part gaming lair, part sewing/crafts space, part studio, part extra TV room, part wardrobe overspill, part antechamber of death for all the crap in the house.

It is of course wonderful to have this spare space, but it can be hard to make it look like anything other than a depressing dumping ground for everything that doesn't belong anywhere else. Because it is impossible to commit to the room's purpose, which is ever-changing, it ends up looking sad and feeling unloved, which puts you in a slightly bad mood every time you set foot in it. Also, nobody coming to stay the night in June especially wants to sleep next to the dismantled Christmas tree from last December, or next to the cage of your late guinea pig, or near a binbag full of old clothes you keep meaning to sort through.

I can't show you how to impose perfect order on chaos, alas. But I can show you how to make a guest room feel wonderful, how to make a work space – even a multipurpose one – feel serene and pleasant, and how to hide domestic debris in a hurry. Having a spare room is a luxury. Let's make it feel like one.

DECLUTTERING

There is no magic formula: you hide spare room crap by getting rid of it. As a lover of clutter (see page 142), you would not necessarily assume that decluttering was one of my specialist subjects, but you'd be wrong. I am ruthless. I show no mercy. This is because I want my home to look a very specific way, and since space is finite, I can't have my efforts buggered up by random bits of cluttery old tat (the *wrong sort* of cluttery old tat) that have nowhere to go. No room should be an orphanage for junk.

The principle is the same whether I am sorting out my wardrobe or any other room. I ask myself the same two questions. They are:

DO I LOVE IT?

Be brutal here. 'I'm fond of it' doesn't cut the mustard. I'm fond of lots of things but it doesn't mean I want them in my house for all eternity.

(The exception here is art of any kind if your spare room walls are bare – assuming that you bought the prints, posters or paintings, or had the photos framed and printed, because you loved them, and that they're in here because you swapped them out for something else, or got tired of them. Hang this art. Hang all of it, if you like, from floor to ceiling if you have loads. There is no better way of making a room feel warm and populated: you've basically redecorated it in one go. Don't worry too much about the art being mismatched or a jumble, because that is exactly the look you're going for. You can measure things out neatly or do it by eye – you get two very different looks. Which one you choose is up to you. The beauty of a jumble of this kind is that it doesn't terribly matter if the individual components aren't first, or even second, rate – the overall effect is of liveliness and warmth that is pleasing to the eye.)

THE SPARE ROOM

HOW LONG SINCE I WORE IT/USED IT/DISPLAYED IT?

With clothes, unless you have a museum-quality vintage collection or are a fashion obsessive with an archive, and assuming we're talking normal clothes – so not your wedding dress or your late grandma's favourite shawl – then if it hasn't been worn for a year or more, it's out. No excuses. I don't care if the item reminds me of a person or an event: that's what photographs and memories are for. OUT. To Vinted, eBay or the charity shop, thank you for your service and goodbye.

As we have seen, I am a great believer in retiring objects/art/cushions/etc. to the loft and then rediscovering and redeploying them later – shopping my house, essentially. But the things in the spare room aren't these sorts of things, otherwise they wouldn't have been dumped in there in the first place. So I chuck them. I still have these conversations with myself, though:

- 'It's perfectly fine, it just needs to get mended.' If it's still sitting there six months later, it may be perfectly fine but you obviously don't need or want it, because if you did it would have gone to be mended straight away.
- 'It might come in handy.' If it hasn't come in handy yet, it's not going to. You get an exemption if the item in question would be astronomically expensive to replace and you genuinely feel you are likely to use it in future – a telescope, say, or a diamond tiara.
- 'I'm saving it for when I have grandchildren.' The hypothetical grandchildren won't be going for a stroll in a Victorian-looking pram that doesn't even fold, or travelling in that antique (and probably unsafe) car seat.
- 'It was a present, I feel bad chucking it.' You don't like it, but somebody else will, so replace guilt with joy by giving them a gift they will love (and appreciate, unlike you).
- 'Not sure what these old cables/chargers are for, but I might need them.' If you needed them, you'd be using them. They probably became extinct five years ago anyway.

- 'It was really expensive!' Maybe, but now it's sitting dejectedly in the spare room of doom – so not just a waste of money but a waste of precious space to boot. Sell it on.
- 'It might come back in fashion.' Most things do, yes, eventually. But it's a top from Next.
- 'The children might want it when they set up house.' Ask them. Say, 'Do you think you, a twenty-five-year-old moving to a tiny city flat, will want Auntie Irene's fire guard with the embroidery of the spaniel on it?'
- 'It's good quality, we should hang on to it.' Why, if you're not using it and it's been sitting gathering dust for months? To what conceivable purpose?
- 'Oh yes, I'm saving that for X or Y, they might want it, they like sunflower motifs. I'll ask when I next see them.' Phones exist. Ask them right now.
- 'But I loved surfing/skiing that one time fifteen years ago. I might like it again.' Take the impulsively purchased salopettes/wetsuits to the charity shop, or resell them. You can hire equipment in the unlikely event of ever taking these activities up again.
- 'That's a really good tent.' It's also a nightmare to put up because it's twenty-five years old. Things evolve. Also, you hate camping.
- 'Hey, put that back! I'm going to start working on my abs really soon.' Use it or lose it, pal.
- 'But I love it!' If you loved it, you wouldn't even begin to think of it as clutter. It wouldn't be in this room in the first place. Look at it clearly. Tell yourself the truth. Maybe you loved it once and don't love it any more. These things happen. Out it goes.

I told you – ruthless. It's the only way.

CREATING A LOVELY SPARE ROOM

So the clutter is out, either on its way to new owners or recycled or tidied away somewhere else (I know, least fun job in the world, though ultimately deeply satisfying).

Don't try and cram a bed into your spare room if it's going to take up the whole room. It will look squashed, dominate the space and throw out the proportions. Also part of the point of a spare room is that it should be a nice room for *you* to spend time in regardless of whether you have guests staying or not. It's much harder for the room to be multipurpose if the bed just squats there hogging all the space. I would always go for a sofa bed (double) or a daybed (single) instead.

You can dress up either of these to look inviting, but it means the room won't spend its time looking like a bedroom until you need it to – good news for the other activities that may need to take place there. (If you do have a bed-bed in there, always use a bedspread – sheets get dusty. You can't make anyone sleep in a bed where the sheets have been uncovered for more than a week or ten days – they will spend the night sneezing.)

With the smaller footprint of a sofa or daybed, the room will hopefully be able to accommodate some kind of table. It doesn't have to be an actual desk, as long as it is the right height for you to sit and work at when the room is unoccupied (I find desks to be very overrated generally). Your guests will appreciate this too, whether it's to sit and work at themselves or just to spread their makeup out on. Don't forget a waste paper basket, and to leave a note of the wifi password.

Put a decent and good-sized mirror on the table if there isn't one on the wall, perhaps a light-up one if the lighting in the room isn't brilliant; a table lamp or two – depending on the size of the table – for atmosphere, and a stack of well-chosen books. I have a formula for this, much like I have a formula for a cheeseboard (one soft, one hard, one blue, one goat, chutney, butter, crackers). It is: one recent popular fiction, one thriller, one cosy crime, one Jilly Cooper, one local interest, one P. G. Wodehouse. This covers all bases, at least in my house.

If there's space, I also like a pretty tray with a tin of biscuits, a small kettle and some teabags in a nice jar. Guests can help themselves to milk from the fridge – provide a little jug which they can refresh as needed. Being able to make yourself a cup of tea in private is a true pleasure, even if you are staying with your favourite people in the world, especially first thing in the morning and last thing at night. You could, if you have a vast surface at your disposal, give them a small coffee machine, but then it starts feeling very like a hotel (all you need are those gross UHT milk pods). The whole point of staying in someone's spare room is that it *isn't* a hotel but someone's home, and I think emphasizing that – the homeliness – is really nice. But we can nick a few hotel tricks.

Aside from the tray, it is heaven to go and stay somewhere and find that there's a hairdryer in the room. You could expand this into tongs/straighteners if you have upgraded yours and have a spare one (it was probably on the floor of this room in the first place). Give your guest your two best, fattest, fluffiest towels, a flannel and a dressing gown. A freshly laundered cast-off will do nicely, but make sure it smells of laundry and is neatly ironed where applicable – nobody wants a rumpled-looking fleecy robe that's seen better days.

If there is no wardrobe in the room, provide a small rack to hang clothes from. These are inexpensive (mine at home are from Argos). Give the rack some nice hangers – I like the padded, slightly ruffled fabric ones, but wooden ones look good too. If there's no space even for a small rack, put a row of wooden pegs on the wall and, again, hang attractive coat hangers from them (as opposed to wire ones from the dry cleaners).

If this room is a proper spare room and has its own bathroom, a basket of bath/shower products plus nice shampoo and conditioner go a long way to making someone feel pleased to be there. If there is no separate bathroom and if there is space on our table (or obviously on another surface, or in a drawer or cupboard), providing these essentials is still a good idea; for girlfriends, I often add an unopened tube or pot of cleanser too.

I sometimes tailor the items I provide to the occasion, so that for example if someone is coming to stay because they have an event to go to, I might leave a tray or basket with a sleep mask, hangover remedies, headache pills and bottled mineral water in it. If they're staying because they're thinking of moving to the area and are viewing a property, I leave my favourite local guidebook and a list of interesting shops and cafés. Of course this information can all be imparted verbally, but it's nice to look at these sorts of things in bed as you plan the next day.

If your guest has a dog or dogs, provide a water bowl, a bed if you have one and an exciting chewy. If you have an alarm system, be sure to give your guest the code so they can let the dog out for wees as required without setting the whole thing off.

Air the room on the day – stuffy rooms are the worst, or unused-smelling ones that are slightly musty. Don't use air freshener, it smells hideous and like you're trying to hide something – fresh air is the best. Make up the bed with fresh bedding a few hours before the guest arrives, plump up the pillows (enough of them to enable bedtime reading/scrolling without getting a cricked neck) and provide an extra blanket/throw or two if your guest feels the chill, in which case I would also put a hot water bottle within reach. In spring and summer, I always add a jam jar of garden flowers to the room. In winter I have been known to whip out the odd piece of holly and ivy. I put a carafe of fresh water with an upturned glass as a lid on the bedside table (which can be anything: a stool, a stack of magazines, a trunk, even an upturned crate).

If you have an old house with an insufficient number of sockets given how many rechargeable bits of tech we all carry about, provide either an extension lead within easy reach, ideally with USB hubs in it, or one of those very neat tower-shaped charging stations.

If your guests are staying for a while, or if they're staying but very much doing their own thing and your paths aren't going to cross that often, it can be nice to leave a little notebook with good local addresses and taxi numbers. You don't have to write a whole guidebook, but jotting down some highlights is a friendly thing to do, e.g. 'the blue café on the High Street has better coffee than the one with the orange signage,' or 'the emptiest beach is at xyz'.

One of the things I hate when I am a guest is never knowing what I am allowed to eat. Can anyone help themselves from the fridge if they're peckish, or if they get back late, or if they wake up early – or is everything in there earmarked for specific meals, meaning you've ruined tonight's mac 'n' cheese by helping yourself to a chunk of Cheddar? And what about these biscuits? They look quite posh – are they being saved for a particular occasion, or are they up for grabs?

It is impossible for the guest to know unless you tell them. This is less of a thing if your hosts live near shops, since you can obviously run out and replace anything that needs replacing (unless the thing is too fancy to be stocked by a corner shop). But out here in the wilds of the country, the nearest shop is half an hour's drive away – so while I wouldn't call it *ruining* tonight's mac 'n' cheese, the demolition of half a block of Cheddar is indeed going to put a spanner in my works, or at least delay dinner by a good hour while someone goes and gets more. Wherever you live, it is always best to tell guests what is and isn't available for them to eat and what they can and can't help themselves to. For absolute avoidance of doubt, it can be an idea to make a separate shelf in the fridge saying 'help yourself to anything from here'. I would also have good snacky things in there, like ready-made picky bits, in case of snack emergencies.

HOW TO MAKE A GUEST SOFA

I used to love doing this when we lived in London and had lots of visitors but no spare room. Whether your sofa is in your now-decluttered spare room or whether it is your main sofa in your sitting room, exactly the same principles apply: you try to be maximally thoughtful and anticipate most needs. People are really delighted by this, because they take 'Can I sleep on your sofa?' to mean 'Yes, I'll chuck you a random duvet and you'll have to make do.' But this isn't fun, and it makes the poor guest feel like you're tolerating their presence rather than welcoming it.

Instead, you make up the sofa with a crisp, fresh flat sheet, you provide plump pillows instead of expecting them to sleep on scatter cushions, and you dress the duvet in a charming cover. You find a stool or small side table and put it by where the person's head is going to be; on this you place a jug or bottle of water, a glass, a pair of earplugs (essential if you have children and/or live somewhere noisy) and something really fun to read, like a gossipy diary – a published one, I mean, not your fourteen-year-old daughter's. At the foot of the sofa you put two fluffy towels, whatever bath or shower products you have about you, a dressing gown (clean, ironed) if you have a spare one and, if you are in the habit of taking unused complimentary towelling slippers from hotels, as I am (specifically for this purpose), a pair of those too.

Sleeping on the sofa can make the guest feel quite uncertain about when they're expected to get up – you might need your sitting room back early in the morning, especially if you work from it. So let them know, either by telling them or by leaving a note.

HOW TO BE A GOOD GUEST

- **Take a present**. Having people to stay always involves a certain amount of work, even if your hosts make it all seem effortless. If you've forgotten the present and your only remaining option is a petrol station, avoid the flowers and take a sackful of crisps and sweets instead. Nobody doesn't like crisps and sweets. But hopefully you'll have had a bit of time to think about a better and more considered gift: petrol station presents spell out very clearly that you have given the matter zero thought. If you are very chic you might send flowers *in advance* of your stay.

- I have a friend who comes absolutely laden, even if she's just staying one night – really good snacks, a cutting or two from her garden or a plant she thought I'd like, an eBay copy of a brilliant novel she thought I'd like, a sweet, funny, day-brightening little thing she's found online, drinks. Obviously the thoughtfulness of the gift shouldn't really make a difference to the host, but I'm afraid it really does. Something personally tailored to your host is always going to be more appreciated than two bottles of mid-priced wine (still nice! But boring).

- **Bring enough**. If you know there are going to be eight of you in the house that weekend, don't bring a doll-sized cheese or 125g of olives.

- **Don't be tiresome about food**. Obviously say if you're vegetarian or vegan, but beyond that the correct answer to dietary queries is, 'I/we eat everything.' If you carry an EpiPen because your allergies cause you to go into anaphylactic shock, then obviously say so well in advance of your arrival, ditto if you have other medically-based dietary needs. But don't say, 'Is there any gluten free bread?' or 'I'm off the carbs, actually' out of the blue just as you're sitting down to dinner. It is really rude. If you are bringing children who are finicky eaters, bring food they like with you. It is not fair on the hosts to ask them to cook separate meals for your kids.

- **If you're effectively using the house as a hotel**, make it clear in advance that you'll be in and out and won't have time to participate in anything much. This is an absolutely fine thing to do, but it needs to be by mutual agreement, so that your hosts aren't sadly waiting for you to come back and join them for dinner.

- **Lavishly compliment the cook and lavishly compliment the house**, even if neither are to your taste.

- **Always be polite and ideally actively loving to the animals**. If you have to pretend, pretend. There is nothing worse than a dog or cat hater making it clear that they don't love the pets that your hosts consider to basically be their children. You are unlikely to be asked again.

- **Always be polite to the actual human children.** Even if they are quite wearying and never seem to go to bed. It's the law.

- **Fall in with the vibe of the house, even if it's not your vibe.** Everybody takes their shoes off as a matter of course in the country, so as not to drag mud and worse across the floors. Don't be the person going, 'Oh God, haha, is this one of those woke houses?' (good rule of life: don't ever say 'woke'). If people get up early, don't tell them they disturbed your sleep with their stomping about. If they get up late, just crack on with your day; refrain from remarking on the lateness of the hour ('What time do you call this, haha? All right for some!').

- **Don't expect to have your day organized for you.** Nobody likes guests standing about gormlessly in the kitchen saying, 'What's the plan for today, then?' If there is a plan, which there might well be if it's the weekend, then it will already have been shared. If there isn't a plan for whatever reason, the guests should either take themselves off somewhere interesting or hunker down on the sofa with their book – or mill about companionably, or help the hosts with jobs or whatever.

- **Offer to cook a meal.** This is always appreciated, assuming you can cook. Please don't offer to cook a meal if you really can't cook – but do perhaps offer to take everyone to dinner at the pub, if that's an option, or for fish and chips, or for breakfast. NB 'A meal' can also be a cake to have with tea, or a breakfast or picnic.

- **Don't drink too much unless everyone is drinking too much too**; consider not drinking at all if you know you are a bad and un-fun drunk. A lone really drunk person, soliloquizing nonsensically and crashing into things, is a really tiresome

- **Don't overstay your welcome**. Your hosts will be utterly delighted that you're visiting. The length of your stay will have already been agreed between you. Don't suddenly announce that you're extending your visit unless you are a really, *really* beloved family member or intimate friend. Especially don't do this on the day you are due to depart. Having people to stay is lovely. The moment they go home is also lovely. No exceptions. Be aware of this. My former husband has an excellent rule regarding weekend guests. He says, 'Come for cocktails, stay for brunch,' so 6pm on a Friday evening, big jolly dinner, probably a late night, big sleep, big jolly brunch, au revoir – and everybody has Sunday to themselves. It's perfect.

guest. Also applies to drugs. But if you know it's going to be a drunken sort of evening, bring good drinks.

WORKING FROM HOME

If you have a dedicated office, I have nothing to offer except the usual exhortation to decorate it like you would any other room, so that it is as pleasurable to be in as your sitting room or bedroom. My other piece of advice is that the people you live with often don't respect or particularly understand the idea of working from home – if it's not something they do themselves, they can sometimes think that it's sort of *playing* at working, and that you can interrupt yourself any time you like, perhaps to go and do something fun with them, or to come and see a hilarious thing, or to have lunch. But putting on a work head in a domestic space is actually quite a tricky thing to manage, and – for me at least – requires absolute concentration. It's a good idea to make this crystal clear, including to any visitors.

Do not accept lesser working from home spaces if you are a woman! The better space is often hogged by the man, almost unthinkingly. I can't stand the 'my man work is more important than your lady work' assumption – well, more like millennia of unconscious conditioning – that leads to this sort of situation. If you only have one great working space, take it in turns to work from it – one in the proper desk chair, one at the kitchen table, and then swap round. Also whoever needs the sober background for their video call – so not a sink with a ton of washing-up in it – gets to pick a room, which the other person must then vacate.

Speaking of work video calls: if you are bothered by the idea of people scrutinizing your bookshelves or spending their time squinting at your décor, or if you are not quite sure of what kind of story you want to tell your colleagues about how you live, whack up a pre-loaded beach or forest screen scene. It may be naff, but it's also quite funny and it saves you from the overly intimate feeling that someone you may not especially like is having a good old nose at your furniture choices. Which can feel a bit like an invasion of privacy. Our homes are such special places – if you don't want to offer part of it for consumption/discussion by colleagues, I think that's fair enough.

RECOMMENDATIONS

– Cunning storage solutions: **Not A Boring Box**, notaboringbox.co.uk. **Muji**, uk.muji.eu, is full of really ingenious, space-saving storage equipment. I like **Hay**'s, hay.com, recycled plastic, stackable storage crates, from Selfridges and others. **Harris & Jones**, harrisandjones.co.uk, do beautiful storage boxes, keepsake boxes, box files and so on in various sizes, covered in various decorative papers and fabrics. **La Redoute**, laredoute.co.uk, has good metal trunks. See the hallway chapter for basket recommendations.

OUTSIDE

I am the product of an entirely urban upbringing.[4] From 1965 to 2015 I lived in cities and 'the countryside' was a mystery to me. I didn't have the kind of childhood that ever involved lolling about under the apple tree, or golden afternoons in cottage gardens with hollyhocks, or the thwack of ball on willow on the village green. I wouldn't have known what a village green *was*.

When I was growing up we lived opposite the Heath in Hampstead. I loved the wildness of it and how it made me feel, but it never occurred to me that you could replicate some of that feeling in a domestic garden. My experience of gardens as a child and young woman – this was the 1970s and into the 1980s – was that people had a lawn they tended to obsessively, and then very neat borders of mysterious flowers, some prettier than others, in primary colours. Sometimes I came across quite grand gardens, and they seemed so formal and stiff – chilly, somehow. I had no interest in any of it.

---

4. The bones of this piece of writing was first published on Jo Thompson's newsletter, The Gardening Mind. I have updated and adapted it here. The Gardening Mind is a must-read newsletter by one of the country's foremost garden designers (and Chelsea Flower Show gold medal winner) – Jo is unbelievably generous when it comes to sharing her hard-earned knowledge. You will find it invaluable whether you are an experienced gardener or completely new to the very concept. Her beginners' guides are especially useful. Find at jothompson.substack.com.

I do have one very vivid garden memory, though – I lived in Brussels as a child and one of my mother's friends lived in an ultra-modern white house with acres of negative space and sculptural, minimalist furniture – quite avant-garde at the time – that had this completely wild, huge garden (no lawns!) which looked like she did nothing to it, though in retrospect I bet she did, a bit. But I remember lying on my stomach in the long grass aged maybe seven or eight and inspecting various insects, feeling pure happiness and an exhilarating sense of total freedom.

As an adult I lived in London for forty-five years. All the outside spaces I had were very small and mostly paved, apart from at a house we lived in in Stoke Newington when I was in my early thirties. But by then I had two small children, so that particular garden – which in hindsight had huge potential – was all about sandpits, toy diggers, a slide, a particularly crap and perilous swing and a Little Tykes Cosy Coupe.

The next garden was a small paved square in Dalston, and by that point I was interested enough to get a gardener in. He made a tiny lawn, planted up the borders with big things like climbers, introduced me to the joy of pots and built a treehouse for the boys in the one not very big tree in the garden. He also put a Japanese maple in a pot, which I still have twenty-seven-ish years later (also two Dicksonia, tree ferns, which later grew massive but sadly perished in the Beast from the East). There was a wooden table to sit at, and a bench my mother gave me, and I think that was the point at which I thought, 'This is really nice, sitting here with these beautiful, delicious-smelling things around me.'

But I wouldn't have known where to start in terms of adding to the garden *myself*. I was massively intimidated. I'd never grown anything apart from mustard cress on a tissue at school, and I was too scared to start. I thought it was a really, really specialized, almost magical skill that you had to study for years, if not decades. And all the Latin! So off-putting to a novice.

Also around about this time, my former husband's stepmother worked at a famous garden called Great Dixter, in East Sussex.

She took us round it one day. It totally blew my mind – but, again, it was like visiting a magical foreign country. It wouldn't have occurred to me to come away with ideas I could apply in miniature to my own minuscule, outside city space.

The garden after that was also a small paved square, north-facing, in Primrose Hill. This is when I started planting up my own pots, nervously and with no idea of what I was doing. It was pretty hit-and-miss, with heavy emphasis on geraniums, because my granny loved them and I'd observed that they didn't seem challenging. Eventually my pots became quite nice and I started growing salad and herbs on my windowsill.

Then I moved to Suffolk ten years ago. We were tremendously lucky that the previous owners' gardener agreed to work for us (seriously, thank God). At first I just left her to it, working her mysterious magic in her mysterious way, but after a while I became curious about what she was doing and why. I also have a friend who is a very keen and competent gardener and she very patiently explained everything to me without laughing at my questions or gawping incredulously at my ignorance.

I knew *nothing*. I didn't understand that you couldn't plant something in October and expect a flower explosion in December – I mean, I was idiotic. I did biology at school, but if I ever learned it then I didn't remember that the purpose of a plant is to procreate and that it dies back afterwards. I didn't know you had to keep picking, and that this was how you got more and more flowers or beans. Literally – no idea. But I became more and more fascinated by plants. If you were drawing a graph, this is the point at which the line very quickly becomes vertical.

Gardening is not scary, it turns out. You plant something, and then, provided you water it and put it where it can get light, it grows. I found the gardening books I eagerly purchased during this period intimidating – they wanted me to test the sort of soil I had, they said that specific plants needed specific placements, they got very techy very quickly, they talked in a kind of shorthand that I didn't understand. All the things they said are true, of course, but it felt like reading *Larousse Gastronomique* when I just wanted to boil an egg.

If you are a total novice and want to get started with gardening, whether in pots or in a small space or in a bigger one, just buy some seeds, stick them in some soil, give them a drink and take it from there. Seeds are cheap (and miraculous: it continues to blow my mind that one tiny, tiny, speck-sized seed contains within it all the information it needs to turn itself into a sunflower, a dahlia or a tomato plant. I find this almost more amazing than human reproduction). Go to garden centres in summer and buy things you like the look of, or make a note of them so that you can order seeds of them the following spring. Gardening is a bit like cooking, in that you can get fancy or keep things very simple and still be satisfied. You can experiment, you can unleash your creativity (gardening is also very like painting, I think, in terms of combining colours and effects), or you can be more matter of fact and just feed yourself/fill the empty spaces in your garden or the pots on your windowsill. It is really, really fun and also madly exciting because, even if you take it up aged fifty, as I did, you'd have to be dead not to be filled with wonder every time a little green shoot transforms itself into something spectacular. Or something that will keep you in flowers all summer. Or something you can eat! Many somethings, in my case. I have three raised metal beds I got online, each measuring 90 x 90cm, and in these I grow asparagus (it takes two years to come to fruition), cavolo nero, Swiss chard, spinach, aubergines, beetroot, radishes and potatoes. In some old cattle troughs I have butternut squash, pumpkins, seven different sorts of salad leaves, and all the herbs. Tomatoes and aubergines work best in a heatwave or in a greenhouse, but everything else grows lavishly and abundantly with minimal interference from me. I also grow green and runner beans in two old metal dustbins with teepees in them, which they scamper up. There would be enough space for these on even the smallest balcony.

When we first moved here I spent a few years growing absolutely everything – leeks! four types of corn! radishes! onions! – just

because I could and found it thrilling. But it turns out that it is really important to grow what you actually love to eat. After the first couple of ears, I can take or leave corn, for example, whereas freshly dug potatoes rinsed, boiled and buttered within fifteen minutes of being picked are ambrosia to me. I also don't see the point of growing stuff that doesn't taste noticeably better home-grown than it does from the shops, so I don't find e.g. onions a good use of space. Salad leaves, on the other hand, taste miraculous when they are freshly picked. I would dearly love to grow brassicas but I can't cope with them being devastated by caterpillars and wood pigeons, so that's not happening, ditto peas (peas are romantic, but Bird's Eye do a pretty good job).

Have a go, is what I'm saying. You might really surprise yourself.

My favourite books about gardening

Gardening solely in pots, no actual garden needed:
- My pot bibles are Arthur Parkinson's *The Flower Yard* (Kyle Books), along with his earlier book *The Pottery Gardener* (History Press) and his later one, *Planting a Paradise* (Kyle Books). Not only does he have a dazzlingly good eye, but everything is planted with wildlife and pollinators in mind. (His book *Chicken Boy* (Particular Books) is the one to go for if you're considering keeping hens.) The other absolutely brilliant one is *A Year Full of Pots*, by Sarah Raven (Bloomsbury). Both are suitable for complete novices. For veg, I like *Crops in Pots*, by Kay Maguire (Mitchell Beazley).

More general gardening books that helped me:
- More Sarah Raven: *Grow Your Own Cut Flowers*, *A Year Full of Flowers* and *A Year Full of Veg* (Bloomsbury). *The New Kitchen Garden*, by Anna Pavord (Dorling Kindersley). *Your Outdoor Room: How to Design a Garden You Can Live In*, by Manoj Malde (Frances Lincoln).

For absolute beauty and inspiration *and* for practical advice:
– *The New Romantic Garden*, by Jo Thompson (Rizzoli) and *Outside In* by Sean A. Pritchard (Mitchell Beazley), *Designing with Plants*, by Piet Oudolf (Conran), *Dream Plants for the Natural Garden*, by Piet Oudolf and Henk Gerritsen (Frances Lincoln), *Pastoral Gardens*, by Clare Foster and Andrew Montgomery (Montgomery Press, divine, and a perfect present for garden obsessives), and the wonderful *Creative Vegetable Gardening*, by Joy Larkcom (Mitchell Beazley), for veg-filled as well as flower-filled borders.

DECORATING OUTSIDE

It is very tempting to overthink – and overstyle – this. We've all seen images of patios, courtyards and garden spaces that have been transformed into what is essentially another sitting room, complete with sofas, rugs, coffee tables, floor lamps and all the accoutrements of indoor life. They look amazing, and I'm not knocking them, but they are quite far removed from... well, from nature. Which is kind of the point? I think that if you are lucky enough to have an outside space, all you need is somewhere to sit and have a long lunch, and somewhere comfortable to lounge when it comes to digesting it. If you have a barbecue, fire pit or other means of cooking outdoors, then as far as I am concerned you have reached nirvana.

My issue with very 'done' outside spaces is my issue with very 'done' anything: I feel they badly lack charm. There is no magic. There is no poetry. Outdoors, especially, I prefer a kind of gentle, slightly home-made ramshackleness to a £20,000 outdoor kitchen made of concrete and banks of bafflingly expensive outdoor sofas (the bafflement partly comes from the fact that they are made of plastic – the nerve of companies charging those prices is permanently amazing to me). Still, each to their own. But I do think there are a few non-negotiables if you're trying to create a magical atmosphere, especially after dark. Mine are:

- **Fairy or festoon lights.** They are just so ridiculously pretty in the evening. If you're covering a large area, you can get connectable ones which can be any length you like. But even one string of fairy lights glinting away in the dark is magical. As ever, don't ruin the effect by going for the ones that are so white they are practically fluorescent.

- **Somewhere to sit at and eat.** It could be a foldable metal bistro table (I find these so pretty) and a couple of matching chairs, or if you have the space it could be a full-sized dining table. One of the first things I did on moving to the country was have one of these made locally out of oak. Ten years on, it is beautifully weathered and gnarled, and even lovelier than the day we got it. I've never done a single thing to it, not even oiled it. It gets a good scrub with water and Fairy Liquid in the early spring, and that's it. That table is one of my very favourite possessions. I think we've had more fun at it than even the beloved kitchen table. Everything feels more fun if it's happening outside on a sunny day or a warm night, even if it's just playing backgammon with a cold drink in hand (and some crisps).

BEING OUTSIDE WHEN YOU DON'T HAVE AN OUTSIDE OF YOUR OWN

Please note that portable, solar-powered fairy lights exist, and so do picnic rugs. When I lived in London I made ample use of both in our local parks and was an enthusiastic picnicker (see below for picnicking food suggestions).

Here are five other tips for feeling rural in the city:

1. **Slow down.** Nature aside, the main difference between country life and city life is speed. But taking things slowly is an attitude that anyone can tap into, regardless of where they are. If you think of a French, Spanish or Italian city at lunchtime in summer, the vibe – languid, unrushed, *dolce*

far niente – is almost rural, despite the mopeds, the traffic, the noise, the urban-ness of the location, and the fact that everyone has things they need to do and places they need to be. People who live in the country have as much to do as their townie cousins: work, appointments, meeting up with friends, going to the gym, attending events. It's just that the vibe is completely different. Tune into it, and you're halfway there.

2. **Make use of any scrap of public outdoor space.** Sometimes they're a bit of a faff to get to, especially if you're dragging a picnic or some minor equipment with you, but they are always, always worth it when you get there. Outdoor spaces are magical. Being surrounded by nature, whether it's to do with trees or to do with sand (or with the sky – I'm a big fan of flat roofs), does something profound to your mood, even if you think you're not interested in nature. Some of these places can often get very crowded, so always walk as far as you're prepared to walk to get as far away from people as humanly possible. Or make your peace with the fact that your intimate picnic is going to be more of a communal event, with other people's picnics happening six feet away from you in every direction. It's not always a bad thing. I know someone who met her husband that way.

3. **Go to quasi-rural events, like markets, fêtes and local fairs.** Again, it's as much about the vibe – relaxed, intimate, slow, community-minded – as about the actual event.

4. **Cook and eat outside if you possibly can.** There's more on this below.

5. **Reduce your consumption, even if only temporarily.** Another major difference between rural and city life is that I am not surrounded by tempting shops selling attractive

things I don't actually need. I don't go past them all day. They are simply not on my radar. This frees up a lot of mental space, as does not constantly checking out what everyone is wearing.

EATING OUTSIDE

Nice as it would be to be having lunch on a terrace by an Italian lake, for me very few things beat being in your own outside space on a hot summer's day, bare-footed, wearing what you like, sun shining, birds chirping, flowers flowering, dogs pottering about contentedly, and cooking exactly what you feel like eating.

There are a few things that help make this situation optimal, and for me they involve cobbling together some sort of outdoor cooking area. In an ideal world you'd have a barbecue, plus a space next to it for a worktop-height table or shelf for food preparation. On this table or shelf, you might have a portable induction hob, a kettle, your crockery, and an extension reel nearby to plug things into. It can be really basic. A clever friend made me just such a shelf – the top is granite offcuts and the shelves are scaffolding boards. The unit itself is a reclaimed industrial thing, repainted in weatherproof red oxide. But IKEA has everything you need if you're cobbling together an approximation of an outdoor kitchen, since all you really need is a barbecue and a little prep area. (I am devoted to my portable hob, which was cheap, is genius – it also comes in very handy indoors at Christmas when you're trying to coordinate the veg – and is in daily use all summer if the weather is playing nicely).

If I'm barbecuing anything at all, Helen Graves's book *Live Fire* – it's the one I mentioned in the Kitchen chapters – is my bible. Before I found Helen Graves and while I was still trying to learn how to barbecue properly, I watched dozens of how-to videos made by gruff men with enormous beards. They were obsessed with meat, to the point of seeming almost turned on by it, and clearly just really liked setting fire to stuff.

HOME

I find the idea that barbecuing is men's work very annoying – if the men don't otherwise cook, it's how you end up eating sausages that are burned on the outside and creepily pink within. By contrast, Helen Graves will kindly and patiently explain everything you want to know, give you recipes for vegetables, fish, seafood and delicious sides as well as for meat, and is a very likeable, witty and reassuring presence. The recipes are fantastic and do-able even if you're a total novice. Also, the quality of the charcoal you use has everything to do with the taste of your food. Avoid garage forecourt options if at all possible unless you want your dinner to taste of lighter fuel. You want natural charcoal with nothing else in it – no chemicals or accelerants. I like Whittle & Flame and House of Charcoal. Your local farm shop, should you have such a thing, will likely be able to help too. My other barbecuing top tip is to coat meat and fish in mayonnaise. I am aware of how gross this sounds, but you can't taste it at all. All it does is make your food miraculously non-stick.

Away from the barbecue, here are a few of my favourite things to make for an outdoor lunch – whether you've climbed out of the window to get on to the flat roof, are picnicking in a park, or staying in your own garden – aside from enormous salads. There is a Substack newsletter called The Department of Salad and it is my first port of call for all or any salad recipe needs, whatever the occasion, season, salad heft level or mood. It's full of amazing dressings, too. Here's what else I like to make:

- As ever, any kind of trusty no-cooking assemblage from the deli + crusty bread. A dish of crunchy radishes on the side is never a bad idea.

- My assemblies often involve a separate platter of burrata, sometimes with tomato and basil, sometimes with anchovies, sometimes with grilled vegetables, sometimes with shaved strips of perky raw courgette and lemon zest, sometimes with figs, always with olive oil. I also like the idea of it with grilled peaches and Parma ham.

- Speaking of which, never underestimate the retro deliciousness of Parma ham and Cavaillon (round, orange flesh, very scented) melon. No-cook lunch in 2 minutes.

- Ajo blanco, which is chilled almond soup and so lovely on a hot day. I use Felicity Cloake's recipe, which is available online.

- Skye McAlpine's second book, *A Table for Friends*, is full of really low-effort, really delicious summery recipes, one of which is for Poulet Anglais – a charmingly old-fashioned recipe, as she says in the book, but none the worse for that. It's cold poached chicken in a cooling, soothing yogurt and tarragon sauce and is exactly the thing to make (in advance, oh joy) on the sort of day when it's too hot to eat. 'God, it's boiling,' people say. 'I'm not sure I'm hungry,' before having seconds.

- When the tomatoes are really good and really ripe, I make kachumber pretty much every day. Toast ½ a teaspoon of cumin seeds. Chop 500g of tomatoes, peel and dice a small red onion, and combine them with the cumin seeds plus the zest and juice of 1 lime and the finely chopped leaves of a small bunch of coriander. Drizzle with extra virgin olive oil and season with salt and pepper.

- I also make labneh all the time. Get some Greek yogurt (it must be full fat), scoop it out into a clean muslin or J-cloth, add a bit of salt, and tie the muslin or J-cloth into a knot, so the yogurt forms a ball. Put it into a sieve or colander and perch this atop a bowl. Leave in the fridge overnight – longer if you want it very firm (at which point you can roll it into balls and roll the balls in spices/herbs). I like it still creamy, as a dip. When you want to eat it, scatter it with dukkah, za'atar, toasted cumin seeds, chopped herbs, chilli flakes or whatever else you like the idea of. Cheat's labneh for instant dips: mix 150g of cream cheese with 500g of Greek yogurt, scatter toppings (which really can be anything you like), and eat with flatbreads or pita.

HOME

- Fruit for pudding. If you're having a barbecue and the barbecue is on but not too hot, I sometimes roast peaches in a tray with butter and sugar in the hollow, which turns into a sort of toffee sauce as the edges of the peach char and caramelize, and have vanilla ice cream on the side. I learned this from (again) the brilliant Jane Lovett.

If all this outdoorsiness is making you hanker for a home where you're closer to nature and further from the city or town – it's a conversation many of us have had with ourselves over the years – the following chapter might help.

RECOMMENDATIONS

- **Fairy lights:** my number 1 favourites in the world are **Canterbury Belles** by Noma. They are multicoloured and are for you if the vibe you're after is 'Granny's house when I was five'. You can just about still find the extra old school filament ones (which do get hot, so bear that in mind), but the LED iteration is pretty great too. These are not weatherproof, so take them down when you come in from supper if rain is forecast. For **all other outdoor fairy light and festoon light supplies, including solar lighting**, you can't go wrong with **Lights4Fun**, lights4fun.co.uk. They do very good connectable ones, so that your fairy lights can span a long distance if you need them to and still only use one socket.
- **Affordable garden furniture:** I have never been able to understand why so much garden furniture is both shockingly ugly *and* astronomically expensive. Mine is almost all second- or third-hand, so that's one option, but if you want something new you'll have to spend time online ferreting out the good stuff, which frustratingly seems to chop and change from year to year. **Wayfair** and **Dunelm** have their moments, **George at Asda** usually has at least a couple of under-the-radar gems, **Habitat** is hit-and-miss but great when it's good (excellent sun loungers),

and **Sklum**, sklum.com, have lots of attractive and well-priced things, but they're in Spain so shipping takes a while and is not cheap.
- **Bits to cobble together an outdoor kitchen:** Salvage yards, ingenuity and **IKEA**; see also **Elfin Kitchens**' mini outdoor options (cute and tiny, won't dominate the space).
- **Picnic rugs:** Obviously you can use anything, but **The British Blanket Company**, thebritishblanketcompany.com, have old-school woollen blankets with weatherproof backing that roll up and fasten with leather straps. **Tweedmill**, tweedmill.com, have several different types of very pretty picnic rugs, both wool and quilted, also rollable and with carrying straps. I especially love their tartan Eventer range.

MOVING TO THE COUNTRY – EVERYTHING USEFUL I'VE LEARNED OVER THE PAST TEN YEARS

As I've said, I'd only ever lived in cities before moving to Suffolk. I remember the day of the move so well – the huge brown removal vans, saying goodbye and thank you to the London house that had served us so nobly, the long journey to our new home, and 'One Day Like This' by Elbow on the radio as we came down the lane, so that the chorus exploded as we turned into the drive. It felt so auspicious. I remember the exhilarating feeling of being at the start of a whole new adventure. It was a grey day and the meadow had just been baled for hay ('What do we *do* with all that hay?' 'No idea. What actually *is* hay? Is it the same as straw?').

Perhaps curiously, in the chaos of those first few days – it is so odd to dismantle a life and then reassemble it in a whole new place – I didn't once think, 'What have we done?' I just *knew*. And I was right. Living here is always a privilege, and in bad times it has been an extraordinary comfort.

Here are some findings that might be useful if you're considering this sort of drastic move yourself. For reference: I live properly in the sticks – like, a twenty-minute-drive-for-a-pint-of-milk sticks – and so the below applies to the sticks. Things will be a little bit different for the lesser sticks, and different again for the semi-sticks.

Decide on what kind of life you want. Really think about it. Recognizably like your old life, but with more space and fresh air? Or something completely, wildly different, more like a new chapter? If it's the former, don't necessarily move to the country-country. Market towns and especially cities (here's my usual shoutout to Norwich) may be the perfect solution: lovely housing stock, a ton more space, plus restaurants, coffee shops that do a decent flat white, exhibitions and theatres, good shopping, interesting, like-minded people, welcome multiculturalism (as opposed to none – more on that below), but also wide open spaces fifteen minutes away, and if you're lucky the sea not far beyond that.

As a rule, avoid the chocolate-box village or the charming spot where you like to spend your holidays. Both are often stuffed full of second-homers, meaning that not only can local people never get a foothold on the housing ladder, but also that those places are completely dead out of season (and then heaving at weekends and during school holidays). You get rows of gloomy dark empty houses and then one poor sod with the lights on because he drank the Kool-Aid and thought the place was idyllic and agreeably busy twelve months a year. My advice would be to live somewhere outside those places, and somewhere with a mix of housing stock, because 'ordinary' houses have normal life in them all year round, meaning active, lively (and youthful) communities regardless of the season.

You'll be worried about loneliness. Don't be. It is of course much easier to meet new people at the school gate, but don't let that put you off if your kids are grown up or you don't have any. People are incredibly friendly and chatty, plus they will be curious about you (new blood). So if your fear about moving is feeling marooned and friendless, I would park that one – it's unlikely unless you deliberately make a point of keeping yourself to yourself.

What I would say is, **have a party as early as you can** and invite every single person you've met, from the postman to the nice woman in the shop to your potential new best mate. If that's still not many people, ask them to bring a friend along. It won't (probably) be like the parties you had in the city or town you lived in before, but it will be a huge amount of fun and make you feel grounded in your new world.

The countryside zings with activities. Try some, even if you don't think of yourself as an activities-type person. If you've ever fancied swing dancing but considered yourself too cool to hoof about with strangers, now's your chance.

I am bad with numbers and fairly impulsive – not the best combo in this context. So I've always **bought the most house I could afford**, leaving zero pence for any work that needs doing or items that need buying (a ride-on mower, say, which still costs thousands second-hand). It's a good idea to set aside a sum of money for these rural necessities when you're doing your calculations.

The idea of having **a bit of land** is insanely exciting to expats from cities, but that land does not look after itself. It costs money – sometimes quite a lot of money – to run. Garden aside – and if it's thrillingly big you will need a gardener in addition to your own (possibly inept, noob-level) gardening – hedges, fence posts, paddocks, fields, external buildings, driveways and so on and on and on, all need maintaining. YouTube exists and it's entirely possible that you will eventually be able to take on some of this maintenance yourself, but probably not from the off, and not without specialist equipment, which, as I've said, is also not cheap. So factor that in, too.

Don't go too big out of exhilaration at the idea that you can buy a big old fairytale cottage for the price of a tiny London flat. Or *do* go too big, but be ready for the stiff (vertical) learning curve.

Always ask the current owners **what the house costs to run** – get them to write down figures, and ask them things like 'Do you heat the whole house in winter?' to make sure those figures are realistic, which they won't be if the people in fact leave the heating off and spend December to March in three layers of clothing holed up in the room with the woodburner in it. For example, I'd always had gas and electricity, which we paid by monthly direct debit, but this house has no mains gas supply and runs off heating oil delivered quarterly

HOME

(there's always a co-op of locals who band together to get the best price, by the way – never buy heating oil solo). I didn't really know what heating oil was, or how much it cost.

If you're planning on working from home, and even if you're not, **always check wifi speeds**. These can be creakingly antique even in well-populated places, where for instance you couldn't watch Netflix or your kids' game online without it constantly buffering. The ideal is existing FTTP, fibre to the premises, which is gold dust and bumps the house price up.

Ditto **mobile signal**. Since Vodafone switched off 3G, I have no mobile signal whatsoever for a radius of about fifteen miles.

The countryside is incredibly white, with everything that suggests. When I see another brown person – locally that's the man who has the nearest takeaway plus his family – we catch each other's eye and nod silently. I find this constantly challenging, sometimes claustrophobic, and also deeply weird. So there's that.

Don't romanticize everything, though I fully understand the temptation. Know that if you keep chickens, they will 100% attract rats. Know that sheep get hideous diseases like fly strike, which is even worse than it sounds, don't google it. Ducks make an incredible mess, plus, distressingly, male ducks are basically rapists (ducks are the only birds to have penises, as Jassy explains in my novel *Darling*). A couple of sweet piglets is a charming idea, but they turn into 300lb+ chunkers that can knock you over and will turn their enclosure into a sea of mud.

Beware of biting off more than you can chew when it comes to poetic notions of self-sufficiency. Grow your own veg, by all means, but beware of growing your own meat. When push comes to shove the idea of killing your pig friends might become monstrously horrible, which is fine – but then you have giant pet pigs crashing around for the next eight years or so.

Know, as I'm sure you already do, that **not all farmed animals have a nice life**. I'll leave it at that and point you to Compassion in World Farming. Maybe look into this if you are buying somewhere near anything related to intensive farming. Also, check for local meat processing plants. There's currently a beautiful house for sale vaguely nearby that makes no mention of the fact that the air there is unbreathable two days a week – you literally gag.

Also know that **farming is brutally hard**, and that farmers have a very high suicide rate – again, it doesn't do to romanticize other people's lives, particularly as an urban incomer. Rural poverty is horrendous, just for starters, not least because of physical isolation from sources of help or relief. There's poor, and then there's rural poor.

Living in the country is not Instagram, Pinterest or wherever else specializes in 'curated' lifestyle envy. It is incredibly beautiful and rewarding, and you are struck by the beauty in an almost trippy way several times a day. But if the life you envisage involves idyllic images from social media – maybe skipping about twirling your gingham-lined basket and milking passing cows borrowed from smiling yokels – then adjust your expectations.

Rewilding takes a lot of hard work. You don't just leave everything and wait for the storks and beavers to turn up.

You will have to learn to cope with **dead things**, or rather with their removal. When home alone, I used to do this using really long barbecue tongs with my face averted, making retching noises, even for a tiny mouse, let alone e.g. a rabbit (or deer, or fox, once, which was so sad). I'm more sanguine these days, though still not at all keen.

Mice: yep. Always.

Moving to the country is not **marital glue**. If you're having a tough time, a change of scene will not cure it and may well make it worse. Because family life is one thing, but if you have no kids or are older, you have to really enjoy each other's company. If you move to the sticks, you will spend the bulk of your time together, just the two of you, far away from other human beings and far away from other sources of entertainment. If you're happy reading your books companionably, great. If your relationship relies heavily on external stimuli – trips, weekends away, hotels, restaurants, parties, etc., etc. – then that could become an issue. Better maybe to move to the semi-sticks.

Though of course **it is possible to still do all those things** even in the middle of nowhere – but it's much more of an effort when the restaurant involves a forty-minute drive and isn't quite the happening scene you were expecting when you finally get there, or when the party always consists of the same people.

You also have to **enjoy your *own* company**. For me, this is central to the whole thing. I love my own company, I write and read and potter about for days on end, I've always got a satisfying little job to do in the house or garden, and if I have to go out I moan about it for days in advance (and then have a lovely time, of course). I say all this because THE WINTERS ARE VERY, VERY LONG. I know two couples who threw in the towel recently. One now just go abroad for the duration – hardly an option for everyone – and the others are moving back to town because they just can't hack the sea of mud, the howling winds, the rivers of rain, the pitch blackness at 4pm, for months and months on end. You'll be fine if you like hunkering doing nothing much, but you may find it highly challenging if you like always being on the go.

Of course, the winters are more than made up for by **the heavenly springs and summers** (usually). And the ravishingly beautiful autumns. Conversation last week: her, 'Are you going anywhere this summer?' Me, 'No, are you?' Her, 'No, we never do. Why would you, if you lived here and had a garden?'

Contrary to popular belief, the countryside is **very far from a cultural desert**. It, or at least my bit of it, is hugely creative. There is always something extremely interesting going on – to look at, to sit down and watch, to listen to, to visit, to experience.

You'll know your house when you see it. We bought the first house we viewed. I knew with absolute certainty that it was the right house. We live in a grotesquely consumerist culture that constantly makes us feel like there is something better just around the corner, whether it's a t-shirt, a lipstick, a handbag or a property, and that we must have it because then our life will finally have meaning. Spoiler: it won't. Being like this slowly drives people mad, because it makes them permanently dissatisfied and lunatically acquisitive.

You don't need to look at dozens of houses if you don't want to. Go with your gut.

Including if your gut insistently tells you **the house is creepy** or has a weird vibe. Never force yourself to like a house because it's ideal on paper but strange in the flesh. This sounds obvious, but it's really easy to override the little voice going 'step away' based on just a vague woo-woo feeling when everything else is technically exactly what you were looking for.

Also: you *make* the house your dream house by being in it and loving it and caring for it: that philosophy is the whole point of the book you're holding. But it's not necessarily always the dream when you first walk into it. It needs good bones, though.

Once you've moved, **don't be too nice or acquiescent** because you're desperate to 'fit in' and not be lonely. You are now part of the community you've moved to and it belongs to you too, just as much as to the people who have lived there for generations. There's no need to affect a change of personality.

Church is still central to many people's lives. If you're not religious, don't cackle sarcastically if someone asks, 'Will we see you at church on Sunday?'

The parish newsletter is always worth reading.

Don't be a wanker from London (or wherever, but ex-Londoners are particularly good at it). But equally, don't be pointlessly keen to denounce London now you've moved away, with that sort of convert's zealotry. London is one of the world's greatest cities. It is amazing, evolved and diverse. There's no need to knock it because you've just discovered honesty stalls.

You will become **obsessed with the weather**, and download every available weather app. Just accept it. I talk about the weather all the time, like a parody of an incredibly boring person. At least, I hope it's a parody.

TAKE IT TO THE TIP

The things nobody needs

In interiors as in life, some things are just a pointless waste of money. Here is my very subjective list of them – you'll have your own to add.

What not to waste your money on

1. Buying all the things from the same brand. Whether it's makeup or furniture, just because they do a good blush or headboard doesn't mean they do a brilliant foundation or bedside table. Also it's not 1985 – you don't need your sitting-room furniture to be 'matching'.
2. Anything faux that isn't 100% convincing. But you could probably have bought the real thing second-hand.
3. Posh baked beans.
4. Posh crisps, with the exception of olive oil ones from Spain. And even then, in my heart of hearts my number 1 is still Walkers ready salted, with salt and vinegar hot on the heels.
5. Cheap scented candles. The smell is nauseating after five minutes, plus breathing that stuff in is really not good for you. Also they burn incredibly quickly (true of any cheap candle, including in a candlestick). False economy. Try incense.
6. Thin binbags.

7. First class train tickets, unless the journey is especially long and arduous.
8. Vintage champagne. 99% of people buy it to show off. 1% can tell the difference (see also wine above a certain price point).
9. Cheap Botox/fillers. Expertise and a good eye cost money.
10. Ready-made salad dressing.
11. Bargain animals, e.g. puppies. Please, please, either rescue or reputable breeders. Never an online ad and a meeting in the car park.
12. Expensive gloves or mittens. You will lose them.
13. Expensive umbrellas, ditto, though I do have a soft spot for James Smith & Sons.
14. Expensive moisturizer. It feels lovely to use, but it is absolutely, 100%, not necessary.
15. Deluxe coffins.
16. Bottled water.
17. Personal trainers. Get them to show you and then do it yourself.
18. Complicated, expensive barista-style coffee machines. Use a Moka pot or a pour-over thing and a paper filter – perfect coffee every time. The whole of Europe can't be wrong.
19. Little piddly jars of spices. If you use something often, buy a big sack and decant into jam jars.
20. Men-only skincare.
21. More than one or maybe two TV streaming subs.
22. Expensive mascara. High-street brands are brilliant.
23. Expensive nail polish. Chemical gloop is chemical gloop. You're paying for the pretty jar. Wear a top coat if you're worried about chips.
24. Fabric softener. It's really chemical and really bad for your clothes.
25. Expensive cufflinks.
26. Expensive shampoo (pointless) and conditioner (marginally less so). Spend the money on K18 – you won't need conditioner at all and your hair will thank you.

27. Pan sets. You never need that many pans and the sizes are weird.
28. Pointless, space-taking electric kitchen gadgets, e.g. omelette makers.
29. Knife sets. I do everything with a cook's knife, a bread knife and a little all-purpose knife.
30. Sonic rodent repellers. They might work for two weeks, if you're lucky. Mouse traps are gross but work every time.
31. Dry cleaning, though there are (rare) exceptions. Most things can be hand-washed with Stergene.
32. Expensive hoovers. Henry all the way! Miele Pet gets an exemption if you have dogs/cats.
33. Posh tiny chocolate. Everybody loves Cadbury's Dairy Milk, which comes in huge 850g bars for parties.
34. Posh teabags. Most people, myself included, want either Twinings Earl Grey or PG Tips. Leaf tea is different, but most people don't drink leaf tea unless you actively set out to convert them.
35. Exorbitant pasta, unless you have a white truffle to hand.
36. White truffle in restaurants. A ghostly grating over your spaghetti for £60 extra – I don't think so.
37. New season extra virgin olive oil, because it's a total lottery (olive oil bottles could really do with explanatory stickers). It's either ambrosial or so crazily peppery that it makes you cough – no way of telling which. Too risky.
38. Wildly expensive weddings.
39. Unnecessarily powerful, top-of-the-range tech. You don't need the latest Pro Max iPhone unless you're a film director who's going to shoot a movie on it. Tech dates, fast, or gets unusable updates – bear it in mind before installing a complicated sound system in your home.
40. Expensive ear buds. I borrowed a friend's £25 ear buds recently, mocking them cruelly as I inserted them. I couldn't tell the difference once they were in.
41. Celebrity chefs in recherché restaurants with waiting lists. They never cook what I want to eat.

42. Expensive TVs. They're all the same now. Technology is great, but the human eye can only see so much.
43. Most stays at most hotels.
44. And 'experiences' in hotels. A bit of cava and some ugly flowers, yours for an extra £100, happy Valentine's day.
45. ££££ puffy winter coats. None of them are flattering, so that's that, and none are as good as Uniqlo's. Save your money for a proper wool coat.
46. 80% of beauty treatments. Maybe 90%.
47. Spas, unless they're those brisk, un-fun medical ones abroad.
48. Most concert tickets. You end up watching a speck on a giant screen. It's a lot to pay for a communal vibe.
49. Expensive wellies. Pointless, plus no faster way of looking un-local.
50. Membership to private clubs. They had their moment, and it has passed. Why pay to be squashed in a corner being brayed over by the world's worst people?
51. £5 coffees that just taste *bad*. Most shop coffee tastes bad. It's a massive con.
52. Anything 'limited edition'. Who cares?
53. Lip balm. Nothing is as good as Vaseline.
54. Wildly expensive lampshades, unless you are going to be sitting very close to them.
55. Expensive knickers.
56. I am repeating myself, but it's important – saving anything 'for best' is the ultimate waste of money.

And, while we're at it, here is some life advice that can go to the tip too.

TAKE IT TO THE TIP

TERRIBLE LIFE ADVICE THAT SOMETIMES GETS PRESENTED AS WISDOM

- **Never give up.** No, do. Knowing when to give up is a brilliant life skill – it's what keeps you from stagnating in place. If you're bad at something, or if it is killing your soul to stay put, and if giving up is viable, then give up! Of course give up! Ditto bad relationships, ditto trying to grow lavender in December, ditto breakdancing at the Olympics when you're crap at it (remember poor Raygun?). Give up! Stop wasting your time! There are always alternative paths – ones that might even make you happy. The sibling of that platitude is **winners never quit**. Wrong again. They quit all the time. That's what makes them find the thing they win at.

- **Be yourself.** Well, yes, obviously, of course be yourself most of the time. But also no, don't always 'be yourself'. If you never have anything nice to say, be someone else. If you're never pleased when something good happens to somebody, hide it. If your natural state is sourness, conceal it (none of these things are really anyone's natural states, so maybe also consider getting help with whatever's eating you up. Often it's to do with not feeling heard). Not being yourself saves you from saying, 'Your baby pictures are unbelievably boring,' or 'I can't stand cats so I'm not finding it cute.' See also **never apologize for being you**. Personally I would always apologize for the cat/baby remarks.

- **You are magic.** Yeah, you're not. There will be aspects of you that are indeed absolutely and perhaps even uniquely wondrous. But no, you are not magic. You do not have power over the universe – the universe has power over you. I am quite woo, so I think it may *sometimes* be possible for the two of you to work together. Wishing is fine, but you have to back it up with action. (In my experience, the only people who think they're magic are extreme narcissists.)

- **You get back what you put in**. True of soup, less true of humans. Some people get a feast without having put much in at all, some people devote a lifetime to gathering the finest ingredients and still end up with gruel. Also, life works better if you put in the stuff because you want to, not in expectation of untold rewards.

- **You're never too old**. Sometimes, you really are. For example, I am too old to routinely address people as bruh, or to twerk. Just because you can do it doesn't mean you have to, as I used to tell my children when they had burping competitions.

- **Nothing is impossible if you want it badly enough.** Loads of things are impossible. It is a kindness to help people not waste years of their precious life chasing them.

- **When they go low, we go high.** Sounds nice, is rubbish advice that loses elections. When they go low, we go lower, right into the gutter if needs be. Or we laugh at them – that might work too. But if someone's about to punch us in the face – literally or figuratively – we don't recite an improving poem at them.

- **There's no such thing as failure**. There very much is. But the silver lining is that you can usually learn from it.

- **Be fearless**. In times of crisis human beings are wired for two responses, fight and flight. It's really important to be able to tell the difference. There's nothing wrong with fear, or caution, or thinking, 'I could fearlessly do this, but then I'd lose my job/wife/driving licence/self-respect.'

- **Don't stop when you're tired, stop when you're done.** Are you a robot? If not, have a rest. A refreshing siesta helps with everything, including focus and clarity.

- **I don't chase, I attract** (or any version that suggests powerful charisma is enough). This might be true in a sexual context if you are unbelievably hot – though I would find someone who thought like this powerfully un-hot – but it is an absolute disaster anywhere else. Chase stuff. Have ambitions. Go after things. Don't just sit there going:

- **I am enough.** There are circumstances in which I believe in this one. For someone with low self-esteem, or someone broken by life, to come to this realization is a massive win. But for some ploddy person to sit there on their bottom all self-satisfied *because they are enough* is merely comical.

- **Respect, don't judge.** No, do judge sometimes. For example, I judge racists, misogynists and other people who are simply horrible to be around.

- **Everything happens for a reason.** Missing out on the shoes you wanted in the sale, maybe. Someone being hit by a truck, no. It is enormously comforting to believe that the world is not random – I get it. But also, nobody could accuse the world of being shy about its randomness.

- **It's all good.** No. Sometimes it's all bad beyond belief and endurance, and being in denial about it isn't going to help you heal.

- **Age is just a number.** I mean, so's your bank balance. I understand the sentiment, but the number kind of matters. **You're as old as you feel** can be true mentally, but is not true physiologically or biologically. (A thing that really weirds me out about people who have had a lot of cosmetic work is that they look a slightly peculiar version of forty-five but are still the full sixty-seven on the inside.)

- **Family is everything.** Ideally, yes. But it very much depends on the family.

- **You've got this**. Sometimes you do got this, but sometimes you don't, in which case it is super unhelpful to tell yourself you do.

- **The best is yet to come**. Very possibly, and hurrah for that, but what if the best is *right now* and you're missing it because you're waiting for the better best that might or might not turn up in the future? Enjoy the present. Right now, in the home that you love.

FOUNDATION 7
IN PRAISE OF IMPERFECTION

Wonkiness is a virtue

For my final foundation, I come to praise imperfection, and I do so with all my heart. Because if we want warmth, life and soul in our homes, we have to let go of the idea of some imaginary perfect ideal that is always frustratingly out of reach. It's the 'if only' thing: if only I had more money, if only I had more hours in the day, if only I had a small, discreet pair of wings I could avail myself of as required. But we don't have these things, and that's okay: we work with what we've got. People aren't perfect, life isn't perfect, God knows the state of the world isn't perfect – and neither are our homes. And do you know what? That's *perfectly* (sorry) okay.

Besides, perfection kills charm absolutely stone-dead. It also often translates into a kind of chilly, impersonal sterility that's not much fun to live in. Imagine constantly fretting about every spill and scratch and freaking out if somebody left their socks lying about, spoiling the look. And ask yourself: what kind of room can be undone by an innocent sock? What kind of interior is sent immediately off-kilter if someone accidentally leaves a takeaway carton lying about for a bit?

Imperfection brings character, history, stories, life and joy into play, and as we have seen throughout this book, those are the things that make a house a home. The seen-better-days rug, the burn mark on the kitchen worktop (so what? it's a worktop, not a displaytop), the ghost of red wine on the side of the sofa are evidence of a life that has been – is being – lived and enjoyed. A skew-whiff picture frame, a wonky stack of well-thumbed, well-loved books, furniture arranged for comfort rather than symmetry, a bit of dust: all of these tell you that you are in a space that is for living rather than for admiring, and tells you everything you need to know about the people who live there and how comfortable you will feel in their home. You wouldn't necessarily whip off your socks and fling them gaily on the floor, or start chucking takeaway cartons about, but isn't it nice to know that you technically *could* without destroying the entire aesthetic in one fell swoop?

Look at all the things – handcrafted, hand-made items, natural materials, art, old things from junk shops and auctions – that we value specifically *because* of their imperfections. I love ceramics for many reasons, but the main one is that a human person took (well, okay, probably bought) some clay from the earth and turned it into something with their own two hands – hands whose imprint I can sometimes still see on the finished item. In the right/wrong mood, this moves me almost to tears. Recently I felt briefly dizzy standing in the British Museum in front of a case containing pottery from about 2200 BC.

The antiquity was more than my brain could compute, but the hand marks and the imprints from the implements they must have used to make patterns on a cup was almost more than I could bear (also the desire of Bronze Age man or woman for *decorating* the cup, for wanting to embellish a functional everyday object, is very moving). I feel the same way about modern pottery – marginally less weepy, but really it could have been made yesterday. It wouldn't alter the facts. THEY MADE IT WITH THEIR HANDS! I want to shout. ONLY THIS VERY ONE LOOKS EXACTLY LIKE THIS!

That's how I want us to feel about the insides of our houses, too. Like we're standing in front of a magnificent painting and can see the brushstrokes, down to traces of individual bristles. Who wouldn't be

FOUNDATION 7: IN PRAISE OF IMPERFECTION

charmed? What sentient being would choose to stand in front of a 'perfect' AI replica instead?

The best houses, like the best people, are never done. They do not reach a stage of 'Finished! That's it!' They evolve for ever, sometimes in big ways, sometimes in minuscule, infinitesimal ones. This constant process of evolution is the opposite of stagnation (or death by boredom), and I find it thrilling and energizing, in houses as with people. We are, rightly, highly suspicious of anyone who appears too good to be true, because we know that human beings are flawed, fallible, odd, eccentric, messy – and beautiful and endearing not just despite but *because* of these things. Because they are real, and their real-ness touches our hearts. Acknowledging their, and our, imperfections is what makes us all feel connected, what make us like each other – love each other, even. We moan and groan and share struggles and funny stories about cocking up, and in doing so bond with others and become more empathetic ourselves. Meanwhile, the 'perfect'-seeming person sits off at a flank, unrelatable and unapproachable, unknown. And as with the perfect person, so with the perfect house.

And that is a truly wonderful thing.

LIFE ADVICE

We're standing by the garden gate now, ready to say goodbye. Thank you for accompanying me on this tour of my home. I have loved every minute of showing you around, and I hope to have given you ideas, inspiration and above all the confidence to make *your* home a place where joy and contentment are at least a possibility. None of us can skip about being joyful and contented all the time, of course, and as I was just saying, our homes and our selves are constantly evolving. Still, a good mattress is a good mattress.

I would like to press a pot of home-made jam into your hand as we part, but I don't actually make jam. So here is another kind of present, in the form of some of my best, most hard-earned life tips to see you on your way: less sweet, but perhaps more useful.

1. Some people are a bad vibe. Don't try and charm them into not being a bad vibe, or try to befriend them. They are a bad vibe. Move away.
2. You can make an okay soup out of frozen vegetables.
3. Humour is born as a coping mechanism long before it becomes a defining characteristic. Understand that funny people are complicated.
4. If you're having a shit day, it's much easier to acknowledge it – 'Today is shit' – than to keep on expecting it to become less shit and keep on being disappointed.
5. Women don't say no enough. Don't feel you have to make up elaborate excuses. Just say, 'Ah, no, I can't.' I sometimes say, 'Ah, no, I really don't want to,' but you have to know the person pretty well.
6. Don't say yes to things you don't want to do because they're six months away. You still won't want to do them in six months' time.
7. 'Quietly happy' is a really good place.
8. The friend you always dread seeing is not really your friend. You already know this. Consider doing something about it.
9. A second language gives you a second life. It's never too late to learn one.
10. I, a Sagittarius, believe in bluntness. If it's important, say exactly what you mean. Not everyone understands nuance, understatement or vague metaphors.
11. Know what triggers you. That way you can stop yourself reacting disproportionately when you encounter it.
12. People sometimes outgrow each other. It's normal. It's fine.
13. Marcella Hazan's tomato sauce recipe, which you can find online, involves only tinned tomatoes, an onion and some butter. It is a good one to have up your sleeve.
14. You don't have to be the most at anything – the best, the happiest, the specialest. You just have to be content.
15. Difficult decisions aren't always difficult. Often you already know the answer in your gut. You're just trying to talk yourself out of it.

FOUNDATION 7: IN PRAISE OF IMPERFECTION

16. The best skincare serum from midlife onwards is Skinceuticals C E Ferulic.
17. If you pee straight after sex, you never get cystitis.
18. Don't waste your life fretting about petty crap. None of it matters.
19. All anyone wants in a relationship is to feel heard. Listen. Don't interrupt. Don't say 'yes, but'.
20. If you screengrab or photograph a few new recipes you like the sound of, you won't ever stand in the supermarket thinking, 'Oh. I've gone completely blank.' Or come home with two cans of tuna, a mop and a banana for dinner.
21. Karma is real. Don't be awful.
22. A messy kitchen looks significantly less messy if the sink is pristine. Grubby sinks are sordid, only one up from terrible loos.
23. Try and stay friends with your exes if you have children together. If two people who were close now have a yawning chasm between them, children can fall into that gap and become lost. This never manifests in fun ways.
24. Green Fairy Liquid gets any stain out of anything, even fragile Dry Clean Only things. Squirt a tiny amount directly on to the stain, leave for three minutes, rub in with a little hot water, rinse as best you can, leave to dry naturally.
25. Don't define yourself to yourself – 'I am like this, I like X and Y.' Stay open to possibilities. Only terminally dim people never change their mind.
26. That empty feeling inside you can't be filled by sex, food, alcohol, drugs or shopping. Or money, success, power, possessions. But therapy does it. Eventually.
27. If you dislike a friend's child – not nice, but it happens – make sure to give them fantastic and thoughtful birthday presents. It alleviates parental suspicions as well as your conscience. This is a Machiavellian tip, I realize.
28. Accept compliments and give them lavishly, including to strangers. It's such a small thing and it spreads happiness.

29. Sometimes older people who appear to have gone completely gaga just have a UTI, so always check for that first.
30. Related: drink enough water.
31. Don't rely on work or partners to make you happy. Find *your* thing and do it, often.
32. Positive thinking works.
33. Negative thinking works even better.
34. None of us is the person we were ten years ago. We'd be doing something wrong if we were. We'd be stagnant. Cut people some slack. We all evolve.
35. If you ever think, no matter how fleetingly, 'I'm not sure I should press send,' don't press send.
36. Rein in your cynicism/bitching. A little bit is funny. A non-stop stream makes you sound insecure and unhappy.
37. If it ever becomes viable to work for yourself, do it. Be the only person telling you what to do. Having control of your own life matters.
38. Always ask for help, but from the right people. Sometimes the right people will be professionals.
39. Here's a quote from James Baldwin in *Life* magazine in 1963: 'You think your pain and your heartbreak are unprecedented in the history of the world, but then you read. It was Dostoevsky and Dickens who taught me that the things that tormented me most were the very things that connected me with all the people who were alive, or who ever had been alive.'
40. Other people are not better at adult life than you. Most of us are just making it up as we go along, and that is fine (I include marriage/children/parenting in this). Don't assume that you're a lone outlier and that everybody else is a thousand times more competent than you. Yes, some people *are* highly organized. It's a control thing, an attempt at imposing order on the unpredictable chaos of human existence. But steering your ship with a very light hand is also an option.

FOUNDATION 7: IN PRAISE OF IMPERFECTION

41. Your version of events is not definitive. It is your version. The other person/people will have their own version, interpreted through their own eyes, lives, feelings and experiences – their truth, to use a phrase I don't love. Both versions are valid.
42. If something is good, don't pull at tiny little threads. All there is to gain is unravelling.
43. Your life is now, today. A lot of people feel dissatisfied because they are always imagining a future where X or Y problem has been addressed and solved. This is like always looking over someone's shoulder at a party, except in this instance you are looking over the shoulder *of your own actual life*. Constantly thinking, 'I will be happy once X happens' is a fool's errand. X might happen, or it might not. Whatever. Meanwhile you only get one 16 October 2025 in your whole entire existence.
44. Be who you actually are. This is easy until you start school, and then difficult until middle age.
45. Calm down. Very few things are catastrophes. The writer Jessica Fellowes remembers a relative saying that most things we think of as massive dramas at the time wouldn't make a paragraph in our autobiographies – most of them wouldn't even make a sentence.
46. And even catastrophes are eventually surmountable, because:
47. You are much more resilient than you think you are. You have no idea. (And hopefully won't ever have to find out.)
48. Emotional games are really boring and weird for everyone else.
49. There is too much choice. Pare back. Edit what you consume. Nobody needs thirty handbags or twenty white t-shirts. Excessive consumption is a disorder of late capitalism, an exhausting search for perfection that can never be satisfied. I sometimes think that shopping obsessively, particularly for clothes people don't need, is the last socially acceptable addiction. It stems, like all addictions, from a not-great place. It is strange that we admire it.

50. There is never just one mouse. Sorry.
51. 'Comparison is the thief of joy,' Theodore Roosevelt said, and he was right.
52. Don't haggle abroad. It is awful, and no, 'they' don't 'expect it'. They're unimaginably poorer than you. Pay the price being asked.
53. It's cool to be a beginner, a learner, inexperienced, inexpert, unsure. Learn something new. Don't be embarrassed! Also, being crap at something and then becoming marginally less crap feels interesting, since most adults only really do things they're already reasonably good at. It's quite freeing.
54. In social situations, don't perform a version of yourself that expired long ago for the benefit of others. Or in professional situations, for that matter.
55. Everyone becomes a child again in family settings; it's almost a reflex. But you don't have to play your designated role – bossy eldest, spoilt baby youngest, or whatever – if you don't want to. You can choose not to play. You can choose to be seen as you are now, today.
56. You don't have to tell everyone what you're doing all the time, whether it's stopping drinking, being on a diet, the intimate details of a new relationship, or whatever. Respect your own privacy. You're not a performing seal. Your own validation is enough.
57. Some people don't want the solution, only the drama. The drama is the point. Stop offering solutions and you'll feel less irritated by them.
58. When you've done your face, put the remaining sunscreen on the backs of your hands.
59. It is never too late to change your mind about anything.
60. Happiness *is* a warm puppy.

BONUS CHAPTER: CHRISTMAS FOR THE BUSY, AND CHRISTMAS FOR THE QUIET

Because there's no right way

I know, we already said goodbye (I've written about guests who won't leave – the *host* who won't leave is a new low). But the Substack post below was wildly popular when I published it, and I wanted to reproduce it here because I feel it needs saying. There's more than one way of doing Christmas, and more than one way of it being a joy.

TINY CHRISTMAS

About halfway through last December, I bumped into an acquaintance on the train, and so obviously I asked them what they were doing for Christmas. They sort of winced and said, 'Nothing much, very quiet, just the two of us at home,' in a way that was almost apologetic. What they went on to describe – roast ham rather than turkey, a two-day list of films they were planning to watch, a walk they were going to take in Norfolk to see pink-footed geese, a specific M&S trifle – sounded like heaven.

I don't like it that people's lovely Tiny Christmases can get downgraded in their own minds by the imagery of what Christmas is supposed to look like – extravagantly well populated, lavishly over-catered, with rosy-cheeked children/grandchildren gambolling in matching pyjamas, course after course of feasting, and mountains of presents.

All of these things are nice, if not entirely realistic. But none of them are obligatory, and I hate the idea that some people might feel that their smaller-scale Christmas is somehow not enough. Because Tiny Christmas is great too. Tiny Christmas is charming. Tiny Christmas is the definition of quiet contentment, and who doesn't want that?

As a veteran of Giant Christmas, I can't tell you how many times I have longed – longed – for Tiny Christmas. I love our family Christmases, but I'd be lying if I said that the idea of spending the day mostly supine, bingeing TV, with nary a turkey in sight, was wholly without appeal. To barely get dressed. To eat fried eggs and parathas and Turkish Delight and have catnaps and read. To do as little as possible, either solo or with one other person.

The idea is to have a nice day – whatever that means to you. It's rather like getting married: running to the register office in your lunch hour is no more or less romantic, no more or less meaningful, than getting married in front of 300 guests and then having a lavish party somewhere grand. Or you could not get married at all. You don't have to do anything.

Lots of people who have children also have divorces, and take it in turns to have the children with them on the day. Lots of people don't have children. Lots of people have difficult families who they'd rather not pretend to want to see. Lots of people are old enough to finally say, 'No thank you, we find you all exhausting and we'd rather it was just us and a cottage pie.'

I think at least as many people have Tiny Christmas as they do Giant Christmas, and that an awful lot of them equate the day more with happy pottering than with raucous chaos. Possibly at this time of year they forget that happy pottering is what everybody yearns for, not just on Christmas Day but in actual life.

The older you get, the more this sort of contented quietness becomes a magnificent achievement, because it means you're still contented in your relationship with another person or – just as impressive – contented in your relationship with yourself. So celebrate yourself if your Christmas is Tiny. No apologizing! You are envied and admired by very many people.

And just in case having a lovely Tiny Christmas is not on the (Christmas) cards:

GIANT CHRISTMAS

Here are some things that have made my life easier in thirty years of hosting Christmas. (Every time I write something like that down I do the maths and think, 'Hang on, that can't be right.' But it always is.)

- Making gravy on the day is madness – there's enough going on. Just do it at some point in December, one evening after work when you have time, and freeze it. This also allows you to make a superior, flavour-packed gravy, which makes a huge difference to the whole meal. I swear by Jamie Oliver's Get Ahead Gravy, the recipe for which is online. Once you've made it, add THAW GRAVY to your phone calendar for the morning of December 24. Then sit back and feel pleased with yourself. This gravy means that the foundation stone of your Christmas dinner is laid.

- On another day before Christmas, make and freeze the bread sauce. This is extremely low-effort and satisfying. Leave out the butter and add on the day. Again, remind yourself to thaw it the day before. You may need to add a dash more milk when reheating.

- You can also freeze parboiled roast potatoes up to a month ahead. I knew that people swore that this not only worked but made the roasties crispier, but I hadn't dared try it myself until last year. I can report back with the glad tidings that it works *perfectly*.

- You can do the same thing with parsnips (parboil for 2 minutes).

- Red cabbage actively benefits from being made in advance, and you can also freeze it.

- You can freeze home-made or shop-bought pigs in blankets.

- You can make cranberry sauce weeks in advance, if you're making rather than buying, and it just sits quietly in the fridge, biding its time.

- And brandy butter.

- At this point you have gravy, bread sauce, potatoes, parsnips, cabbage and pigs good to go. I mean, you're practically there.

- Remember that a cold car makes a perfect second fridge.

- Guests will (hopefully) ask what they can do to help. For me there is only one answer, which is to take charge of the washing-up/dishwasher whenever they're passing. Loading and unloading the dishwasher is the most helpful thing a guest can do at Christmas. It makes such a huge difference to morale not to have to clear up as well as cook, especially if you're eating in the room you cook in, i.e. the kitchen. Obviously don't make one poor lone guest be the dishwasher Dobby – ask everyone who's staying to help too.

- Another guest needs to be in charge of wrapping paper, roaming the land with a binbag at regular intervals. For me, dishwasher + binbag action = festive serenity.

- More jobs for guests: put out an enormous drinks tray and make someone in charge of ice and mixers. Handy tip: you can freeze tonic water, meaning the drinks stay cold for ages. Also if you have some lemons that need using, slice them up and freeze them to use as ice cubes.

- Deploy guests for peeling duty on Christmas Eve (and have enough vegetable peelers on hand to make this effective). We do peeling to *Carols from King's* and it's extremely jolly.

- Don't feel wedded to the idea that you need a starter, a main course and a pudding. I rarely do starters in life, and never at Christmas. I refer you back to page 75 for hearty snack ideas like shop-bought charcuterie, cornichons, butter and good bread, a huge cheese plate with crackers or squares of smoked salmon and soda or rye bread. The hearty snacks keep people going happily for hours.

- Unless you are vegetarian, get, or make, a ham, or half a ham. No one is ever hungry when there is ham. The ham is Christmas. The ham is joy.

- A turkey is a big chicken. Most people can successfully anoint a chicken and bung it in the oven with some aromatics. Stay calm.

For me the main issue is oven and counter space, and the endless mess. Here's what I do:

1. Get up and take the turkey out of the fridge as early as possible – we're talking two hours at a bare minimum. It wants to be comfortably at room temperature before you start cooking it. Go back to bed.

2. Get up again at a sensible time – the reward of having adult children – and make quite a hearty breakfast; for us it's usually smoked salmon and scrambled eggs or frozen parathas with eggs and green chilli.

3. I like a nice old movie at this point on the kitchen telly.

4. Ask someone else to clear the breakfast away and load (and empty) the dishwasher. Turn the oven on.

5. Turkeys are often really overcooked. The easiest way to ensure optimal doneness is by using a meat thermometer, either a Thermapen or a little £5 one of the kind some butchers give you when you buy your bird. Your turkey is done when it reads 70 degrees, though check with your butcher or the label because it slightly depends on the type of turkey. The cooking is highly unlikely to take more than 3–3½ hours max unless you're feeding thirty people.

6. YOU NEED TO REST IT FOR AN HOUR, and longer is fine (less if it's small, obviously). This is so important, otherwise it will be tough because the meat will have contracted (from the heat) rather than relaxed, meaning tough rather than moist. All the juices will run out when you carve it, instead of reabsorbing and making the meat tender. So rest, rest, rest. Cover it loosely in foil with tea towels on top. It absolutely won't get cold. It will be warm and your gravy will be hot – perfect. This is my main piece of turkey advice. It makes all the difference.

7. Do the other oven things while the turkey is resting. It is hopeless to cram everything in and hope the potatoes cook properly. They won't. Insufficiently crispy potatoes ruin Christmas.

You don't have to serve everything piping hot. We've already discussed the turkey. The vegetables can be warm or room temp. All that needs to be really hot is the gravy and the potatoes. Bearing this in mind really helps with not getting stressed out.

Whether yours is big or tiny, if you're reading this in December I wish you a very merry Christmas.

Now it really is THE END! Goodbye! You can always find me at indiaknight.substack.com for much more of this sort of thing.

ACKNOWLEDGEMENTS

I really do want to thank my Substack subscribers. I'd wanted to write a newsletter for ages, but the terms of my then work contract didn't allow it. Then, luckily, I lost one of my jobs. It did not feel remotely lucky at the time – it felt catastrophic and threw me into a complete panic, because mortgage – but you know how it is: when life gives you lemons, you make the best lemonade you know how to make. So I thought, 'At least I can start that Substack now.' (I had signed up to the platform five years previously: the newsletter had been brewing in my head for a looooong time.)

It took off, and at the time of writing it is the number one global bestseller in its category. Of course, that won't always be the case, but I don't care: it's the most fun I've ever had putting finger to keyboard. So to anyone who pays for a subscription: really, thank you, from the bottom of my heart. You've given me the best job I've ever had. What a thing! THANK YOU.

At Penguin, I especially want to thank Helen Garnons-Williams, my publisher, who is much too grand to have involved herself as intimately as she did with the mechanics of this book. Wrangling tens of thousands of words when they don't tell a linear story can feel a bit like quite a complicated jigsaw puzzle for the author (me). But not for Helen. It was her brilliant idea to shape the book like a house, and once she'd thought of that, everything started to flow. You know when someone just comes in and says, 'That goes there, this goes over

ACKNOWLEDGEMENTS

here, this straggly bit goes there, and also I've fed the dogs, made the bed and hoovered'? That was what it felt like: if my manuscript was (appropriately enough) a messy house – why are the socks in the bathroom, sort of thing? and what's this lightbulb doing next to the dishwasher? – she came in like a mixture of Mary Poppins and Diana Athill and imposed order with laser-like focus. In fact, she sorted out the entire structure of the book in one afternoon at Durrants Hotel, armed with nothing but a laptop and egg sandwiches. I was, and am, in awe and I am monumentally grateful.

Thank you to Annie Lee for her eagle-eyed copyedit. At Penguin, huge thanks to Dan Jackson for the beautiful cover design and for the collages; to Stephen Hickson for the text design and for making my bullet-pointed lists into something lovely; and to Pete Pawsey for making the inserts look gorgeous. Thank you to Ellie Smith and Emma Brown for steering the ship to safe waters. Thank you to Savreet Virk and Ella Harold, Team Fig Tree, for everything, including Ella's handwriting on the page with the pink paint swatches on it. Thank you to Sara Granger in production, and to Caitlin Knight, Sam Fanaken and Rohan Hope in sales.

It is lovely to work with Julia Murday on publicity again after all these years. Thank you to Natalie Chapman, marketing dynamo. Thank you to Harriet Russell for the enchanting chapter illustrations.

My beloved agent's beloved husband – himself my beloved friend since our second day at university forty-odd years ago – died shortly after I started writing *Home*. He and she and their three daughters were very insistently in my head as I typed. I briefly considered dedicating the book to him – his name was Roger Gillett and he was wonderful – but then I could imagine him puzzled, laughing, going, 'Uh, why? It's about *cushions*, Ins.' When I think about houses, I also think about the ones we all holidayed in together over so many golden-seeming summers when our children were small. I'm so happy and proud that we still work together all these decades later. I love you, Georgia Garrett.

Finally, I'd like to thank my mother for showing me, from infancy to this day, what a confident aesthetic looks like. She taught me from very early on that how you live in a space – what you choose to surround yourself with, to eat off, to look at – not only *matters*, but changes the way you feel. She was pretty bold in her design choices: we had a navy-blue rubber floor in our flat in Brussels when all my primary school friends had 1970s swirly carpet, and modernist Danish tea cups (still in use) when everyone else's parents had blue-and-white china. These things leave their mark, and although her taste is far more refined than mine, I'm forever grateful for the lessons in knowing how to live – then and now.

INDEX

Abbott and Holder 140
Addison Ross 139
age
  'is just a number' 239
  parties and mixture of 82
ajo blanco (chilled almond soup) 221
algorithms 10, 65–6, 67, 158
Alvar Aalto stools 160
animals
  buying bargain 234
  farmed 228–9
anti-friction stick 196
appliances, kitchen 34, 35, 38–9
Arlo & Jacob 139
armchairs 32, 117–18, 130, 190
art 19, 20, 98, 119–27, 199
  bedroom and 162
  dark rooms and 98
  framing 123–6, 139–40
  kitchen and 37
  layering and 112
  meaning of 119–23
  pink walls and 106
  plates as 126–7
  spare room and 198

bad vibe 244
baked beans, posh 233
Baldwin, James 246
Basket Room, The 95
baskets, pretty 21, 79, 95
bathroom 189–96
  bath mat 193, 196
  bathroom cabinet, useful products for 195–6
  bath things, favourite 194
  natural cleaning materials 194, 196
  pottery basins 196
  recommendations 196
  sanitary ware, coloured 193
  shower curtains 193
  sink 193–4
  Sylvia Plath on 189

INDEX

bathroom – *cont'd*
  taps and shower heads, changing 194
  tiles, regrouting 194
  towels 191–3
bed 157, 158, 159, 162–81
  bedding 176–81
  duvet 166–7
  mattresses 167–76
  pillow fillings 164–6
  pillows 163–6
  sleep 162–3
  spare room 201, 203
bedding 176–81, 203
  bamboo 179–80
  brushed cotton/flannel 179
  colour 161–2
  dry cleaned 176–8
  Egyptian cotton 178
  linen 178
  microfibre 179
  polycotton 178–9
  sexes and 161–2
  silk 179
  thread count 180–81
bedroom 14, 109, 110, 155, 157–81
  bed *see* bed
  bedding *see* bedding
  bedside tables 161
  blackout curtains or blinds 162
  books 161, 181
  duvet 166–7
  furniture 160–61
  lighting 159
  mattresses 167–76

  Old Married Couple and 159
  pillows 163–6
  sexes and 161–2
  sexy, potential to feel 159
  sleep and 162–3
  stools 160–61
  tech ban during the week 157–9
  wall colours 160
'best is yet to come' 240
Betjeman, John 68
'be yourself' 237
be who you actually are 247
binbags 233
Birdie Fortescue 139
blackout curtains or blinds 162
blender, stick 63
bluntness 244
books 181
  bathroom and 189–90
  bedroom and 161
  coffee table 136, 137–8
  cookbooks 61–2
  gardening 213, 215–16
  hallways and 19
  on interiors 186–7
  kitchen and 32
  loo 154–6
  spare room 201
botox/fillers, cheap 234
bra liners 196
Braided Rug Company 38
brand, buying things from the same 233
Braun 63
British Blanket Company 222

INDEX

cabinetry 34, 35, 36–7
calm down 247
candles 33, 36, 80, 83, 112, 136, 137, 160, 191
  candlesticks 10, 26, 32, 72, 103, 130, 133, 135, 136, 233
  scented 153
  shavers 72–3, 95
Canterbury Belles 222
Caradok 43
Carter, Helena Bonham 142
casserole dish 51, 56, 63
celebrity chefs 235
champagne, vintage 234
changing your mind 248
character, evolution of 246
charm 4, 8, 9–12, 216, 241, 250
Charvet 39
chicken 228, 253
  Epic Tarragon Chicken 74–5
  Poulet Anglais 221
  roast chicken 49–50
children
  art/photos and 120, 143
  Christmas and 250
  disliking a friend's 245
  parties and 82, 85
  play and 183–6
  politeness to 207
  sitting room and 112, 115
  staying friends with your exes if you have 245
chocolate-box village, avoiding 226
chocolate, posh tiny 235

Christmas 41, 48, 49, 56, 61, 79, 86, 94, 127, 154, 155, 176, 177, 197, 219, 249–54
  décor 83
  Giant 251–4
  Tiny 249–51
church 231
cleaning materials, natural 194
Cloake, Felicity 221
clutter 141, 145–6
  decluttering 146, 198–200, 204
coats
  parties and 84
  puffy winter 236
cocktails 81, 83, 208
  cocktail napkins 85
coffee
  machines 234
  shop coffee 236
coffee table 68, 73, 112, 118, 121, 128, 130, 131, 134, 135–6, 216
  books 137–8
coffins, deluxe 234
Colefax & Fowler 69
collagerie 139
colour 143
  bathroom 190, 193
  bedding 161–2
  bulb colour temperatures 19, 32, 41–3, 127–8, 190
  choosing 97–9
  clothing 141
  flowers and 89
  food 78
  hallways 20

INDEX

colour – *cont'd*
  importance of 36–7
  kitchen 33, 36
  neutral 69, 98, 99, 100, 101, 102, 103, 127, 130, 141, 144–5, 196
  paint and *see* paint and colour
  pink 106–7
  pots 56
  room soup 101–3
  scared of 99–101
  similarity in 145
  sitting room 115, 121, 123, 125
  wall 158–60
  wardrobes 160
'comparison is the thief of joy' 248
compliments 245
constipation 196
content, being 244
Cooper, Jilly 81–2, 181, 201
coriander chutney 85, 87
Corston Architectural Detail 44
CosmoCol 196
country, moving to the 225–31
  activities 227
  biting off more than you can chew 228
  chocolate-box village, avoiding 226
  church 231
  creepy houses 231
  cultural desert, as 230
  dead things 229
  farming/farmed animals 228–9
  house, affordability of 227
  house costs 227–8
  house, knowing it when you see it 230–31
  Instagram, living in the country is not 229
  kind of life you want, deciding on 226
  land 227
  loneliness 226–7
  mice 229
  mobile signal 228
  parties 226–7
  race and 228
  rewilding 229
  romanticizing everything 228
  springs and summers 230
  weather 231
  wifi speeds 228
  your own company, enjoy 230
creepy house 231
crisps 85, 233
crockery 1, 32, 34, 76, 219
cufflinks, expensive 234
curtains 1, 35, 36, 103, 112, 130, 160, 162
  shower 193
cushions 3, 100, 101, 112, 114, 116, 117, 130, 147, 168, 199, 205
cynicism/bitching 246
cystitis 245

decisions, difficult 244
decoration 5, 31–2, 36, 66, 67, 68, 99, 103, 104, 109, 112–13, 123, 125, 141–3, 161, 183, 185, 186

INDEX

kitchen 37–8, 77–9
mixing styles 146–8
outside 216–17
Department of Salad, The
  (Substack newsletter) 220
DHS, Sophie Robinson's range
  for 139
dining rooms, separate 7, 71–4, 153
dinner party 73–81
doors
  front doors 1, 13–15
  kitchen doors 36, 37
Dowsing & Reynolds 43, 44
drama, need for 248
drinking glasses 81
drinks party 81–95
dry cleaning 235
Dualit 38
Dunelm 38, 222
duvet 163, 166–7, 176, 177, 205

ear buds, expensive 235
eating, how to have fun 71–95
  ages, mixture of 82
  baskets, pretty 21, 79, 95
  candles and 72–3, 80, 83, 95
  Christmas décor 83
  coats on departure 84
  cocktail napkins 85
  cocktails 81, 83
  cooking pots on the table 78
  coriander chutney 85, 87
  crisps 85
  dining rooms, separate 72
  dinner party 73–81

drinking glasses 81
drinks party 81–95
Epic Tarragon Chicken 74–5
flowers 79, 89–92
fruits and vegetables as
  decoration 79
invitation templates 82
kitchen and *see* kitchen
lighting 72–3, 82–3
look amazing, tell everyone that
  they 84–5
mini-samosas 75, 85
napkins, linen 80–81
'nice to see you' 84
non-drinkers, drinks for 84
outside 219–22
people, interesting 82
placemats 81
plating 77–8
platters 77, 85
playlists 87–9
pudding 55–6, 74, 76
recommendations 95
relaxing 84
salt/pepper/chilli flakes 79–80
setting the table 76–80
snacks 75–6
sober, partying 92–4
spiced apple shrub 86–7
staining 80
starters 75
tablecloths 80, 95
tablescaping tips 80–81
tarragon chicken 74–5
vegans/vegetarians 85

INDEX

Elfin Kitchens 223
emotional games 247
Epic Tarragon Chicken 74–5
Etalage 139
Etsy 82, 95, 196
exes, staying friends with your 245

fabric
  blackout 162
  cables 43
  cotton 179
  extension leads 43
  lampshades 36
  sofa 115
  softener 234
  texture and 129
  thread count 180
fairy lights 217, 222
Falcon 59, 63
family, importance of 239
farming 229
  farmed animals 228–9
fearless, be 237
Fellowes, Jessica 247
Fer À Cheval 196
first impressions 13–21
flatwoven jute 38
flowers vii, 4, 11, 19, 32, 34, 79, 106, 112, 120, 141, 161, 184
  arranging 89–92
  bathroom 189
  kitchen 79
  outside 211, 213, 214, 215, 219
  sitting room 134, 136, 137, 138
  spare room 203, 205

food processor 35, 57, 63
frames.co.uk 139
framing 20, 122–6, 139, 140
Frazzled Englishwoman 142
French Soaps 153, 196
friction 67–9, 100, 148, 179, 196
fruit
  as decoration 79
  galette 55–6
front doors 1, 13–15
furniture
  bathroom 190
  bedroom 160–61
  colour 144
  door 13, 37
  garden 212, 222
  layering and 112
  matching 233
  placement 131–2

gardens 211–17
  gardening books 215–16
George at Asda 222
get back what you put in 238
Gilbert, Melissa vii
Glassette 140
gloves or mittens, expensive 234
glycolic acid 195, 196
golden rules, sitting room 136–7
Graves, Helen: *Live Fire* 62, 219, 220
Great Dixter, East Sussex 212
grey paint 97

INDEX

guests
  bedrooms and 155, 176, 197, 201–5
  Christmas and 252–3
  drinks party and 82, 85
  how to be a good guest 205–8
  loo and 110, 149, 150
  sofa for 204–5

Habitat 222
Haden 38
haggling abroad 248
hallways 15–21
  recommendations 20–21
  storage ideas for narrow 20–21
  things that work 18–20
Harris & Jones 209
Hay's 209
Hazan, Marcella 244
help, asking for 246
home
  charm and 4, 8, 9–12
  defined 2–5
  as extension of you 3
  first impressions 13–21
  heart of, kitchen as 29
  storytelling and 23–7
  stuff, importance of 3
  you and 5
  See also individual room and location
hoovers, expensive 235
hotels 236
House of Charcoal 220
House Upstairs, The 139

hygiene 30–31

Ibbi 95
IKEA 21, 38, 63, 79, 117, 126, 148, 159, 219, 223
imperfection, in praise of 241–8
  life advice 243–8
ingrown hairs 196
'Intentional Clutter', TikTok 141

Jim Lawrence 44
John Lewis 38, 140, 164, 166, 177
John Oliver 106
joyful, how to make kitchen feel 32–7
Judge Speciality Cookware Skillet Solid Cast Iron Frying Pan 63
Judge Vista Sauteuse Pan 63
Jung, Carl 183

kachumber 221
karma 245
Kime, Robert 146
Kinky Pink 106
kitchen 29–40, 45–63, 71–95
  appliances 34–5, 38–9
  art 37
  cabinetry 34, 35, 36–7
  candles and 72–3, 80, 83, 95
  casserole dish 63
  Christmas décor 83
  cocktail napkins 85
  cocktails 83
  colour 36–7
  cookbooks 61–2

INDEX

kitchen – *cont'd*
  cooking pots 78
  coriander chutney 87
  countertop oven 61
  curtains 36
  decoration and appliances 29–39
  dining rooms 72
  dinner party 73–80
  drinks party 81–94
  Epic Tarragon Chicken 74
  equipment/kit 56–63
  fish and greens, steamed 52–4
  fish slice 58
  flowers 79, 89–92
  food processor 63
  fruit galette 55–6
  fruits and vegetables as decoration 79
  heart of the home 29
  hygiene 30–31
  Instant Pot or similar 59–61
  joyful, how to make a kitchen feel 31–7
  kitchen door furniture 37
  kitchen roll 80–81
  lighting 32–3, 72–3
  living things 34
  mini-chopper 56–7, 63
  napkins 80–81
  open shelves 34
  Our Place 63
  pans 35
  peel-and-stick wallpaper/vinyl wrap 37
  placemats 81
  plating 77–8
  platters 85
  pot, giant 56
  pudding 55–6, 76
  puttanesca 50–52
  recommendations 37–9, 63, 95
  roast chicken 49–50
  roasting tins 59, 63
  rugs 33, 37–8
  salt/pepper/chilli flakes 79–80
  salt pig 59
  setting the table 76–80
  skillet 57–8, 63
  snacks 75–6
  soft furnishings 35
  spiced apple shrub 86–7
  spider 58
  staining 80
  stick blender 63
  suppliers for decorating 37–9
  table, kitchen 71–3
  tablecloth 37, 80, 95
  tablescaping 80–81
  tarragon chicken 74–5
  tea towel 39
  textures 35
  toaster ovens 63
  vegetables 54
  vinaigrette 54–5
  vintage and modern elements 37
KitchenAid 38
knife sets 235

INDEX

Kuhn Rikon All-Round Shallow Casserole 63

La Corvette 196
La Redoute 38, 209
La Rochère Perigord Short Goblet Glasses 81
labneh 75, 221
lamps 19, 32–3, 36, 41, 69, 72, 83, 127–30, 159, 216
  lampshades 36, 128, 129–30, 236
  table lamps 19, 32, 36, 69, 127, 136, 201
Lancaster, Nancy 69
language, second 244
layering 32, 112–13
learning something new 248
leather sofas 116
life advice 243–8
  terrible 236–40
life is now, today 247
lighting 32–3, 41–4, 127–8
  bathroom 190
  bedroom 159–60
  bulb colour temperatures 19, 32, 41–3, 127–8, 190
  candles 33, 36, 72–3, 80, 83, 95, 112, 136, 137, 153, 160, 191, 233
  candlesticks 10, 26, 32, 72, 103, 130, 133, 135, 136, 233
  cool light 42
  drinks party and 82–3
  fabric cable/extension leads 43
  hallways 18–19
  importance of 32, 41
  kitchen and 32–3, 72–3
  lamps 19, 32–3, 36, 41, 69, 72, 83, 127–30, 159, 216, 236
  lightbulbs for atmosphere, best 44
  neutral light 42
  outside 222
  recommendations 43–4
  sitting room 112, 127–8
  spare room 201
  spotlights 32–3, 43, 83, 190, 191
  wall switches in brass 44
  warm light 41, 42, 97
Lights4Fun 222
limewash 108, 108*n*
limited edition 236
Linen Tales 95
Linen Works, The 39
lip balm 236
listening 245
Little House on the Prairie vii, 179
Lola & Mawu 95
Lola's Leads 43
London Basin Company 196
loneliness 226–7
loo 149–56
  Aesop hand soap 152–3
  air freshener 150
  books 154–6
  deodorizers 150–51
  favourites 152
  guest loos 149–50
  hand towel 151, 154
  pot pourri 153
  scented candles 153

INDEX

loo – *cont'd*
  scenting rooms 150–51
  seat, wooden loo 154
Lovett, Jane 62, 84, 86, 222

Magimix 57, 63
Mainstone Press, The 140
Maison Bengal 38, 95
Mann, Charlotte 17
mascara, expensive 234
Mason & Painter 139
mattresses 4, 7–8, 69, 113, 114, 163, 164, 166, 167–76, 243
  budget 169–70
  buying tips 175–6
  materials 172–5
  sleeping position 168–9
  types 170–72
  weight 169
  wriggly partners 169
maximalism 66, 68, 76, 131, 143–4
McAlpine, Skye 79
  A Table for Friends 62, 221
mess 16, 17–18, 25, 31, 33, 99, 116, 131, 145, 147, 228, 245, 253
mice 229, 235, 248
Microplane Colossal Foot File 195
minimalism 129, 130, 143–4, 212
Mitford, Jessica: *Hons and Rebels* vii
mobile signal 228
modernism 68

moisturizer 195
  expensive 234
Muji 209

nail polish, expensive 234
negative space 145–6
negative thinking 246
Netherton Foundry's Prospector Casserole 63
New House 13, 14
Next, Nina Campbell's range for 139
nice things, insignificant look of 134–6
Nisbets 35, 39
nobody needs
  life advice, terrible 237–40
  what not to waste your money on 233–6
Noma 222
Nordic Knots 38
Not A Boring Box 209

O'Keefe's Healthy Feet cream 195
Objects of Use 63
Old House 13
Oliver, Jamie 251
Oliver, Mary 2
open shelves 32, 34
Optrex Brightening Eye Drops 195
ordinary things 23–4
Ordinary, The 195
ottomans 112, 118–19, 132, 139
Our Place Always Pan 63

268

outgrowing people 244
outside 211–22
  books, gardening 215–16
  decorating 216–17
  eating 219–22
  feeling rural in the city, tips for 217–19
  gardens 211–17
  recommendations 221–2
overhead spotlights 32–3, 191
olive oil, new season extra virgin 235

paint and colour 4, 20, 97–108, 108*n*, 109, 114
  colour, choosing 97–9
  colour, scared by 99–101
  grey paint 97
  intensity 104–5
  kitchen 36–7
  limewash 108*n*
  pink 106–8
  room soup 101–3
  sitting room 109, 114, 119, 124–5
paintings 2, 19, 32, 37, 68, 105, 119, 120, 126, 128, 135, 138–40, 146, 183, 184, 198, 214, 242
Pallant House Gallery Bookshop 139
pans 34, 35, 56
  pan sets 235
Papers and Paints 106
Partnership Editions 139
parties

dinner party 73–81
drinks party 81–95
moving to the country and 226–7
sober 92–4
peel-and-stick wallpaper/vinyl wrap 37
Pentreath, Ben: *An English Vision: Traditional Architecture and Decoration for Today* 183, 186
personal trainers 234
Phipps, Catherine: *Modern Pressure Cooking* 61, 62
physical comfort 111–12
picnics 207, 218, 220
  rugs 217, 223
pillows 4, 69, 163–6, 167
  fillings 164–6
placemats 81
Plakatcph 139
plates 69, 77, 85
  as art 126–7, 190
plating 77–8
Plath, Sylvia: *The Bell Jar* 189
platters 85
play room 183–7
Pooky 44
positive thinking 246
pot pourri 19, 153
pot, cooking 56, 63, 78
Poulet Anglais 221
Powell, Anthony 161
Printspace 139
private club membership 236
pudding 47, 55–6, 74, 76, 222, 253

INDEX

Purdy & Figg 196
puttanesca 50–52
Pym, Barbara 142, 181

race/racism 14, 228, 239
recipes 7
  cocktail 83–4
  coriander chutney 85, 87
  Epic Tarragon Chicken 74–5
  fish and greens, steamed 52–4
  Jamie Oliver's Get Ahead Gravy 251
  puttanesca 50–52
  roast chicken 49–50
  salad 220–21
  screengrab or photograph 245
  spiced apple shrub 86–7
  tarragon chicken 74–5
  timings in 60–61
  vegan canapés 85
  vinaigrette 11, 54–5
RE-found Objects 196
rentals 37
resilience 247
rewilding 229
roast chicken 49–50
roasting tins 59, 63
Roberts, Julius 74
Robertson, Debora: *Notes from a Small Kitchen Island* 55
rodent repellers, sonic 235
Roosevelt, Theodore 248
round things 128–9
Rowan & Wren 139
Royal Academy, The 140

Ruggable 38
rugs 4, 27, 32, 69, 112, 143, 216, 217
  bathroom 190
  imperfection and 241–2
  kitchens and 33
  picnic 217, 223
  sitting room 128, 129, 131, 140
  washable 37–8
rural in the city, tips for feeling 217–19
Russell Hobbs 38

Sage 38, 63
salad 46, 47, 48, 49
  dressing 233
  recipe 220
  vinaigrette, classic 11, 54–5
salt pig 59
Salter 38
sanitary ware, coloured 193
Santa Maria Novella 19, 153
Scandi Compact 38
Selfridges 209
setting the table 76–80
sexual health 195
shampoo, expensive 234
shelves
  hall 19, 21
  open 32, 34
  outside 219
  vintage 190
shower 189, 190, 194, 195, 202, 205
  curtains 193
sink 27, 37, 151

INDEX

bathroom 193–4, 196
kitchen 209, 245
sitting room 15–16, 26, 41, 107,
    109–40, 204–5, 208, 216, 233
  armchairs 117–18, 130
  art 119–27
  backdrop/paint/wallpaper 119
  coffee table books 137–8
  framing 123–6
  furniture placement 131–2
  golden rules 136–7
  layering 112–13
  lighting 127–8
  objects 132
  ottomans 118–19, 139
  physical comfort and 111–12
  plates as art 126–7
  play room 183–5
  recommendations 139–40
  round things 128–9
  sofa 111–19,
    128–32, 204
  squish 111–13
  Stoke Newington, IK's house in
    109–11
  styling surfaces 132–3
  texture 129–31
skincare
  men-only 234
  moisturizer *see* moisturizer
  serum/Skinceuticals C E Ferulic
    245
skillet 57–8, 63
Sklum 223
Slater, Nigel 62, 74

sleep 25, 26, 111, 142, 157–81, 201,
    203, 205, 207
  bed *see* bed
  bedding *see* bedding
  mattress *see* mattress
  position 168–9
snacks 75–6, 206, 253
sober, partying 92–4
sodium percarbonate 192, 196
sofa 1, 16, 23, 32, 35, 69, 84, 101,
    103, 139, 141, 144, 207, 242
  classic sofa/classic shape/classic,
    relatively neutral upholstery 117
  cushions 114
  delicate, avoiding 115
  fabric 115
  guest 204–5
  leather 116
  leg height 116
  Martindale rub test 115–16
  measuring your space 113
  outdoor 216
  removable, washable covers 115
  side table and 113
  sitting room 111, 112, 113–19,
    128–32
  spare room 201
  swatches 115
  testing/sitting and lounging on
    114
  trends, don't buy into 116–17
  vintage, check 114
soft furnishings 35
Soho Home 139
souls, houses need 24

INDEX

soup
  ajo blanco (chilled almond soup) 221
  out of frozen vegetables 244
spare room 14, 84, 176, 197–209
  creating a lovely 201–4
  decluttering 198–200
  guest, how to be a good 205–8
  guest sofa 204–5
  recommendations 209
  storage solutions 209
  working from home and 208–9
spiced apple shrub 84, 86–7
spices, jars of 234
spiders 58
spotlights 32–3, 43, 83, 190, 191
squish 111–14, 118
staining 80
  Green Fairy Liquid and 245
stick blender 63
Stoke Newington, 109–11, 212
stools 160–61
storage 17, 20, 21, 56, 118, 128, 143, 160, 190–91, 209
storytelling 23–7
stuff 5, 141–8, 186
  clothing 141
  clutter 141, 145–6
  decorative styles, mixing 146–8
  Frazzled Englishwoman 142
  importance of 3
  'Intentional Clutter' (TikTok) 141

maximalism and minimalism 143–4
negative space 145–6
styling surfaces 113, 133–4
sunscreen 248
Susan Deliss 139
Swan 38
Swoon 139

tables
  bedside 161
  coffee table 68, 73, 112, 118, 121, 128, 130, 131, 134, 135–6, 216
  cooking pots on 78
  lamps 19, 32, 36, 69, 127, 136, 201
  setting 76–80
  tablecloths 1, 37, 80, 95
  tablescaping 80–81
taps 194
taste 64–70
  algorithm and 65–6, 67
  consistency and 67–8
  friction and 67–9
  'ghastly good taste' 68–9
  judgement and 66
  neutral interiors 68–9
  surrounding yourself with things you love 69–70
  trends and 65
  trust yourself 70
  unifying theory of 67
teabags, posh 235

INDEX

tea towels 26, 35, 36, 39, 78, 254
tech
  banning in bedroom during the week 157–9
  unnecessarily powerful, top of the range 235
texture 35–6, 60, 66, 67, 78, 118, 124, 127, 129–31, 133, 144, 145, 148, 162
therapy 245
tiles, regrouting 194
Times, The 81–2, 146
Tinsmiths 140
toenail clippers 195
Tolstoy Edit, The 139
tomatoes 38, 47, 48, 49
  kachumber 221
  puttanesca 50–52
  sauce recipe 244
Tosca & Willoughby 154
towels 190, 191–3, 202, 205
train tickets, first class 234
triggers 244
Turshen, Julia 55, 62
TV
  expensive 236
  streaming subs 234
Tweedmill 223

Ulster Weavers 39
umbrellas, expensive 234
Urban Cottage Industries 43

Vanish 38
vegans/vegetarians 62, 75, 85, 86, 206, 253
vegetables 32, 46, 54, 56, 57, 58, 60, 77, 220, 253, 254
  as decoration 33, 34, 79
  cooking 54
  soup out of frozen 244
vinaigrette, classic 11, 54–5
vintage 136
  art 139
  clothes 11, 122, 124, 199
  frames 124
  jugs 147
  kitchen and 37
  mini-cabinets 20
  ottoman 119
  shelves 190
  sofa 114, 116
  texture and 131

walls
  colours 106, 160
  wall switches in brass 44
  wallpaper 1, 37, 43, 45, 119, 160
water
  bottled 234
  drinking 246
Wayfair 222
weather 16, 97, 219, 222, 223
  living in the countryside and 231

INDEX

Weaver Green 37–8, 139
weddings, wildly expensive 235
wellies, expensive 236
white truffle 235
Whittle & Flame 220
wifi speeds 228
Wilson Stephen and Jones 139
Wolfe, Thomas 5
women
  'intimate' deodorants 150
  kitchens and hygiene, attitude to 30–31
Woolf, Virginia 149
working
  for yourself 246
  from home 159, 208–9, 228

Zara Home 95, 139
Zico lightbulbs 43, 44
Zinsser 36–7